Hot Plants for Cool Climates

Hot Plants for Cool Climates

Gardening with Tropical Plants in Temperate Zones

Susan A. Roth and
Dennis Schrader

Photographs by
Susan A. Roth

Timber Press
Portland • Cambridge

Paperback edition published in 2005 by
Timber Press, Inc.
The Haseltine Building
133 S.W. Second Avenue, Suite 450
Portland, Oregon 97204-3527, U.S.A.

Timber Press
2 Station Road
Swavesey
Cambridge CB4 5QJ, U.K.

www.timberpress.com

ISBN 0-88192-719-8

Printed in the United States of America

Cataloging data is available from the Library of Congress and the British Library.

Contents

Introduction

If you're a gardener hungry for something new, tropicals, subtropicals, and tender perennials may be just what you're looking for. If you've ever traveled to the Caribbean region or another tropical area, you'll especially appreciate learning how to re-create a tropical paradise in your own garden, no matter where you live. Many tropical plants flourish, growing and blooming with abandon, in the hot, humid summers of the Southeast, Midwest, and Northeast and in the mild climate of the Pacific Northwest. Some tender plants produce more flowers in a single summer than a long-lived hardy perennial does in its entire lifetime. In many areas of the country, subtropicals extend the season of the autumn garden because by summer's end they have grown into huge specimens that continue blooming splendidly until a hard freeze cuts them down. You can grow tropicals as you do annuals, for only a single season outdoors, or overwinter them and return them to your garden for additional summers.

The natural jungly look has taken hold of people's imaginations—particularly in the garden, where it's possible to create your own private Eden. A garden almost anywhere can evoke the splendor of Hawaii, Tahiti, St. Lucia, or Costa Rica—a splendor redolent with exotic flowers and tangled greenery. The look is sumptuous and over-the-top. The scale borders on monumental, and color combinations are bold and daring. The aim is to create a riotous exuberance of growth and brilliant colors in the context of restrained abandon. Here, more is better because it's an exotic, wild look that is the hallmark of tropical-style gardens. No strict rules apply—almost anything goes. The design secret lies in choosing and combining the right plants: vines whose trailing branches drip from overhead trees; glossy-leaved shrubs whose foliage screams with vibrant, color-splashed patterns; and wild-looking flowering plants whose grand blossoms perfume the air with delicious scents.

In *Hot Plants for Cool Climates* we describe how—even in a northern site such as Pennsylvania, Oregon, or Minnesota—you can create a luxuriant, tropical-looking garden where the sweet perfume of jasmine floats in the sultry, summer-night air and where a sudden downpour plays a drumbeat on heavy foliage. This is easily done by integrating tropical and subtropical plants (and even a houseplant collection) into a traditional garden and by including cold-hardy plants that boast beautiful leaf textures, fantastic colors, and lavish flowers in your landscape.

Tropical-style gardens rely heavily on foliage, playing up the contrast between bold glossy leaves and fine ferny leaves, but on a big scale. And then there's color. Many popular tropical plants display variegated or colorful leaves that deliver striking, season-long contrasts. The combinations look wild and riveting when done with a calculated eye. The deep purple leaves of 'Dark Star' coleus (*Coleus blumei*) become even moodier when juxtaposed with the golden glow of the leafy 'Margarita' sweet potato vine (*Ipomoea batatas*). Flowers, too, appear large-scale and luscious. Mandevilla vine (*Mandevilla* spp.) scales to the top of a pillar, then sends its twining branches cascading downward to display 6-inch-wide, shocking pink blossoms. Angel's trumpet (*Brugmansia* spp.) bears its foot-long, creamy trumpets, sometimes a dozen at a time, and these scent the garden with an incredible fragrance during moonlit evenings.

It's possible to change the look of a traditional garden and make it more tropical by artfully placing just a few plants in the right place—such as by framing the entrance to the garden with a large potted palm, draping a vine to tumble from the branches of a tree, or planting daring combinations of brightly hued foliage plants such as bloodleaf (*Alternanthera dentata* 'Rubiginosa'), croton (*Codiaeum variegatum* var. *pictum*), or copperleaf (*Acalypha wilkesiana*). This garden style relies on using true tropical plants as well as tropical-looking, Temperate Zone plants to re-create the wild, untamed feeling of a tropical setting.

Tropicals in gardens aren't really anything new—plant enthusiasts have grown and collected them for centuries as conservatory plants and houseplants and have bedded them out in lavish (and outlandish) displays of flowering annuals, such as impatiens, wax begonias, and geraniums, all of which are actually tropical plants. Fifteen or twenty years ago, garden centers stocked few tropical shrubs that were more exotic than a rubber tree, and

This Pacific Northwest garden features hardy versions of tropical plants: Tasmanian tree fern and Japanese fiber banana, which live year-round in this mild temperate climate.

these hibiscus or banana plants would invariably end up in someone's living room—never in their flower garden. Recently, however, innovative gardeners have begun to think of tropicals as garden subjects. What is new is the trend of using these exotics in great quantities outdoors to re-create a sumptuous tropical feeling in the garden—and the availability of exotic plants has grown as fast as the popularity of this garden style.

About this book

We've organized the book into two parts. The chapters in the first part concentrate on the various aspects of gardening and designing with tropicals in temperate climates. The first two chapters tell you how to go about creating this exuberant style in your own garden.

The third chapter details how to grow tropicals in containers—because most are perfectly suited to being grown as living bouquets in large, ornamental pots. Tropicals are naturals for container plantings, flourishing in summer's heat and producing season-long foliage and flower effects. A sumptuous tropical container sets the mood of exotic splendor. You can use container groupings in a small garden or on a patio to create an intensely intimate, tropical-looking setting. And containers can be rearranged and moved to change the effect. They even work well placed within a garden bed, where they add dramatic color and serve as a focal point.

The fourth chapter delves into the art of using cold-hardy plants that look tropical to create the desired ambiance in your garden. By going that route—at least partially—you won't need to dig up and replant your tropical-style garden every year to protect it from the cold climate. Many familiar cold-hardy perennials, such as hosta (*Hosta* spp.), golden ray (*Ligularia* spp.), heart-leaf bergenia (*Bergenia* spp.), and gunnera (*Gunnera manicata*), evoke a tropical feel because they feature large, glossy leaves. Other cold-hardy foliage plants such as ferns, yuccas, bamboos, and ornamental grasses lend a tropical air because of their large size and lush, lacy textures. Certain temperate trees, shrubs, and vines summon the mood of the tropics by their stature or leaf and flower textures. The mimosa tree (*Albizia julibrissin*), with its powderpuff flowers and large, lacy leaves, resembles acacia, a common tropical tree. Rambunctious hardy vines such as wisteria (*Wisteria* spp.), trumpet vine (*Campsis radicans*), and anemone-flowered clematis (*Clematis montana*) can be trained to grow up high and drape sinuously low. You can rely on these and other cold-climate woody plants that have a tropical look to create an enduring backbone for your tropical-style garden design.

The final chapter is a practical one that tells you how to keep these tender plants alive from year to year. Because by definition tropical plants cannot withstand freezing temperatures, they are one-season plants in temper-

Most tropical plants, like this red passionflower, know no seasons and bloom throughout the year because they are native to areas with a year-round growing season.

ate gardens unless you take steps to overwinter them. Gardeners outside of the tropics routinely dig up the tubers and corms of popular garden plants such as gladioli and dahlias, so some of the techniques are not new, even if the plants are. But we have included many new tricks on how to overwinter these heat-loving plants in a cold-winter climate. We'll tell you how, even if you live in Vermont, you can grow a banana tree or other frost-tender tropical outdoors in your summer garden, year after year, so that it grows ever larger with each passing year.

The encyclopedia section—part two—details choice tropical and subtropical plants that you can successfully grow outdoors from spring through fall in temperate climates. We don't by any means include all the exotic plants that you might try in your garden—but the ones we do include are sure performers. They are plants that Dennis has tested and grown in his garden, or ones that other gardeners we know succeed with in temperate areas. Some tropicals don't adjust well to conditions outside of their normal habitats—they may shed leaves or go dormant at the slightest chilly breeze or in humidity levels that are less than jungle-like. So if you're just starting to garden with tropicals, begin with the reliable plants we've described here. Then after you've become proficient, you can start seeking out rarer types. The plant lists and mail-order source list in the appendixes offer a quick and easy reference for when you begin to design your garden.

What makes a plant a tropical?

Now that you want to grow these exotic plants, you might be wondering exactly what a tropical plant is. Strictly speaking, a tropical plant originates in the tropics, and that means from the geographical region on both sides of the equator, bounded by the Tropic of Cancer to the north and the Tropic of Capricorn to the south. This includes much of Africa, South and Central America, Australia, India, and Indochina and all of the Caribbean and South Pacific islands. The tropics are unlike any other place on Earth. They know no seasons. For all practical purposes, the daylength is the same every day of the year. Because the sun lies almost directly overhead, an incredible amount of sunlight strikes the earth here, heating the air to what we would consider summery temperatures each and every day, with only minor fluctuations during the year.

Seasonal weather patterns can and do occur, but these are variations mainly in the amount of rain that falls at different times of the year. We often think of the tropics as a region of very high rainfall, and indeed much of it is rain forest; however, the tropics also include deserts and grasslands called savannas. A tropical rain forest receives 100 or more inches of rain a year, either spread out evenly over the year or in a seasonal pattern. Wet and dry seasons may be created by the trade winds as they travel across warm and cool ocean waters, picking up moisture and depositing it as rain as they go. Rainfall in the tropics compares not to a drizzling spring day in New York but more to a July thunderstorm—the precipitation can come in the form of a monsoon that delivers deluges of rain day after day, or predictable heavy showers every afternoon for months, with beautiful clear weather before and after the cloudbursts.

Elevation comes into play here, too, for the tropics aren't all flat. Mountains in the equatorial region change the climate drastically. For every 1,000 feet of elevation, the temperature drops about 3 degrees Fahrenheit. Volcanic mountains in the Caribbean, for instance, can soar from sea level to 3,000 to 5,000 feet, so the temperature at the summit might be 15 degrees cooler than at the bottom. Plants adapted to these mountainous slopes acclimate to seasonal rain patterns but also grow in relatively cool temperatures year-round—which means that not all tropical plants love heat.

If the dry season in a particular tropical region is long enough and dry enough, plants may go dormant and lose their leaves. The dramatic lush landscape of some tropical rain forests looks brown and dead for a few months. As often happens in temperate forests, with the return of moisture the trees burst into fabulous bloom. Some rain forests may be cloaked with mists and clouds at certain times of the year, and this damp shroud slows evaporation, so the plants remain evergreen even though actual rainfall may be scarce. On the other hand, some regions of the tropics are deserts because rain is scarce at any time of the year—a rain shadow created by a mountain or other factors puts these areas out of reach of the trade-wind-driven rain.

Subtropical plants hail from the regions bordering the true tropics—an area that varies, due to the influence of cooling mountains and ocean currents, from 300 to 700 miles north or south of the tropics. Here frosts do occur, but only rarely and only lightly. Rainfall can follow any of the same patterns found in the tropics, and balmy regions of low rainfall are termed "Mediterranean." Many exotic plants flourish in the subtropics, which is defined by the northern limit for growing citrus and olives.

Tropical plants are varied, with different sorts adapted to all these various conditions. Their only common trait—with the exception of those mountain-peak dwellers—is that they cannot survive freezing temperatures, which is the criterion that most horticulturists and gardeners use to define these cold-sensitive plants. Most tropicals simply die if exposed to freezing temperatures, and some cannot even survive temperatures in the 40s or 30s. Some tropicals and subtropicals, however, when grown in colder areas, die to the ground if hit by a freeze and then regrow from their surviving roots, so they act like perennials. Gardeners often call these plants "tender perennials" even though they are programmed to grow as evergreen plants.

Variegated leaves, which create a bold color impact, continue their spectacle for months on end. This Long Island garden includes *Coleus* 'Saturn', *Manihot esculenta*, a hibiscus relative, lemon grass, and angel's trumpet.

Whatever is novel and new has the capacity to captivate people, and so it is with plants. People throughout history have lusted after plants—either for their medicinal and practical purposes or for their beauty and rarity. During centuries past, when the major European nations were colonizing other parts of the world, every ship had a botanist who collected and brought back new and unusual plants to grow at home in display gardens and conservatories. During Victorian times, tropicals were all the rage. Today tropical plants offer gardeners in cool climates the opportunity to include some very dramatic and strange-looking vegetation in their plant palette. If you're just beginning to use tropicals in your garden, you might enjoy visiting local botanical gardens, public gardens, or zoos, most of which feature tropical plantings. Wave Hill (in Riverdale, New York) and Chanticleer (in Wayne, Pennsylvania) are two notable, small public gardens with national reputations and are a must-see for anyone interested in tropical plants. These two gardens are in the forefront of garden design and offer imaginative displays that combine all types of plants, hardy and nonhardy alike.

*I*n preparing this book, we traveled all over the country, journeying as far north as Vermont and as far south as South Carolina, and west to Washington, visiting with enthusiastic gardeners who are at the forefront of this gardening trend. We picked their brains and photographed their gardens—tropical-style landscapes that are the proving grounds of this hot new style of gardening. We hope that the photographs of these tropical-looking gardens and the exotic plants in them will rejoice your spirit with their beauty as much as these gardens did ours. But we also hope that after reading the book and looking at the pictures, you'll have learned enough to venture into your garden and begin to transform it, creating the sumptuous, lush look that is tropical-style gardening. Most of all, we want you to have fun in your garden.

❖ ❖ ❖

Hot Plants for Cool Climates

CHAPTER ONE

Tropicals Catch Fire

The canna–banana-plant palette has caught fire, sending gardeners everywhere into a frenzy of planting everything and anything big and bold, lush and leafy, extravagant and exuberant. It's a rebellion of sorts among gardeners who have been controlled too long by the fussy doctrines of English garden design and the dictates of rigid native-plant advocates. These guerrilla gardeners are revolting against excessive good taste and seriousness, striking back with vibrant foliage colors and unrestrained growth, all in the spirit of good fun.

Perhaps this trend toward the exotic is also a result of how well traveled we now are. Our pioneering sense of adventure knows no bounds; we cast off eagerly on Caribbean vacations, Hawaiian honeymoons, and Mexican holidays; trek through the cloud forests of Costa Rica and the rain forests of the Amazon River Basin; and set off on safari in Kenya and Botswana. Gardeners returning from these adventures bring back an extensive new set of favorite plants and a very different sense of garden aesthetics.

The tropical look

The tropical-style gardens that are sprouting across the land are not really naturalistic gardens—they are not meant to mimic the jungles, rain forests, and desert islands of the tropics. Although they often possess a wild, jungly appearance, they capture only the untamed mood of the natural tropical landscape. They imitate in a more northerly climate the real gardens that bloom around the elegant homes and resorts that abound in equatorial regions. In these true tropical gardens—whether they're in Martinique, Bali, Thailand, Costa Rica, Hawaii, or even Florida—the showiest and most glorious hot-weather plants from around the world flourish together in a riot of color and texture. Since growing conditions vary little from one part of the tropics to another, plants native to the Philippines will happily adapt to a garden in the West Indies. And gardeners in the tropics are just like gardeners everywhere else—they lust after what is showiest, new, or different. The gardens of the tropics are collections of the best tropical plants from around the globe, not necessarily gardens made exclusively with local flora.

A tropical-style garden is a visually exciting place to be. Here, an array of tropical and hardy plants surround the pond and grow with controlled abandon to mimic the popular jungle look.

Actual tropical gardens, like this one at Blancaneaux Lodge in Belize, feature the showiest plants and are much more colorful than the surrounding jungle, which is predominantly green.

What gives these gardens such great appeal to gardeners in the Temperate Zone is their exotic look—a look unlike anything we have back home. Exploding with fireworks of color and growing into exuberant leaf, these tropical paradises capture our imaginations. The gardens' scale is grand, almost monumental, with leafy fronds of palms and bananas casting a shifting, shadowy shade. Trickling fountains, palm-thatched huts, and ancient ruins are not just whimsy but the real thing, the finishing touches that give the garden a sense of place, history, and culture. When re-created back home with tender tropical plants or with cold-hardy tropical-looking plants, this look can transport you to vacationland.

Tropical greenery

First-time travelers to the tropics are often surprised by the overwhelming greenery of the rain forest, and by its lack of bright color and seeming dearth of flowers. It's really not at all what they expected. Because the growing season in the tropics is often twelve months long, the landscape lacks seasonality. Plants don't need to make a mad dash to grow and reproduce in a few weeks or months. The beauty of the rain forest comes more from leaf textures and plant forms than from colorful flowers and fruits. Although many tropical plants are beautifully colorful, they are so widely dispersed through the surrounding greenery that their effect becomes diluted. When we reproduce a tropical-style garden in more northerly climes, however, we can concentrate the most colorful foliage and flowers the tropics have to offer in one setting, creating a vibrant effect not found in the natural tropical landscape.

The tropical rain forest is the most diverse ecosystem on Earth. It contains so many different kinds of plants that almost every plant you see on a hike through the forest is a unique species. Unlike the maple, beech, and pine forests of the northeastern United States, a tropical rain forest contains perhaps four hundred species of trees. This vast diversity translates into an astonishing variety of textures, forms, and shades of green, which you can use to good effect in a tropical-style garden. The wonderful contrast of all these elements is what we try to imitate.

The path running through this New York garden is shaded and defined by several *Musa zebrina* (bloodleaf banana), which are dug up each year and overwintered indoors as dormant corms.

Because so much rain falls in most regions of the tropics and subtropics, plants there have adapted to deal with an abundance of moisture. Their leaves, for instance, are cleverly designed to shed water: either they are very large and slickly glossy (think of a rubber tree), so water runs off them in sheets, or they are cut into lacy segments like a snowflake (think of a tree fern or palm), so torrential rain passes right through them. Most big, solid leaves are further equipped with long, pointy tips, called drip tips, to funnel water right off them. Desert dwellers, on the other hand, have needed to develop other means of coping with their harsh conditions in order to preserve whatever water they can scavenge. Often they either have thick, succulent, water-storing leaves or lack leaves altogether. Some have evolved a hairy coat on the leaves and stems to provide some shade from the burning sun.

Along with possessing a wonderful bold or ferny texture, most tropical leaves display fascinating outlines that make the tropical-style garden an intriguing place to explore. Besides being rounded or fernlike, tropical leaves can be deeply lobed, sharply serrated, thin and wiry, ferociously thorny, curly, or spiky. All these attention-getting forms add to the exotic look of a tropical-style garden, and combining various leaf shapes to contrast with each other will accentuate each leaf's special design.

Plants in temperate climates typically have small or moderate-size leaves in comparison with those of tropical plants, which can reach gargantuan proportions. Tree-fern and palm fronds, for example, while usually fine-textured, sometimes grow to 12 feet long or more, making an indisputable statement that says "tropical" in anyone's book. Banana leaves can measure 10 to 12 feet long. Where it grows wild, the giant taro (*Alocasia macrorrhiza*) produces shield-shaped leaves that can reach 4 feet wide and 6 feet long and are held aloft on 4-foot-long stems. The yard-long leaves of candle bush (*Cassia alata*) are beautifully cut into lacy segments, but their sheer size lends a dramatic presence.

Left: Senna alata leaves are 3 feet long but cut into blunt lobes, creating a lighter texture. Right: The huge fur-covered gray leaves of Argreia nervosa stand out dramatically from stout vines.

Tropical forms and colors

The form of some tropical plants is so intrinsically exotic-looking that including these plants in your garden immediately transports you to a far-off land. Conjure up the image of a sinuous-trunked palm tree topped with a whorl of 12-foot-long fronds and you are automatically carried to a sunny, tropical island. Visualize the dense rosette of succulent, blue-green, thorn-tipped leaves of a century plant (*Agave* spp.) and you're in the desert. Imagine the lacy, translucent, green fronds of a giant tree fern spreading out overhead and you're in a misty cloud forest imbued with the earthy scent of moss. Picture the gigantic, heart-shaped leaves of elephant's ears (members of the genera *Colocasia, Alocasia,* and *Xanthosoma*), which can grow so tall and large that a child can stand under them, and you're hiking through a South American rain forest.

The tropics and subtropics offer an astounding array of colorful foliage plants, from the mottled red-and-green leaves of copperleaf (*Acalypha wilkesiana*) to the striped green-and-gold leaves of the variegated spiral ginger

(*Costus amazonica* 'Variegata'). These and other notable tropical foliage plants such as *Coleus* exhibit colorful leaf patterns in the wild, but their garden forms are even more flamboyant. These garden varieties have been chosen for their intense color patterns or exaggerated size and texture, attributes that may exist in nature but that have been further enhanced by selection and breeding.

With such a bounty of distinctively colored and textured tropical foliage plants, your design possibilities are limitless. You can create combinations that are bodaciously outrageous if you wish, or use a bit of restraint and come up with more sedate, but still vibrant, color schemes. The success of any design depends not just on using leaf color wisely but on contrasting leaf size and form. Play off the ferny against the solid and bold, the fine-textured against the coarse-textured. Then add the element of color and you've got a tropical-looking garden. (These topics are covered in more depth in the next chapter.)

Tropical flowers are often giant trumpet-shaped affairs, like this *Brugmansia* 'Ecuador Pink', that attract humming-birds for pollination.

Tropical flowers and fruits

A flower's main job in life is to attract pollinators to fertilize it, in order to ensure seed set and thus reproduce the plant. This vital task is an especially difficult one in the tropics, where competition between plant species is fierce and where individual plants of the same species may be located a quarter of a mile apart. To ensure survival, the flowers of tropical plants have evolved into very specialized—and often gorgeous—structures meant to attract the creatures that pollinate them. For unlike many Temperate Zone plants that spread their pollen helter-skelter on the wind, most tropical plants rely on birds, insects, and mammals for pollination.

Many of the showiest flowers in the tropics are large tubular red, orange, or pink affairs that depend on hummingbirds for pollination. With their craving for nectar and excellent vision, hummingbirds are significant pollinators of tropical plants. Red and orange blossoms attract them the way a lightning rod attracts lightning. Plants that use hummingbirds exclusively for pollination produce tubular scarlet to pink flowers with a rich store of sugary nectar in the depths of their throats, where only this long-tongued bird can reach. Often perched at the tips of lengthy stems, these blossoms stand away from any tangle of leaves, to allow the birds to fly from flower to flower and hover without hindrance. The vibrantly colored blossoms are typically scentless, because they need no additional help in attracting the birds.

Large, nectar-rich, night-blooming white flowers rely on hawk moths, not hummingbirds, for pollination. These night-flying insects hover, sprint, and sip nectar in hummingbird manner, but they visit different-type flowers. Because these moths fly at night, the flowers they find attractive must be easy to locate in the dark and so are invariably a luminescent white and have a heady fragrance. The moths' 6-inch-long tongues can probe deeply into tubular flowers to reach the nectar, but these insects also feed on shallower blossoms.

And then there are flowers that are pollinated by bats, which abound in the tropics. Despite popular belief, not all bats are blind. Flower- and fruit-feeding bats enjoy excellent vision, unlike insectivorous bats, which navigate by a kind of radar called echolocation. The nectar-laden flowers they visit must be easy to see at night and so are commonly white or pastel and quite large, with a dense puff of anthers that rubs pollen onto the bats' snouts as they probe the flowers in search of their sugary riches. The bats' specially developed sense of smell helps them find their way to the flowers that are designed for them to pollinate—bat-pollinated flowers possess a musty odor reminiscent of fermented fruit, which is not exactly pleasant.

Bees and butterflies are also important flower pollinators in the tropics, as are many other kinds of insects. As with insect-pollinated plants in temperate regions, tropical versions attract their pollinators with color and fragrance as well as by devious mimicry. Some flowers, notably orchids, resemble colorful female insects and insidiously draw their male counterparts to enjoy their attractions, all the while taking advantage of them as inadvertent pollinators.

Some plants, particularly those in the aroid family (Araceae), employ carrion beetles as pollinators, a specialty that endows them with the repugnant aroma of rotten meat. Fortunately for tropical-plant lovers, these often bizarre-looking flowers usually don't stink for long, nor does the odor carry for much of a distance, but you are well advised not to stick a curious nose into such a flower.

Once pollinated, most of these fabulous flowers ripen into juicy, edible fruits, which serve to attract hungry monkeys, parrots, and other creatures, which then carry off the seeds and disperse them far away from the parent plant. Because they need to be found and eaten, the fruits often turn bright red when ripe, a color that is easy to spot against the forest's prevailing greenery. Not only do they taste delicious, they look beautiful, too.

With all these wonderful flowers and fruits, it's surprising that the tropical rain forest remains so predominantly green. This is partly because in a frostless environment the growing season is year-round and there is no need to make a great show of flowering and fruiting before unfavorable weather sets in. The insects and birds that pollinate the flowers or spread their seeds are in attendance throughout the year, so flowering trees, shrubs, and vines usually bloom—with notable exceptions, such as the spring-blooming royal poinciana tree (*Delonix regia*) and the golden bell tree (*Tabebuia caraiba*)—sporadically, a few blossoms at a time, throughout the entire year, rarely making a floral splash. Fruits also ripen a few at a time all through the year, thus ensuring a plentiful food supply for the birds and animals that the plants rely on to spread their seeds. However, some flowering plants do put on exquisite shows of blossoms, but they do so high up in the forest canopy, where visitors to the forest cannot see them from the ground.

When it comes to using flowering tropicals in a garden, you will of course seek those that flower most freely, such as flowering maple (*Abutilon* spp.), mandevilla vine (*Mandevilla* × *amoena*), bottlebrush ginger (*Hedychium coccineum*), or firecracker plant (*Cuphea ignea*), or those, such as flamingo flower (*Anthurium* spp.) or lobster claw (*Heliconia rostrata*), whose individual flowers are so dramatic that quality makes up for any deficiency in quantity. Night bloomers, such as thorn apple (*Datura inoxia*), belong close to the house—along a moonlit path, next to a lighted patio, or under a window—where the delights they offer won't be missed.

No tropical-style garden is complete without fragrant plants to add to the romance. The heady fragrance of the night-blooming jessamine (*Cestrum nocturnum*) is so strong that it can permeate an entire backyard. The sweet perfume of ginger (family Zingiberaceae), gardenia (*Gardenia jasminoides*), and angel's trumpet (*Brugmansia* spp.) can transport you to the tropics as the scent lingers in the sultry summer air. Locate fragrant plants where you'll be sure to enjoy them, whether in a container set on a patio, deck, or terrace or planted next to a hammock or an outdoor dining area. You can also bring containerized plants indoors to act as fragrant living bouquets.

A free-flowering and easy-to-grow tropical, *Hibiscus* 'Jason' delights gardeners with its dinner-plate-size yellow blossoms with red centers.

Tropical vines and epiphytes

Luxuriant vines twisting their way into the treetops and sending down a drapery of leafy branches define the dense, uncontrolled growth that typifies much of the tropics. Probably as much as 90 percent of all the vine species in the world grow in the tropics, where their predatory growth is fueled by abundant warmth, sun, and moisture. With their roots firmly in the soil, vines drink up plenty of moisture and nutrients, but they keep their heads in the sky, where they bask in the sun and spread out in a smothering blanket across the plants they climb. Because they cannot support themselves, vines need something to grow on and a climbing strategy.

Two types of vines abound in the tropics. The woody, long-lived, high-climbing lianas, such as the Swiss cheese plant (*Monstera deliciosa*), germinate in the debris on the dark forest floor and immediately begin to grow upward, seeking light. Their stems wrap and twine around the tallest tree they can find, rapidly twisting themselves high into the canopy and grasping the tree trunks they climb in a fierce stranglehold. Their woody bases can grow to a massive size, as big around as a man's leg. As a liana climbs upward, it may weave from one tree to another and tangle with other vines. But once it has achieved the top of the forest canopy, its leafy branches sprawl out every which way to soak up the sun and can eventually grow to 1,000 feet long. This great, weighty vine can ultimately topple a tree or impair its health by blocking life-sustaining sunlight.

Other less mammoth vines, such as morning glories (*Ipomoea* spp.) and passionflowers (*Passiflora* spp.), scramble their way over low shrubs and small trees at the edges of a forest, along a riverbank, or in a sun-drenched clearing opened up by a tree fall. They grow rapidly in the sun and stay much lower, climbing by slender twining stems or clinging tendrils that grasp onto their host's narrow twigs and branches. These opportunistic vines live shorter lives than the massive lianas, because their sunny site inevitably closes in upon them.

Tropical trees serve as the home base for many other types of plants besides vines. In the moisture-laden equatorial regions, mosses and lichens encrust tree bark, wallpapering it in intricate patterns. Epiphytic ferns, bromeliads, cacti, and orchids cling to tree branches, sprouting from every nook and cranny like hats tossed onto a hat rack. None of these plants are actually parasitic, only opportunistic. These smaller plants use the host plant for support to put them in reach of sunlight and rainfall.

An epiphyte sacrifices a lot in trade for a boost skyward. Its roots, which are not anchored to the ground but are lodged in debris that collects in the crotch of a tree branch or in a crack in a rough-textured bark, cannot do much by way of absorbing water or nutrients. So epiphytes live constantly on the verge of dehydration or starvation. The roots absorb what moisture and nutrients they can from the decaying litter they are rooted in, or if they are attached directly to a branch and suspended in midair, they rely on rain and mist to bring them moisture and nutrients.

Some epiphytes have adapted to their situation by other novel means. Many bromeliads catch water and litter in tanks formed by the cuplike arrangement of their leaves. The litter and insects in the water decay into a

An opportunistic vine that twines itself into shrubs and trees in sunny clearings in the tropics, moonflower has gorgeous, sweet-scented, night-blooming blossoms.

nutrient-rich broth that feeds the plant. These vessels not only benefit the bromeliad but also provide water for thirsty rain-forest dwellers and even are home to insects, frogs, and other amphibians. Epiphytic cacti and orchids store water in their pseudobulbs to call upon during dry periods.

The abundant presence of vines and epiphytes further adds to the tropical forest's chaotic lushness, a lushness reflected in layers of tangled vegetation. This layering is one aspect of designing a tropical-style garden that should not be overlooked, because it is so important in creating a tropical ambiance. To do it right, you must add several vines to scale up a tree trunk or twine around a post or trellis, so that their dripping branches create a bit of a jumble. You can go so far as to attach actual epiphytic plants, such as air plants (*Tillandsia* spp.) and orchids to the trees in your garden, or just suspend hanging baskets of ferns and vines to create the layered look.

Tropical vines flourish even in Boston gardens like this one, where *Mandevilla* 'Alice du Pont' has been trained to grow up a support. *Colocasia esculenta* basks in a water-filled trough.

Tropical plants move north

It's easy to create a dazzling display of tropical foliage and flowers even in seemingly inhospitable climates such as those found in Vermont, Pennsylvania, or Oregon, far from the Tropic of Capricorn. Summers in most parts of North America bring plenty of sun, heat, and humidity, along with thunderous rainstorms. These conditions fuel tropicals into high gear, so that even if the plants start off the summer small, they grow by leaps and bounds and turn into impressive specimens in a matter of a few weeks. Overwintered specimens are large to begin with and use this head start to great advantage, claiming an immediate presence in the garden as soon as they are set out in spring. By late summer and fall, tropicals are at their best.

The tropics are the most fecund and diversely vegetated region of the world, boasting, by some estimates, as many as three-quarters of the world's plant species. Only a relatively small number of these exotic plants are available to gardeners outside the tropics, and fewer still adapt to being thrust into a garden in Delaware or Minnesota. Many tropical plants need specific temperatures with hardly any fluctuation from day to day or wilt unless the humidity hovers around 100 percent. Others require specific nutrients or have an essential symbiotic relationship with another plant or fungus. Yet despite these restrictions, you can still choose from countless exotic plants to incorporate in your garden.

The ones that perform best in temperate gardens grow undaunted by the climate's normal fluctuations of temperature, humidity, and rainfall during the summer and fall. If they can also adapt to houseplant culture or to one of the many types of overwintering techniques (see chapter 5), they become even more valuable as garden subjects because they'll only get more beautiful with size and age. Many common and popular houseplants, such as rubber trees, diffenbachia, spider plants, prayer plants, Chinese evergreen, and pothos, rescued from the dark corner of a living room, perform fabulously out-of-doors in warm weather and make authentic additions to a tropical-style garden.

You can grow tropical plants right in the ground or in containers outdoors in cold climates during the frost-free months of the year, creating entire tropical-style gardens from these tender beauties. For the most natural appearance, you might wish to plunge the pot of a large container plant right into a hole dug in the ground in a bed of tender or hardy plants. You might also site the container aboveground, but camouflage its base with dense plants.

Going native

Although some native-plant enthusiasts are purists and might disapprove of growing tropical plants in gardens where they are not endemic, this is really a matter of style and personal preference. Certainly when exotic plants—and in this case we define "exotic" not as a tropical plant per se but as any plant not native to a given region—are planted in a garden, they can escape its confines. Some escapees run rampant in the natural landscape, posing a threat to native vegetation that's like a disease let loose on a susceptible population. Countless incidences of imported plants turning into terrible pests fill gardening folklore. Kudzu—that infamous vining weed from Japan—is the most notable example. It's literally eating the South, smothering trees and houses in its advancing path.

You need feel no guilt or worry whatsoever in planting tropical plants outdoors in climates colder than the limits of their hardiness. Since they would perish if they spent a winter outdoors in such a climate, they pose no danger of escape. Even if a tropical sets seed, the seed will not germinate.

However, some exotic tropicals and subtropicals should not be planted outside in areas where they are cold-hardy—in zones 9–10 and 8–10, respectively—because they do present a threat. This is especially true of certain exotic grasses that disperse their windblown seeds far and wide and can thus become terribly invasive. Plants that pose such a problem are indicated in the encyclopedia section of this book.

Tropicals defy the seasons

In July and August in temperate regions, when temperatures and humidity are at their most insufferable, many traditional garden plants start to wilt and sulk, but tropical and subtropical plants shout for joy. It's their kind of weather. A garden planted densely with tropicals and subtropicals gets better

and better as the growing season progresses, and it does not falter in mid- or late summer, or even in fall until it's too cold to care anyway.

Because they are genetically coded to keep on growing all year and don't plan for frost, when grown in a temperate climate many tropicals obliviously continue growing and blooming in fall. Putting on a fantastic show of foliage, flowers, and form at a time of year when few northern plants are looking all that good, tropicals seem like miraculous season extenders. In autumn, our northerly perennial gardens more often than not look tired and worn; not much is in bloom, and leaves begin to shrivel and drop off, preparing for dormancy. But when tropicals, subtropicals, tender perennials, and cool-season annuals occupy a cool-climate garden, the show only gets better as summer advances into fall.

Although some tropicals make good season extenders, subtropicals usually do a better job of it, because they are designed for cooler temperatures and a relatively long growing season. By late summer they have grown to their full size and are ready to bloom and put on a floral show. Some variegated or fancy-leaved tropicals have been strutting their stuff all summer and then take curtain calls by beginning to bloom late in the season. Leaf colors of many foliage plants intensify with the advent of cool, crisp nights, so they become only more striking. Princess flower (*Tibouchina urvilleana*) even develops rust-orange autumnal foliage hues. (For a listing of tender plants to extend the fall season, see page 200.)

Many of these plants, especially the ones that you want to die back and then store as dormant plants over the winter, can and should be left out until frost. Still others, even though they may not be destined to be overwintered, have an attractive presence in the autumn border. Use lion's ear (*Leonotis leonurus*), castor bean (*Ricinus communis*), and shower bush (*Senna* spp.) for their bold architectural appearances, which are especially welcome in fall.

You can spruce up containers by removing faded annuals or plants that don't perform well in cool temperatures and leave in the fall performers. Use New Zealand flax (*Phormium tenax*), gingers (family Zingiberaceae) and honey bush (*Melianthus major*), and then add a few ornamental cabbages or kales, fall-flowering perennials such as asters (*Aster* spp.), and cool-season annuals such as pansies (*Viola* × *wittrockiana*), blue daisy (*Felicia amelloides*), and pot marigold (*Calendula officinalis*). Your aim is to make a design statement, so why limit yourself by using only traditional fall plants such as chrysanthemums?

A few tropicals are so cold-sensitive that they may lose their leaves when the nights start getting into the 40s—these plants must be protected from cold. But most tropicals take night temperatures even into the high 30s in stride as long as days are warmer, into the high 40s or 50s. They don't begin to falter until a light frost turns their leaves brown.

Most tropicals keep on performing outdoors well into autumn, as they do here on Long Island in September. This beautiful mixed border effectively combines cold-hardy shrubs and perennials with tropicals.

Most plants that thrive in a subtropical climate carry on even through light frost. Gingers (family Zingiberaceae), flowering maple (*Abutilon* spp.), fuchsia (*Fuchsia* × *hybrida*), fancy-leaf geranium (*Pelargonium* × *zonale*), princess flower (*Tibouchina urvilleana*), and firecracker plant (*Cuphea ignea*) keep pumping out their blossoms even when the surrounding landscape blazes with fall color. A butterfly ginger (*Hedychium coronarium*) out-blooms a garden mum any day. Not until a hard freeze blackens the tops do these plants stop performing. Tender ornamental grasses hold onto their wispy good looks and fluffy seed heads long after they've been hit with frost and can play an important part in the fall garden—and in the winter garden if you're willing to treat them as annuals.

When a light frost or the first hard freeze makes its mark on a tropical, it's time to dig it up and store the roots in a state of dormancy until spring. You can also protect some tropical or subtropical plants—and even borderline hardy plants for that matter—from winter by burying them under mulch or wrapping them in insulating material. This way you can often carry them over in the ground from season to season in areas one or two zones colder than they would normally survive. (See chapter 5 for details on how to get tropicals through the winter in a northern climate.)

Even if you aren't creating a tropical-style garden, you'll find that using tropical plants here and there in a traditional landscape extends the gardening season well beyond what you're used to. These equatorial wonders find a place in almost any garden setting, bringing color and volume to the late-season garden.

An exotic-looking urn is fashioned into a trickling fountain and surrounded by luxurious foliage and flowers to create the atmosphere of a garden from some far-off land.

Creating a tropical style

Tropical ambiance comes not just from the plants you use and how you combine them but also from the accouterments you bring to the garden. The ornaments—containers, fountains, lanterns, fences, furniture, and statuary—that find a home in the garden put the final flourish to its tropical spell. Even a single large Asian urn used as a focal point adds a foreign flavor. Statuary, artifacts and ruins from earlier cultures, huts and other garden buildings all bring a sense of place to the garden that makes it distinctly individual.

You can punctuate your tropical-style garden with tasteful ornaments or go at it with a bit of humor. Have some fun and approach this aspect of your garden with tongue in cheek. Try mounting

tiki torches along the length of a path through the garden, for instance, or erect a faux temple ruin among the vegetation. You might suspend Yucatán hammocks from tree to tree or hang a parrot cage, perhaps with a cascading plant inside, among the tree branches.

Water plays a key role in a tropical-looking garden, and if possible you should include a water feature—either large or small—somewhere in the garden. You'll enjoy watching the ripples on its surface and listening to the music of its trickling flow. The water feature can be as simple as a water-filled urn fitted with a recirculating pump or as elaborate as a naturalistic boulder-strewn stream—whatever fits your budget and your imagination.

Formal pools and fountains surrounded by tiled courtyards defined Byzantine Middle-Eastern gardens. Reflecting pools were also important features in the gardens built by the colonial powers in Africa and South America. Rocky naturalistic pools and waterfalls adorn gardens in the South Seas and Thailand.

Not all tropical-style gardens look jungly. Mediterranean gardens are usually more controlled, with a lushness that comes from massing containerized plants within a walled courtyard, although vines such as bougainvillea spilling over the walls can add a splendid garnish. These plants may be water-guzzling tropicals nurtured with a watering can or arid types that adapt to the seasonally dry climate. Tropical plants growing in a courtyard in a temperate climate can bask in the warm microclimate the enclosure provides, which encourages their rapid growth and lengthens the time you can grow and enjoy them outdoors.

Tropical impersonators

Some cold-hardy plants, such as these *Rodgersia aesculifolia* (rodgersia) and *Hakonechloa macra 'Aureola'* (variegated windgrass), have the same bold leaves as tropical plants and can be used easily to create a junglelike effect in a cold climate.

Gardeners anywhere in the world, in almost any climate, can also imitate the tropical-style garden by relying not on real tropical plants but on a collection of cold-hardy plants. Many cold-hardy plants, by way of their dramatic size and form, fascinating foliage, and extravagant flowers, possess a tropical air about them. Combine these into a dense planting that radiates an overgrown exuberance and you've achieved the tropical look without having to replant year after year. You can also mix and match the cold-hardy with the tropical, much as you would mix perennials and annuals in a traditional flower bed. (See chapter 4 for details on designing the tropical look with cold-hardy plants.)

When choosing hardy plants for a tropical-style garden, study the foliage first and select those that look as if they belong in a giant, moist terrarium. Choose perennials with big glossy leaves a foot or more across and plant them in clumps to create a tropical look. Like the true tropicals, many large-scale perennials have brightly variegated foliage and make great exotic-looking additions. To give it authentic-looking structure, you can also work into your design trees and shrubs that feature the huge smooth leaves or large lace-cut leaves so common in the tropics. Contrast this big and bold framework with ferny and grassy textures to further enhance the tropical effect.

The big, bodacious look is all the same whether the plants are tender or hardy. By using these cold-hardy impersonators in tropical-looking combinations, you save yourself planting effort each year and also avoid the need to cram your house full of overwintering tropicals for several months.

*B*y adding distinctive tropical plants to your garden design, you expand your plant palette enormously over the more common garden choices. Tropicals work in almost any garden or garden area. They can create a cool green sanctuary or an opulent paradise. The tropical style can characterize just a small oasis in your garden or encompass your entire landscape—fanat-

A tropical effect can be created solely from cold-hardy plants. The layered branches of *Aralia elata* 'Aureovariegata' (gold-variegated aralia) spread dramatically to frame low-growing clumps of variegated windgrass, Japanese iris, and star of Persia.

ics have been known to get carried away by the fun of it all, completely making over their garden. You might want to start off small, with perhaps as little as a pair of containers flanking the front door, and then go more tropical. Hobbyists go to great lengths to defy their garden's climate in attempting to overwinter tropical plants, such as palms, in the ground in regions where they aren't normally hardy. Whatever your gardening personality, the idea is to enjoy your tropical adventure. You're limited only by your imagination and the number of frost-free days in your garden.

CHAPTER TWO

Tropical Style for Temperate Climates

Although every culture has its gardening traditions, and some of these, such as the Islamic gardens of Persia, the villa gardens of the Roman Empire, and the temple gardens of China, date back hundreds or thousands of years, pleasure gardens were historically few and far between in most of Southeast Asia, Africa, South America, and the South Pacific. Until colonial officials, plantation owners, and their cohorts descended upon the tropics, the only ornamental gardens of note that existed in the equatorial regions adorned royal palaces, Buddhist and Hindu temples, and other holy sites in Southeast Asia. Most of these gardens did not sparkle with colorful plants but were mainly architectural in nature. Enclosed within walls and featuring water as a sacred element in formal pools, elaborate fountains, or even naturalistic lakes, these gardens were tranquil places of great religious significance. Trees and fragrant plants thought to possess mystical properties brought these gardens to life.

The tradition of ornamental gardening, especially the exuberant plantings we think of today, was otherwise unknown in these regions. Plants were grown and harvested primarily for food or medicine and used in symbolic rituals. A lush, wild landscape of almost sinister jungle scenery, village and family farms hacked from the natural landscape, and only an occasional few plants grown for ornament or for religious reasons greeted the European colonists to the tropics upon their arrival.

Perhaps out of homesickness and perhaps with a bow to fashion, these European gentry, determined to carry on in the lifestyle to which they had become accustomed, created gardens around their new homes and clubs. The style was based on nineteenth-century European tastes and garden-design principles, but the plants were purely tropical, chosen out of practical necessity and regard for the climate. Eventually, upper-class locals, who were largely Westernized, also adopted the gardening fashion of the day.

The first tropical gardens created by these colonists were probably rather Victorian in style, featuring bedding-out schemes, like those in vogue in England, with colorful flowering and foliage plants arranged in patches of swirling color. Hedges marked boundaries and created garden rooms, and succumbed to the pruning shears by carrying neat and tidy formal lines.

Opposite: Canna 'Tropicana' is planted between cold-hardy Catalpa 'Aurea', which is cut back hard each year to create gigantic leaves, and Miscanthus 'Variegata'.

Groomed lawns protected what would have otherwise been bare earth surrounding the impressive baronial homes, and a uniform row of trees lined the long driveways. More exuberant gardens emulated the pseudo-equatorial scenery of palms and ferns displayed in the great Victorian glasshouses that were all the rage in European cities during the 1800s.

The mighty international trading companies of the era, such as the East India Company, established several amazing botanical gardens throughout the tropics, notably Pamplemousses on the island of Mauritius in the Indian Ocean, Kebun Raya on the Indonesian island of Java, Peradeniya in Sri Lanka, and the Singapore Botanical Garden in Singapore. There they amassed extensive collections of tropical plants, choosing and experimenting with anything that seemed to hold a potential economic importance. But the grounds were also designed for strolling and enjoyment in the grand style of European gardens, with vast lawns, artificial lakes, flowing fountains, and opulent displays of massed tropical plants.

From these botanical gardens the most desirable tropical plants—both ornamental and agricultural—found their way around the world. This.dramatic diaspora of tropical plants means that few tropical regions now possess their own endemic garden flora—the hibiscus so evocative of Hawaii actually came from tropical Asia and southeastern China, and the bougainvillea so popular in the tropics the world over originally came from Brazil.

As English gardeners rebelled against the formal and began to embrace the naturalistic, so too did many tropical gardens evolve toward the more natural. After all, it was only fitting to go a bit more native with the jungle as a backdrop. With no country of origin and no real sense of place, today's tropical and tropical-looking gardens can be anything and everything. But one thing is certain: They are distinctively daring.

Carefully chosen plants give this formal garden a tropical look. The pool's corners are marked by urns of taro, their bright green ears reflecting in the water. Dutchman's pipe, a hardy version of a tropical vine, drips over the arbor.

Creating the look

A tropical-style garden might be classically formal or romantically wild. Its formal overtones might derive from straight hedges and paths that set off burgeoning blossoms and bold foliage. Or its naturalistic look might rely on irregular lines and a tangle of riotous vegetation.

No matter how daring it seems at first glance, a tropical-style garden's audacity works visually only if the garden is planted to the tune and discipline of some very basic garden-design rules—tried-and-true rules to which you might want to give serious credence. But rules, once learned, it must be noted, are meant to be broken. And only tropical plants can break them with such impunity, especially when it comes to color.

Bursting with foliage textures and forms, this North Carolina back yard epitomizes the wild overgrown look that results from plunging potted tropicals into a garden planted with subtropicals and perennials.

To make your garden evoke an exotic climate—no matter its formality or informality—it should be a meticulously contrived extravaganza of texture, form, and color. You can learn to make great plant combinations by manipulating these three plant attributes. Then you can do almost anything else with your garden to make it distinctly individual.

Taming tropical leaves

By and large, no matter how unabashedly colorful it is, a tropical-style garden ought first to be a study in leaf texture and shape. For it's the skillful commingling of the textures and shapes in a garden, more than of any other attribute, that makes it work visually. Use too many plants all of one texture or shape, and the scene looks boring and blah. Use too many different textures and shapes side by side, and the garden takes on a disturbing quality. Even an all-green garden pleases the senses, becoming a peaceful retreat, if the foliage textures, shapes, and sizes work together to create visual harmony. Most tropical plants are foliage plants, so it's their distinctive leaf size and texture—and their shapes—that you need to consider first off when making plant combinations.

The tantalizing textures of tropical leaves

Most tropical plants display big—sometimes gargantuan—solid leaves with smooth outlines, a pointed tip, and a glossy or leathery finish to their surfaces. Such plants bring a commanding texture to the garden scene, which comes primarily from the leaves' size and solidity. The bigger and more solid a leaf is, the bolder its texture. Shiny, glossy leaves reflect light and look bigger and bolder, too. (For a listing of tropical plants with big leaves, see page 201.)

Leaf size and texture play a prominent role in designing a tropical-looking garden. Big, bold leaves, like those of Japanese fiber banana, *left*, add structure, while ferny dissected leaves, like those of honey bush, *right*, make softer contrasts.

If a tropical leaf isn't big and solid, then most likely it is big and dissected into segments (and is known as a compound leaf), so it has a fine-textured quality. (Some tropicals do, however, have small solid or dissected leaves.) The leaf segments (called pinnae) of such compound leaves may be rounded or pointed, linear or circular, adding detail to the texture. Dissected leaves are always more fine-textured than solid leaves of the same size. Fuzzy or hairy leaves look softer and more fine-textured than similar-shaped lustrous ones.

Special terms describe the pattern of dissection. A leaf that's divided so that a row of segments lines up along each side of the midrib (or rachis) is said to have a pinnate leaf pattern, a configuration rather like that of a feather. If the pinnae further divide into their own rows of segments, the pattern becomes double-pinnate or twice-divided, and so on. Ferns are usually doubly or triply pinnate, while palms are typically single-pinnate. The more pinnae a leaf has, and the smaller the pinnae are, the more fine-textured the leaf, no matter what its overall size.

Another observation holds true about texture: The more widely spaced the leaves, the coarser the plant's texture; the closer together the leaves, the finer the texture. This trait is immediately noticeable on tropical plants such as candle bush (*Senna alata*). This species holds its 3-foot-long, pinnately compound leaves at widely spaced right angles from the branches, creating an open effect that gives each leaf a dramatic prominence.

The sexy shapes of tropical leaves

Although most plants of the rain forest have oval to oblong leaves, there certainly is room for a lot of variation from the norm. The overall outline of a tropical leaf may be sword-, lance-, shield-, or heart-shaped; circular; or lobed in the manner of a typical maple or oak leaf. Grassy leaves stretch out into fine linear patterns, forming spiky tufts.

Compound leaves often grow longer than wide, giving them an oblong, triangular, or sword-shaped outline. But some compound tropical leaves have a rounded overall shape that's divided into segments reminiscent of the spread-out fingers of a hand. This beautiful pattern is called palmately divided. The leaves of fan palms divide up this way, creating a lovely composition of shape and texture.

The crazy colors of tropical leaves

Although travelers to the tropical rain forest frequently express surprise and disappointment at its pervasive greenness, no one could ever truthfully accuse a tropical garden of lacking color. The tropical plants selected for ornamental gardens are the most ornamental of the lot, and more often than not they display wondrously colorful foliage. Even though most natural species have green leaves—in one shade of green or another, but nevertheless still green—mutations exist throughout the plant kingdom that serve us up plants whose leaves are deficient in the green pigment chlorophyll. These leaves may be painted sunny shades of bright gold or yellow, if their underlying yellow pigments dominate, or moody shades of reddish or purplish brown, if their underlying red pigments dominate. If the chlorophyll goes missing only in parts of the leaves—the leaf margins, for instance—then the leaves will be gaily variegated, or patterned, with stripes, spots, or mottlings of white, yellow, reddish purple, or other colors. Among tropical-garden plants, colorful foliage versions abound. (For a listing of tropical plants with colorful leaves, see pages 201–3.)

Tropicals with colorful leaves sustain the garden because their alluring colors never wane. Here, the boldness of *Colocasia* 'Jet Black Wonder', *Canna* 'Pretoria', and castor bean is softened by a veil of annual verbena.

Rules for pairing painted leaves

The rules of good taste in traditional gardens admonish us to use colorful foliage, especially variegated types, sparingly. We're instructed to avoid massing the colorful leaves and instead scatter them around the garden to create highlights, or to use a single specimen as a focal point. And, to avoid the scene becoming too colorful (heaven forbid), we're told to use plenty of pure green foliage as a foil to offset the tendency toward brightness.

But in the tropical-style garden these rules ought to be brazenly broken. If you're out to create a garden with a sizzling show of color, then you must rely more on foliage than on flowers, for flowers, beautiful as they are, come and go, but leaves, brightly colored leaves, remain ever constant. So go right ahead and plant masses of the same brightly colored foliage plant. Groups of three, five, seven, or more work well, depending on the size and scale of your garden. The effect can be electrifying, but so as not to actually electrocute the beholder, you might wish to incorporate these colorful leaves according to some of the color rules discussed below. These rules are ones best not broken, even with tropical plants, although the color combinations can get rather outrageous and still be playing by the rules.

All leaves are not the same shade of green. And it's the subtle shades and hues of a leaf—whether it tends toward gold, bronze, blue, or green—that point the way toward the most effective color combinations. So before planting anything in your garden, stop to take a close look and ask yourself, what color is that anyway?

The color purple

Various terms, such as "purple," "bronze," "red"—or even "black"—describe leaves in which the red pigments dominate the green, and these terms are actually not very accurate or, if accurate, are not used with much consistency. Very few such plants, whether equatorial or temperate in origin, are in fact truly purple, except for a few notable tropical exceptions such as purple heart vine (*Tradescantia pallida* 'Purple Heart'), purple velvet plant (*Gynura aurantiaca*), and Persian shield (*Strobilanthes dyeranus*), whose leaves are the lucid color of grape juice. Other plants described as purple, bronze, or red tend to be a reddish or purplish brown, like oxblood shoe polish or polished mahogany, certainly not the dull gold of tarnished bronze metal.

Bronze (reddish brown) leaves can tend a bit toward the dull mud brown, but when planted so that the sun strikes the leaves from the side or from behind, the more reddish ones among them shimmer with glorious red highlights. These reddish brown tones combine with almost any other color of foliage or flowers, the effect either sobering or enlivening, depending on their companions, but they are anything but dull when paired with hot colors.

Purple- and burgundy-tinged foliage adds moody color to a garden and makes stunning combinations with red and pink flowers and silver leaves.

Try using reddish bronze leaves in combinations with rich scarlet, orange, or gold flowers and you'll intensify the blossoms' heat, turning up the temperature by several degrees. One effective pairing is underplanting the spiky mound of bronze-leaved New Zealand flax (*Phormium* 'Bronze Baby') with the fancy-leaved geranium *Pelargonium* 'Vancouver Centennial'—the geranium's star-shaped, brick-red-and-gold leaves echo the bronze hues of the *Phormium,* and its clusters of bright salmon blossoms add an unabashed dazzle to the combination.

Purple-bronze leaves keep peace with every color in the garden, too, but they become stars when you play up their purple overtones with blue-gray foliage plants or with flowers in shades of blue, purple, pink, red, or magenta. These pairings emphasize and deepen the cool red pigments in the purplish foliage. Use the deep wine red leaves of 'Burgundy Knight' rubber tree (*Ficus elastica* 'Burgundy Knight') with luxuriant red or hot pink tuberous begonias for an electrifying matchup.

So-called black leaves, which are actually the rich deep purple hue of an eggplant, are so dusky that they seem to absorb light. Use the beautifully murky leaves of *Colocasia* 'Jet Black Wonder', *Ipomoea batatas* 'Blackie', and *Coleus* 'Dark Star' to enrich combinations with blue, lavender, or purple flowers—or to create shock waves with yellow or red blossoms. These black leaves make bold, almost black-and-white contrasts with the lavender-flushed white trumpets of thorn apple (*Datura* 'Evening Fragrance') and pleasing monochromatic washes with the purple flower clusters of heliotrope (*Heliotropium arborescens* 'Marine').

Golden rays

Sunshine illuminates a garden with a golden light that warms all the colors in it. More northerly climates may lack this golden light, but you can simulate the golden rays of the tropics by including lots of golden-hued foliage plants in your tropical-looking garden. When planted in masses or dropped into the center of a garden, gold-, chartreuse-, or yellow-leaved versions of green plants mimic beams of light, even on a cloudy day.

As with bronze leaves, yellow-hued leaves turn up the temperature of an already hot color scheme, but by many degrees. Orange and red flowers boil over when massed with hot-colored leaves, for a truly tropical effect. Golden shades have a bit of red or orange in them, so they work well with intensely scarlet or orange colors. Chartreuse (yellow-green) is a gleaming, but totally unrestrained, hue that cools down beautifully when given blue or purple flowers as neighbors, and it gets even hotter with orange and red friends. When the boldly variegated, green-and-gold leaves of sanchezia (*Sanchezia speciosa*) are positioned next to the fiery red blossoms of Egyptian starcluster (*Pentas lanceolata* 'Ruby Glow'), the combination really gets cooking. Another rather shocking—but quite pleasing—composition is the pointed, chartreuse leaves of the sweet potato vine (*Ipomoea batatas* 'Margarita') blanketing the ground beneath the red-leaf ginger (*Hedychium greenei*), where it intensifies the red in the ginger's stems, leaf undersides, and large coppery red flowers.

Silver trimmings

Silvery white or blue-gray leaves, which are often cloaked with a fuzzy down coat or a waxy bloom, connote the desert landscape. Like bronze leaves, these light-reflecting leaves make excellent harmonizers in the garden, blending compatibly with almost any other color. Pink, white, blue, and lavender flowers make time-honored elegant combinations with silver foliage, but the look may be cooler than most tropical-style gardeners have in mind. Don't overlook using silver with red, gold, and orange flowers or with bronze or gold leaves—the silvery foliage punctuates the hot-hued garden with a metallic shimmer.

Patterned leaves

Variegated leaves can have subtle patterns or be quite gaudy—and both kinds of coloration have a place in a tropical-style garden. In one com-

The vein pattern of *Canna* 'Pink Sunburst' is echoed and emphasized with pink, gold, and green stripes, creating a brilliant display of both color and texture.

monly found pattern, the leaf margin is either white or gold, creating a halo around the green center. The effect is attractive but relatively subtle if the margin is narrow, but the wider the colorful margin is, the brighter the leaf's color veers from neutral green. The result can be quite striking as the contrasting margin further intensifies the vertical aspect of sword-shaped leaves or the roundness of round leaves. For instance, for a fascinating combination of both shape and variegation choose the gold-and-green-striped, sword-shaped leaves of 'Yellow Wave' New Zealand flax (*Phormium* 'Yellow Wave') for a dynamic effect, or the creamy white-edged, rounded leaves of 'Marginatus' Spanish thyme (*Plectranthus forsteri* 'Marginatus') for a gentler statement.

In another common pattern, the background color of the leaf is green but the veins stand out in a different color, creating a high-contrast effect. A radiating pattern of silvery white veins marks the dark, glossy, metallic purple-black leaves of African mask (*Alocasia × amazonica* 'African Mask'), and the prominent leaf veins of many fancy-leaved caladiums (*Caladium bicolor*) paint a road map across the heart-shaped blades.

Mottled irregular patterns become more complex, with the variegations expressing themselves as speckles or spots, blotches, or swirling patterns. And often these irregular patterns include more than two colors—sometimes, as in the case of coleus (*Coleus blumei*), copperleaf (*Acalypha wilkesiana*), croton (*Codiaeum variegatum* var. *pictum*), and some canna lilies (*Canna* spp.), a seeming multitude of colors. The more colors in a leaf, the gaudier its pattern, and the more challenging it is to use in the garden.

Sometimes hot and cool colors occur in the same leaf—the flame-shaped leaf of *Coleus* 'Olympic Torch', for example, starts out at its base with a deep olive green wash that shades into dark purple-brown, then explodes into fiery red, orange, and yellow flames at the tip. *Coleus* 'Violet Tricolor' leaves feature bright magenta centers surrounded by an irregular violet band, all bordered with a lime green edge. Use these wildly patterned plants effectively by picking up on one leaf color and carrying that hue over into the companion plantings.

A color echo in the garden

You can use plants with variegated foliage as single specimens if they are large enough, locating them as a focal point where your eye returns time and time again, but you can also mass them for a really colorful effect. Whether used alone or grouped, a variegated plant looks best if planted next to, or near, a plant with a similar color in its leaves or flowers. This echoing of a color creates harmony even among plants with screaming colors.

For instance, you might plant the green-gold-and-reddish-orange variegated croton (*Codiaeum variegatum* var. *pictum* 'Andreanum') to flank an arbor covered with a golden trumpet vine (*Allamanda cathartica* 'Hendersonii'). The huge, golden yellow flowers obviously echo the pattern of burnished veins marking the glossy leaves of the foliage plant. Another repetition of color—this time a subtler one—also makes this combination a real winner: the reddish brown flower buds of this cultivar of golden trumpet vine echo the reddish orange markings on the croton's new growth. Double whammy.

These obvious color echoes are easy to create once you take the time to look closely at your plants and think about the intricacies of their colors as you go about incorporating them into the garden. It sometimes helps to take several leaves and flowers and walk around the nursery or garden center—or your garden before actually planting—holding one up against another to try out the color combinations before you make your final selections.

A subtler and very sophisticated color interaction—one that's sometimes hard to notice even though it's working effectively right before your eyes—is achieved by echoing the yellow stamens or throats of a flower with a swath of yellow or golden leaves planted underneath or nearby. For exam-

ple, the graceful white flowers of a skyflower (*Duranta erecta* 'Grandiflora White'), which bloom in lilac-like clusters, feature yellow throats in their centers and are also followed by golden nuggets of berries. Underplant this bushy shrub with the leafy golden mounds of *Lysimachia congestiflora* 'Aurea' to intensify the skyflower's blossoms and berries and to create a harmonious pairing. The color echo may not be noticed for what it is, but the effect will.

Warm and cool combinations

Yellow and blue reside opposite each other on the color wheel, making them complementary colors in the context of artistic color combinations. These natural companions create a riveting contrast of flame and ice. All cool colors have a bit of blue in them, such as turquoise (blue-green); warm colors have a bit of yellow in them, such as chartreuse (yellow-green). Warm and cool colors normally look good together, but only if they are hues from the opposite sides of the color wheel; the closer together they come, the more hazardous the arrangement. This means that you should avoid pairing the cool and warm hues of a color together. Such combinations spell color clash in almost anyone's book. For instance, scarlet is an orange-red, the warm hue of red, while magenta is a purple-red, the cool hue of red. These two colors, even in a tropical garden, look horrendous together—probably because they are so close to each other, yet so very far away.

You can, however, get away with matching up magenta flowers with chartreuse foliage—these hues are, after all, variations on red and green, two complementary colors. The cool-warm combination is anything but subtle, yet it works spectacularly in a rather scintillating way. 'Persian Queen' fancy-leaved geranium (*Pelargonium* 'Persian Queen') creates its own visual excitement when its bright magenta flowers begin to bloom, standing out vividly against the chartreuse leaves.

By using color echoes and minding the warm and cool hues throughout your tropical-style garden, you can tame its often wild colors like a ringmaster taming a lion. You need not fear that even a garden with the full spectrum of colors in it will be garish and unruly: as audacious as they are, you'll learn to partner up plants that work together to create some very compelling combinations.

Putting it all together

Once you begin to appreciate the daring details that tropical plants have to offer, try looking at them not as individual elements in a garden but as pieces of a puzzle that work together to create a garden scene. This, of course, goes for all plants, no matter what type of garden you're designing, but it is especially important with these bodacious beauties.

Contrasting leaf colors and shapes make for a riveting combination. Taro and purple sugarcane pair up for a bold and beautiful effect that spells tropical in anyone's book.

It's all in the leaf contrast

Most Temperate Zone gardens suffer from foliage boredom, but not so when tropical plants enter the picture. Tropicals offer so much dramatic foliage excitement that you might feel compelled to tame them a bit. Avoid like the plague locating plants that have leaves of the same size and shape next to each other. The idea is to create a textural contrast, which makes the bold-textured appear bolder and the fine-textured finer, playing up their inherent qualities and making them stand out.

Once you start thinking about it, the pairings become rather obvious. Palms (family Palmae) planted next to bananas (*Musa* spp.) come to mind immediately, since this combination occurs throughout the tropics. The dissected palm leaves have a linear line and fine texture that, when used against a backdrop of the coarse solidness of the huge, paddle-shaped banana leaves, stand out with startling clarity.

Other imaginative texture and shape combinations spring to mind, such as allowing the fine-textured, linear leaf shapes of sugarcane (*Saccharum officinarum*) to rise up from a mound of the bold-textured, heart-shaped foliage of elephant's ear (*Colocasia esculenta*), the two together evoking the mood of abstract art. Play up this artistic contrast of shape and texture further by varying the leaf colors of one of these same plants from the green of the species, choosing instead a cultivar with colorful leaves. For instance, you might pair up the smoky purple sugarcane (*S. o.* 'Violaceum') with the bright green of the *Colocasia* to heighten the contrast and create a scene brimming with vitality.

Once you grasp the concept, you can easily create wonderful plant combinations. Whether you're using only tropicals or integrating tropicals with the cold-hardy plants in your garden, select plants whose foliage contrasts with that of their neighbors in both shape and texture. That's a sure way to ban foliage boredom from the garden forever.

All flowers great and small

No matter how excellent a plant's foliage, all eyes turn to its flowers, especially when the plant is decked out in some of the bizarre concoctions that the tropics have to offer. Many tropicals excite the imagination with their gigantic flowers, which can become so large that you might wonder if the soil has been laced with steroids. The blossoms of angel's trumpet (*Brugmansia* spp.), for example, can grow 8 to 12 inches long or more, their silky-textured

This Long Island garden includes free-flowering *Brugmansia* × *insignis* (angel's trumpet), *Fuchsia* 'Gartenmeister', canna, and bougainvillea as well as tropical foliage plants.

cornets flaring to 6-inch-wide, fluted mouths. These great big flowers grow in clusters that dangle from the shrub's branch tips like holiday ornaments strung all over. Some hibiscus (*Hibiscus*) cultivars offer up crepe-paper-textured blossoms the size of dinner plates. These come in a rainbow of colors.

You can have a lot of fun playing with gargantuan blossoms, for their very size elicits surprise and wonder. Try emphasizing their extravagant dimensions by combining large-flowered plants with ones that have diminutive blooms; the contrast works to make their size ever greater—almost preposterous—adding a bit of humor to the setting.

When you start to choose plants for your garden, consider all of a flower's attributes—size, shape, texture, and color—just as you do with foliage. The same rules apply. Then begin making combinations of flowers, or of flowers and foliage, that play up the contrasts and echo the similarities between neighboring plants. You might wish to scatter plants with large blossoms throughout your garden, planting them in prominent locations to draw the eye to their voluptuous size and further cast the spell of tropical abundance.

The feathery, fragrant flowers of *Hedychium coccineum* (bottlebrush ginger) draw all eyes with their voluptuous size.

Remember, the more contrast you create between colors and textures, the more exciting the combination; the less contrast you create, the more soothing the combination. Up to a point, that is. Neither too much nor too little contrast is pleasing. The degree of contrast you choose is entirely up to you—after all, it's your garden, and you can make it look any way you want.

Scaling new heights

In the tropics, plants grow to enormous size because the growing season lasts all year, or most of the year, and the abundant rain and sun fuel rapid growth. In your tropical-style garden, your exotic subjects won't get to be anywhere near the size they do in the wild, but you do want to accentuate a sense of large scale and height as part of the tropical look you're after. This means using tall tropical-looking plants in groups to bring height to the garden.

Some of the fastest growers and tallest tropicals you can select for a Temperate Zone garden are banana (*Musa* spp. and *Ensete* spp.), canna lily (*Canna* spp.), palms (family Palmae), and castor bean (*Ricinus communis*). A canna lily, for instance, can grow from an overwintered tuber planted in early summer into an 8-foot giant in a month or so; some cultivars become even more statuesque.

When using tall plants in a bed or border, you'll want to keep the garden's overall scale in mind. A general rule of thumb is to make a border at least as wide as the height of the tallest plant in it, so it looks balanced. Where a building or hedge backs up a border, then the border's width might work at about two-thirds the building's height. These rules are, of course, not hard and fast but general guidelines that will help you use big tropicals in scale with your garden.

An upright clump of 12-foot-tall Zanzibar castor bean (*Ricinus communis* 'Zanzibarensis') might look stunning in a 6-foot-wide bed at the corner of a building, where it has the height of the building to anchor it. But that same plant in a 6-foot-wide bed in the center of a lawn will look lonely and top-heavy, if not downright silly. The castor bean plant needs a lot of lower plants around it in a widely planted area to create balance. Large tropicals look well situated when combined with tall and medium-height grasses and bamboos, to create a textural contrast as well as scale compatibility. You can also use them with other large tropicals or large perennials that have bold-textured flowers or jumbo-size leaves.

Plants as architecture

Keep in mind, too, that these big plants often have so much character that they create an architectural presence. This quality reflects a plant's strong stature and commanding good looks. An architectural plant has clean lines that aren't cluttered with a lot of fussy foliage. It typically exhibits a majestic branching pattern and an arresting leaf shape that contribute to its overall structure and form, commanding attention like a piece of sculpture. An architectural plant draws and holds your eye, acting as a focal point in the landscape. These plants are the prima donnas of the garden and need to be given center stage. (For a listing of tropical plants with architectural shapes, see page 205.)

The gorgeous fan-shaped fronds of *Sabal yapa* (thatch palm) have a strong architectural form, which gives them a commanding presence in the garden.

Focus on focal points

As you begin to compose a garden scene and bring plants together into a wondrous picture, it helps to include various focal points throughout the garden to create a cohesive whole. A focal point is something that catches your eye and holds it, something that you keep looking at over and over. Your eye is usually drawn to anything that looks distinct in its surroundings, something that stands out because it is different in form, color, or texture.

An architectural plant used as a single specimen among a group of less dramatic plants creates a focal point—as does a big, brightly colored one amid a sea of greenery. A garden bench, a big planter, a statue, or a fountain also stands out from its surroundings because it is a unique element. Some garden locations are natural focal points: the bend in a curving path, the end of a straight path, or a point off center in a long bed. Your eye tends to look there anyway, so if you position something striking and individual in that location, then it becomes a successful focal point.

Tropical plants make very good focal points in a garden composed mostly of cold-hardy plants, because many tropicals take to container culture and you can easily place one in the perfect spot in a border, on a patio, or along a path. And because most tropical plants generally have some extraordinary aspect—a dramatic leaf shape, a vivacious color scheme, or simply an overall exotic appearance—they usually draw attention if placed among cold-hardy plants. Their bold leaves or intensely vivid or immense flowers catch your eye, even from a distance, because they stand out so clearly. By drawing on tropicals this way when designing a Temperate Zone garden, you have a larger, more exciting plant palette to choose from when painting your garden picture.

Be careful not to include too many focal points in your garden, however, or it will become busy-looking, which defeats the purpose. Instead of scattering several focal elements throughout the garden, you might try grouping them. For instance, a long wooden bench with a big ironstone planter anchoring one end looks better than the bench and planter positioned about 5 feet or more apart. Your eye jumps from one to the other if they are separated but turns them into a single focal point when they are grouped. Focal points help to eliminate visual chaos in the garden, and they can tame the wildness of a tropical-style garden without compromising its character.

Shape echoes

Echoing colors from one plant to another and from one part of the garden to another works magic when you are designing a tropical-looking garden. So, too, does echoing similar shapes throughout a garden. Repeat, for example, the arching tufts and spiky leaves of a group of pineapple lilies (*Eucomis* spp.) by planting a much taller and larger spiky-shaped New Zealand flax (*Phormium tenax*) nearby. Place the *Phormium* not beside but several feet away from the *Eucomis,* the distance depending on the garden's size. This repeating pattern sets up a visual rhythm that directs your eye through the garden and has a taming influence on the conglomeration of plants within.

Using techniques such as this one is especially important when you are designing a tropical-style garden because it allows you to include a lot of exciting plants. Without some organizing principle, you might feel compelled to limit your choices to avoid creating a clutter, a hard thing to do with so many great-looking subjects to choose among. By echoing leaf and flower shapes (as well as color), you visually organize the plants within your garden, preventing them from vying with each other for attention.

When combining hardy and tropical plants, you can echo the large, rounded to heart-shaped leaves of low-growing perennials such as hostas (*Hosta* spp.) by using taller tropical plants with similar leaf shapes, such as elephant's ears (*Colocasia* spp., *Alocasia* spp., and *Xanthosoma* spp.), in the back of your design. These enormous tropicals can easily grow to 6 feet tall. By using blue, green, gold, and variegated hostas with elephant's ears in different leaf colors, you can create an overall effect that seems friendly and harmonious because of the repeated shapes but that is anything but boring because of the variation in leaf color and size.

In this Pennsylvania garden, a variegated yucca creates a focal point at the end of a walk and repeats the arching shape of the bromeliads in front.

Natural layers

In the natural landscape, especially in a temperate forest or a tropical rain forest, plants grow in layers from the ground upward, occupying every niche and cranny in the competition for light. Nearest the sky are the tallest trees, which can stretch to a height of several hundred feet. Beneath them spreads out a layer of lower trees and tall shrubs, called understory plants. The next layer contains smaller shrubs and large perennials, with the lowest layer consisting of low-growing perennials and ground covers. In a tropical region, the layers are even denser than in temperate regions, with vines and epiphytes invading whatever layers they can occupy. The most natural-looking gardens duplicate this structure and contain several layers of plants.

A tropical-style garden, especially if it is meant to have a wild, untamed air about it, calls out for layers of plants, from the treetops to the ground. Since it would be imprac- tical, if not downright impossible, to grow a true tropical tree to the size needed for the tallest layer in a temperate garden, you should rely on the existing trees in your landscape to provide that layer. The larger the trees you have to work with, the better. And the effect will be most realistic if they are broad-leaved trees such as oaks and ashes, not needle-leaved conifers such as pines and spruces.

Old established trees add an incredible amount of emotion to the gar- den with their rough-textured bark, huge branches, and imposing stature— and even their gnarled, exposed roots. By suspending several hanging baskets of orchids and ferns from the branches and tucking some bromeliads into the branch crotches, you can give any tree a tropical appearance and begin the process of layering the garden.

Add a few banana (*Musa* spp.) and palm (family Palmae) plants be- neath the big trees, and the understory layer starts to take shape with great tropical flair. The banana's oversize leaves not only cast deep shadows, they also rustle in the wind, adding to their credibility. A host of smaller shrubs, such as giant heart-leaved copperleaf (*Acalypha wilkesiana* 'Macrophylla'), croton (*Codiaeum variegatum* var. *pictum*), and Hawaiian snowbush (*Breynia disticha* 'Roseapicta'), make good choices for the lower shrub level at the edge of the jungle, where they get some sun. Or plant them under an opening in the overhead canopy where sunlight can reach them. These shrubs' intense leaf colors work perfectly to add bursts of color where it's needed at eye level.

Many low leafy or spreading plants, such as coleus (*Coleus* spp.), tuber- ous begonia (*Begonia tuberhybrida*), and Cape fuchsia (*Phygelius* spp.), can fill in the gaps below. Golden creeping daisy (*Wedelia trilobata*), lantana (*Lantana* spp.), and African daisy (*Arctotis* × *hybrida*) make great flowering ground covers, blanketing the ground with a colorful display. But foliage color abounds in this level, too. Try parrot leaf (*Alternanthera ficoidea* var. *amoena*), purple heart vine (*Tradescantia pallida* 'Purple Heart'), and sunset plant (*Lysimachia congestiflora*) for a season-long carpet of brilliant leaves. Use these lower plants in groups and large masses, echoing the colors and shapes of the taller plants.

Necessary vines

Your layering is not complete until you've added a curtain of vines to descend from a tree branch or crawl over a shrub. Vines prove to be that nec- essary missing link that once in place says "Presto, it's a jungle." Vines con- nect the layers, lending a rampant atmosphere to the garden. In a tropical- style garden, you don't have to limit yourself to tropical vines if you want a tropical look—the stout, twisted trunks of old hardy vines such as wisteria add immensely to the jungle look and impart an effect that's practically

impossible to achieve in a temperate climate with tender vines. (See chapter 4, page 87, for more about how to use hardy vines.)

Vines add a whole new dimension to small-space gardens because they can grow upward in a narrow space, adding height and an overhead layer where a tree would never have the room. A 10-inch pot can nurture a climbing vine such as passionflower (*Passiflora* spp.), which can scramble up and around to heights of 20 feet or more. Vines provide shade in sunny areas when trained to grow over an overhead structure. A hammock suspended under a vine-smothered arbor gives the impression of a secure nest tucked away in a jungle.

You can plant a tropical vine to scamper up just about anything as long as you match climbing style with the support. Flowering vines planted next to a hardy spring-flowering shrub take over the shrub by summer and then deliver another season's worth of flowers in the same spot. Vines make excellent vertical accents in container plantings when grown on a stake or trellis plunged into the container.

Twining vines need something sturdy to wrap their arms around—they cannot scale a blank wall, which poses no problem to a vine that climbs by suction cups. Vines with tendrils, such as passionflower (*Passiflora* spp.), do best with a more delicate support than those that twist and twine their branches, such as moonflower (*Ipomoea alba*).

Part of the fun in growing vines is getting these recalcitrant plants to climb where you want them. This act is ironically termed "training the vine," but in actuality the vine often trains you instead—trains you not to ignore it. To get the vine started, you may need to tie it with a piece of twine to the tree trunk, arbor post, or base of the railing where you want it to grow. In a few days check the vine again—it may be sending out grasping shoots every which way except where you want it to grow, vainly searching for more support. Gently return the vine to the post or other support and tie it again, up higher, or untangle the branches from the shrub it grabbed in lieu of the lat-

Bougainvillea 'California Gold' and 'Orange King' mingle on a rustic arbor to create spectacular color overhead.

tice fence where you intended it to be and weave them in and out of the slats. Repeat this process every few days when the vine is young, because it will grow astoundingly fast; ignore it for a week and you're dead meat, for it has surely now hopelessly woven itself into a tangle reminiscent of a real jungle—well, that's what you wanted anyway, wasn't it? (For a listing of tropical vines, see page 204.)

Tropicalizing your garden

Skillfully using leaf textures, colors, shapes, and sizes combined in layers with flowering plants to all echo each other in color and form is an achievement in itself. But you can go a few steps further in giving your garden a true tropical personality. The finishing touches you bring to the garden help to conjure up the exotic setting you're after and sometimes, in the process, bring a dash of humor to the whole experiment.

Tropical-style structures and statuary

Every garden needs a place where you can sit and enjoy it—a place where you can dine outdoors, rest, or even nap. So you can savor your tropical-style garden to the fullest, design it around an outdoor sitting area such as a deck or patio furnished with rustic wooden, bamboo, or rattan furniture. String up a hammock between the trees and your tropical spell is cast. Even if you never actually get to use the hammock, the sight of it makes the garden more inviting and creates illusions of relaxation even while you're sweating among the mosquitoes, pulling weeds. You might even add a fire pit to evoke memories of camping out in an exotic place.

The sitting area in this Long Island garden is a tiki hut with a fire pit in front—perhaps for hosting a luau. *Phyllostachys aureosulcata* (golden groove bamboo), a very cold-hardy plant, forms a realistic backdrop.

If it's in your dreams and budget, adding a garden building, one patterned after a bit of tropical architecture, gives the garden a sense of place and further tropicalizes the theme. Try fabricating a thatched dining pavilion or garden retreat in the style of a Caribbean palm-thatched bungalow or a Polynesian tiki hut. Sitting under a thatched roof on a stormy afternoon listening to the rain beat out a clattering rhythm and surrounded by luxurious foliage plants can transport you to a far-off world.

If your garden needs a privacy fence, or a fence to help create a garden room, go for a style with a rustic look if you want to emphasize a tropical motif. Build a screening fence from bamboo poles, split bamboo, or reed matting to make an Asian-looking screen, or erect masonry

This Seattle-area garden owes its ancient-world appearance to the stylized walls and colonnaded pergola that frame the formal garden pool.

walls and paint them in clear bright colors for a South American look. You can install sections of lattice and cover it with fast-growing vines, or erect a wooden plank fence and allow it to fade to a dull natural gray so its color disappears in the background while showcasing the plantings.

Don't overlook the dramatic difference that even a simple piece of sculpture, pottery, or garden art can make in your garden. The right objet d'art in the right place adds an incredible amount of excitement, serving as something of an exclamation point to draw the eye. Choose something evocative of an ancient culture, something old-looking and Asian, African, or South American in style—a moss-covered urn, a massive primitive figurine, a wooden carving, or anything that lends your garden a sense of history and place. Colorful pieces of pottery or painted art might be used to complement a specific plant or color scheme. Place the sculpture among the plants to create the illusion that it has been hidden there for centuries, or that it was buried by the jungle and only recently unearthed.

A far-fetched folly

Some might think that growing tropicals in a temperate garden is folly enough—after all, no one expects to see a palm or banana tree growing in a temperate garden. So you might want to underscore the eccentricity by adding a garden folly to your tropical-looking setting, maybe just for the fun of it. A garden folly created in the fashion of an ancient ruined temple or grotto is a theatrical note that brings a bit of humor to the garden.

In designing your folly, you can let your imagination run away to some far-off land and return with blueprints for something unique and generally useless. Your contrived ruin might consist of a few broken columns and toppled statues, a massive Buddha and blocks of mossy stone, or a primitive water urn and Polynesian sculpture. Or you can purchase a ready-made folly. For example, Haddonstone, a British company that specializes in decorative cast stone, sells a realistic miniature ruin complete with pillars, arches, balustrades, and portico.

Locate the folly at the end of a winding footpath through the foliage, so visitors discover it as they turn the bend. To complete the illusion, plant the ruin so the remnants are overrun with vines and vegetation.

Water, water everywhere

Natural-looking ponds or garden pools with fountains make delicious features to add to a tropical-style garden, enhancing its tranquillity. You can construct a vinyl-lined pond to look quite realistic, surrounded by a combination of flat rocks, a lawn edge, or

This folly at the bend of a leafy path, at Heronswood Nursery near Seattle, makes visitors feel transported to a ruined temple in Thailand or Cambodia.

a gravel beach (avoid ringing it with round, flat stones if you want it to look naturalistic). You might add a small waterfall fed by a babbling brook at one side to bring the music of running water to the scene. A more formal pool might be a concrete square or rectangular structure tiled to reflect a Middle Eastern–style tropical garden. Consider raising it aboveground so that it is easier to tend and so its edge can then double as a sitting area.

Not only is a water feature a magnetic focal point around which to build the garden, it's also a place to grow many unusual tropical aquatics or bog plants. In addition, ponds provide a home for fish, frogs, and turtles as well as much-needed water for birds and other wildlife.

Tropical water lilies (*Nymphaea* spp.) are favorite denizens of tropical-style ponds. These romantic plants come in a vast array of pure glistening colors ranging from pastel pinks, lavenders, and blues to vivid reds and magentas and warm yellows and oranges. Different types bloom during the day or at night. Most night bloomers are intensely fragrant. The flowers of tropical water lilies are larger than those of hardy ones, and their floating leaves are often mottled and spotted with dark burgundy.

Floating tropical plants that do not need to be rooted to any soil include water hyacinth (*Eichhornia crassipes*), which bears showy spikes of lavender blossoms; water lettuce (*Pistia stratiotes*), which has fuzzy, jade green, lettucelike leaves; and fairy moss (*Azolla caroliniana*), a charming floating fern. Papyrus (*Cyperus* spp.) grows with its feet in wet or boggy soil, adding vertical structure to a pond arrangement with its leafy heads.

This pond with its gravel beach gives a naturalistic note to any tropical-style garden. Cannas and papyrus flourish in tubs sunk in the pond. Aquatics include water lilies and water hyacinths.

The best way to grow tropical aquatics is in plastic tubs of soil sunk beneath the water's surface. Water lilies should be positioned so that there is 6 to 18 inches of water above the surface of the soil, depending on the size of the plant. Elevate the containers on rocks if need be so that they are at the proper height. Grow bog plants that flourish with wet feet along the edge of the pond, in special boggy-soil pockets created from the pond's liner. Tropical aquatics can be easily overwintered indoors in a semidormant state or can be treated as annuals. (See chapter 5.)

Some tropical plants that are normally grown in traditional garden beds can also be grown as bog or shallow-water plants, conditions under which they'll reach an enormous size. Many canna lilies (*Canna* spp.) and elephant's ears (*Colocasia* spp.) flourish when grown along boggy pond edges or in tubs submerged in a pond. For the best results, start them in heavy soil, kept very wet, and place them in the pond so that the top of their container is 2 to 3 inches below the water's surface.

Swimming-pool artistry

Planting areas around swimming pools are ideal for lush plantings, perhaps reminiscent of tropical vacations past where you sunbathed to the tune of the

Lush plantings transform a swimming pool into a lagoon that invites swimmers to dive in while keeping an eye out for alligators. Tropical plants grow among cold-hardy ornamental grasses and perennials.

pounding surf and palm fronds rasping in the breeze. A tropical-theme garden seems fitting around a swimming pool that incorporates a bar and lounge and sunning and dining areas. Your swimming pool can be the sparkling turquoise of the Caribbean Sea or the dark navy blue of a Belizean lagoon. The water color derives from the paint hue used on a gunite pool or from the vinyl liner of a lined pool, so choose a color to go with the mood you want to create.

Since a swimming pool gets used most often in summer in temperate areas, it makes sense to plant the area surrounding it with tropicals, which are also at their best during the entire swimming season. Tropical plants can easily be used to soften the pool's edge and give the pool a naturalistic setting. You can further turn a swimming pool into a tropical swimming hole by landscaping it with natural materials such as river-bottom stones and boulders. Instead of a diving board, add a diving rock or hang a stout rope from a tree branch to use as a jumping-off point.

Containers filled with a mixture of sizzling tropicals both dress up and soften the paving surrounding a pool. Foliage plants with intensely colored leaves are especially useful because they don't shed flowers into the water. Use large containers singly or in groups to balance the size of the pool. Here, where swimmers lounge and sunbathe, the planters can really be appreciated up close.

Have fun with fragrant flowers

Many tropical flowers, whether great or small, give off luscious fragrances, attracting pollinators and people alike to explore their beauty. The heady sweet scent of jasmine (*Jasminum* spp.) is so intense that it can almost knock you down as it saturates the garden with its presence. These tropical perfumes hang in the air on a sultry summer's day and waft through the garden whenever a gentle breeze blows. Combine a romantic scent with the rattle of palm fronds and all the senses find themselves stimulated.

Not all tropical flowers are as pervasively fragrant as jasmine, and some may require a searching nose to find the aromatic source. Other tropicals may be disappointingly scentless during the day, holding off releasing their perfume until the evening, when they somehow manage to dispense their scent as if equipped with an atomizer. In order to enjoy these tropical bouquets to the fullest, be sure to locate a fragrant plant where you'll pass by it frequently. Prime locations for best sniffing include along a path or walkway, in a container on a patio or near the swimming pool where you sit during the day or evening, or under a kitchen or bedroom window. Be sure, too, that night-scented flowers find a position close to home where you walk or sit outdoors in a romantically lit area at night. (For a listing of tropical plants with fragrant flowers, see page 204.)

Outdoor lighting lets you enjoy your garden on a leisurely evening. Lanterns and torches cast soft, romantic light.

Light the way

A garden designed to be lit after dark is a garden that can be enjoyed during as many hours of the night as it can during the day—perhaps even more hours if your only leisure time is in the evening. Nighttime lighting in a tropical-style garden is a very important part of its design, because the garden looks its best during the months when you'll want to be outside in the evening. Such lighting on a terrace or patio surrounded by tropical plants increases their drama by deepening the shadows or silhouetting their forms.

Outdoor lighting can take several forms. The best method for overall lighting is to inconspicuously mount floodlights high up in several trees and/or on the roofline of the house, so they shine down from overhead, casting a luminescent light that simulates moonlight. These lights will also cast shadows from palm fronds and banana leaves, adding to the tropical spell.

Avoid bright lights at eye level or just above head height, because such illumination glares into your eyes and looks unnatural. Ground-level lighting for paths may light your footsteps but won't help you enjoy the garden around you, because it leaves the plants in darkness. For a dramatic effect, you can use up-lighting to illuminate the silhouette of a large specimen tree hung with vines and epiphytes. Place a spotlight at the base of the tree and turn it upward, aiming it so it skims along the trunk and heads off toward the stars, not into your eyes. All these types of lighting create a garden that you can see and enjoy after sundown, but keep the wattage as low as possible to simulate moonlight, not midday sunlight.

To add further to the mood, you can use lanterns and candles around the garden. Protect open candles with glass hurricane globes to prevent them from blowing out. Suspend the lanterns from an arbor or from brackets mounted on a wall, or place them on a table or on the ground, as long as they are safely out of the path of pets and children, or even clumsy adults. Torches and tiki lights mounted on posts can be secured into the ground around the garden to create a Hawaiian atmosphere. With their flames licking the breeze, you'll surely hear drumbeats and calypso music in the air.

Tropicals in traditional gardens

Because of their diversity of characteristics, tropical plants integrate easily into most temperate-region gardens—you don't have to use them only for creating a tropical-looking garden or a garden that consists solely of tropical plants. They find a place and look good almost anywhere, combining well with almost all other types of plants. And the combinations are endless.

No matter where you use tropicals, be sure, however, that you meet their cultural needs—some need shade and some need sun. Most, but not all, flourish in heat, so in a northern climate where the summers are hot, a tropical's cultural needs are automatically provided for. But whatever garden situation you have, you can find a tropical to fill the bill.

Tropical houseplants frequently perform better indoors if they've been summered outdoors in a lightly shady, protected location. Conversely, tropicals that you've chosen especially to be prize performers in an outdoor display may need to be overwintered as houseplants so they can grow bigger and lusher over the years. (A cherished mature tropical can often be stored dormant over the winter in a frost-free place; see chapter 5.) You can easily integrate houseplants such as zebra plant (*Calathea zebrina*), ivy (*Hedera* spp.), orchids, snake plant (*Sansevieria trifasciata*), spider plant (*Chlorophytum comosum*), wax plant (*Hoya carnosa*), Swiss cheese plant (*Monstera deliciosa*), philodendron (*Philodendron* spp.), and schefflera (*Schefflera arboricola*) into your garden design, whether you use just a plant or two or a whole collection.

Planting a few tropicals among the perennials in a traditional perennial border—just as you would plant annuals—livens up the planting significantly because these exotics add such wonderful foliage variety to the sameness of a typical planting. You can combine large-growing tropicals, subtropicals, and tender perennials into mixed shrub borders as well. It's as easy as adding a hardy perennial or shrub. The only difference is that you will have to replant them each year.

And because tropicals and subtropicals come into their stride as the growing season progresses, most pay dividends in autumn, blooming continuously until frost or putting on a luxurious show of foliage when the perennials around them are looking tired. Many foliage plants flourish in the cool nighttime temperatures of autumn, which further intensifies their leaf coloration.

You can find tropical plants to fit anywhere in a traditional perennial or mixed border, from low ground-covering ones to towering back-of-the-border types. Tropicals with broad, fleshy, or ferny leaves, or ones that have an herbaceous appearance, work best in the perennial border, because they won't look out of place with the surrounding plants. When using tropicals in a hardy-plant border, it's still important to make them look as if they belong, not as though they were just plugged in to fill a gap. You can easily do this by repeating leaf colors or leaf shapes, as described earlier in this chapter. Use a single large specimen as a focal point or mass smaller ones into drifts, just as you would with any other type of plant.

Most traditional houseplants are tropical plants that benefit from summering outdoors. Gather them together to make an attractive display in a lightly shaded area near the house or under a tree.

First steps

If you're starting with a landscape containing mature trees and shrubs that you plan to keep, then you already have a garden backbone onto which you can build. Plants that have an inherently tropical feeling—such as those with large, coarse leaves—are especially important. Emphasize and accentuate these plants by clearing out areas around them and then underplanting with a ground cover that shows them off. Use existing large mature plants as support for vines or rambling shrubs. (See chapter 4 for more about using tropical-looking hardy plants.)

When adding a new section to an existing garden, you can approach the task in many ways, but it helps to put in the garden's "bone" structure first. You may want to incorporate a water feature, a sitting area, or an architectural element in the beginning stages. From there add the biggest plants—the hardy trees and shrubs—and then the perennials. Finally, integrate the tropicals into the garden, using them in groups or as focal points. Or you can also go all out and plant the entire new garden with tropicals.

A garden structure constitutes part of the backbone of the garden, serving as a prominent focal point that gives the garden form. You can use a gazebo or a summerhouse as the destination at the end of a path and create a patio or terrace around it. Assuming you are starting a garden from bare ground, once you have the garden retreat and patio in place, then plant the permanent trees and shrubs to flesh out the garden's skeleton. Add containerized tropicals to the beds as plunge plants, sunk into the ground, or plant tropicals right in the soil. Set potted plants around the patio and place hanging plants in the trees. Then as a final touch, situate a rampant vine to clamber up and over the garden building.

Remember that you'll probably be looking at your garden twelve months of the year, so consider what it will look like in winter when devoid of tropicals and perennials and deciduous leaves. Use some broad-leaved evergreens as a backdrop for your tropical planting and around the garden retreat, if it's in view from the house, so they can bring greenery and interest to the garden during winter. Borderline hardy plants, which have to be protected for the winter, can be wrapped with some type of insulating material and then covered with burlap or reed matting to make into playful winter ornaments or sculptures. (See chapter 5.)

Creating a dramatic entrance

In a well-designed landscape, the entrances to the house and garden are often announced with significant plantings. A front-entrance planting points the way to the door and greets visitors with a warm welcome. This area makes a perfect place to display something different or to position an eye-catching arrangement so it indicates that this is the way to go. Symmetrical plantings usually flank a formal entrance. Matched pairs of planters containing tropical plants on each side of the door make a wonderful greeting. For a very formal feel, use standards (tree-form shapes) trained to have a treelike trunk and a round head of foliage and flowers. (See chapter 3, page 61.)

If your garden style is to be tropical-looking, herald this theme at the entrance to the garden. A garden's entryway is often marked by an arbor or a gate, which conceals the garden beyond, adding to the mystery of what is to come. An arbor calls out to be entwined with a colorful vine or scrambling shrub. In a more casual setting, bold exotic plantings work wonderfully as exclamation points that signal a transition from one part of the garden to another.

Tropicals in the shade

Gardening in the shade challenges most gardeners, especially those who long for brilliant color. Since many tropicals grow naturally on the jungle

At Heronswood Nursery, a moist area in the light shade cast by high-pruned trees was transformed into a primeval swamp by making islands planted with cold-hardy *Musa basjoo* (Japanese fiber banana).

floor, they are adapted to growing and blooming quite well in the shade, offering bouquets of flowers and rich color to the dimmer areas of your garden. By adding tropicals to your shade garden, you open a new door onto countless possibilities and combinations of plants. You can simply plunge a few brightly colored foliage plants into the shade garden to brighten up your existing mixture of ferns and hostas. Try a few big dramatic plants such as tree ferns (*Dicksonia* spp. and *Cyathea* spp.) and bananas (*Musa* spp.), then use lower shade-tolerant ones such as bromeliads, begonias (*Begonia* spp.), flowering maple (*Abutilon* spp.), flamingo flower (*Anthurium* spp.), fancy-leaved caladium (*Caladium bicolor*), rex-begonia vine (*Cissus discolor*), Amazon lily (*Eucharis* × *grandiflora*), and tabletop fern (*Pteris cretica* 'Albolineata').

Keep in mind, though, that many shady situations are dry and depleted of nutrients, because shallow tree roots quickly suck up the soil moisture. If the soil in such areas is thin and dry, most tropicals may die of thirst if planted in the ground. Better to make an arrangement of containers right on top of the ground, which can be heavily mulched or planted with a ground cover, so you can water them easily with a gentle spray from an overhead sprinkler. That way they won't compete with the trees for moisture but can happily enjoy the dappled light under the tree.

A shady spot under a tree is a great place to transition houseplants into the great outdoor garden. Tropical plants that have been overwintered indoors need to be placed in the shade when first brought outside for the summer or their leaves will burn because the plants are unaccustomed to the light intensity. Even sun-loving indoor plants need to be acclimated in light shade before they can receive full sun. You can add them temporarily to a shade garden in early summer and then move them as the garden gets going and after they have adjusted to their summer quarters.

Creating a relaxing retreat

A sitting area in the garden can be a destination or a stop-off along the way. The site ought to have interesting plantings because you'll spend many pleasant hours there; use it as a staging area for some of your favorite tropical plants, especially fragrant ones, so you can thoroughly enjoy them nearby. A bench tucked into a shady spot along a path makes a perfect place for a container planting of shade-loving tropicals. Adding a table and chairs to a secluded nook in the garden can transform it into an outdoor dining area, even if it isn't a formally paved section. Set up the table right on the lawn or in a mulched or graveled area. Such retreats are often a place to get away from it all—what could be better than to escape to the tropics for an afternoon right in your own backyard?

CHAPTER THREE

Sizzling Container Gardens

On the hard, flat, unadorned expanse of a patio, deck, or balcony, you can give free rein to your creativity by using pots and containers to make a vibrant, gardenlike setting where it would otherwise be impossible because there's no ground to plant in. Tropicals are naturals for this treatment, and you may even already be growing many of them year-round in pots. The sun lovers among them really flourish in the sun-drenched heat of such surroundings and give a nonstop performance of color and texture right where you need it most—up close in a location that you use and enjoy or pass by every day.

Almost any tropical plant adapts to pot culture and grows happily outdoors in late spring, summer, and early fall in a temperate setting. Some perform best in shady conditions and make great choices for bringing leafy touches to porches or shade-cooled patios and decks. Others need full sun to look their most dazzling.

There are two basic ways to design with tropicals in containers: grow them as showy specimen plants or in colorful mixed planters. A specimen plant should be grown alone in its own container or perhaps be accompanied by a cushion of ground cover at its feet. Choose especially large, sculptural plants, or those that are in constant glorious flower, such as honey bush (*Melianthus major*), with its gorgeous, toothed, waxy-blue leaves and zigzag shape, or angel's trumpet (*Brugmansia* spp.), which produces tall, shrubby growth and clusters of impressive, trumpet-shaped blossoms. Specimen plants look best if you grow them in a decorative planter, one whose color or texture complements or accentuates the plant's flowers or foliage. Cover the soil surface with a decorative mulch, such as washed gravel or stone, wood chips, pinecones, or shells, or plant a trailing plant to hide the soil and spill over the edge. For most specimens to reach their full, magnificent potential, you'll need to overwinter them indoors in your house, sunporch, or greenhouse or in some kind of dormant state. (See chapter 5.)

A mixed container holds several different kinds of plants arranged into a beautiful design—rather like a small-scale garden within the confines of the planter. When creating mixed planters, try to choose plants that look attractive when grouped together and that also share the same growth

When grown in containers, tropicals are easy to care for and to overwinter.

requirements. This isn't always easy, but when it's done well, the result is a small garden with splendid dimensions.

Both mixed planters and specimen plants solve design problems in many ways. Because they are so attention-getting, planters are like the icing on the cake when it comes to a garden's design. They are the finishing touch that can bring it all together and meld one part of the garden with another.

Create a living bouquet

A mixed container of tropicals at its peak explodes with concentrated foliage and flower color in the best tradition of a tropical-style garden. It's a complete garden designed on a very small scale, and it should and can be a wondrous study of foliage and flower colors and textures. To create compelling combinations, follow the rules for combining textures and colors described in chapter 2, by marrying warm and cool colors, echoing foliage and flower colors and shapes, and contrasting textures and sizes.

Beyond selecting the right colors and textures, you need to fill in the layers of the pot with the right types of plants. This is the real secret to creating a scintillating container display. Stuff plants into it, placing them very close together, much closer than you would in the garden. The container is meant to look like a lovely living bouquet when you've finished planting it, not as if it needs to grow for a month or two. For a successful combination, you'll need at least three different kinds of plants, one to represent each of the three structural elements: height, filler, and edge. By targeting plants for each of these roles, you're sure to create a composition that works.

Choose a dramatic tall, upright grower to soar up from the container, giving the arrangement height. It can reach up to about one and a half to two times the height of the pot and not look unbalanced. Use a single specimen if it's a big plant with bold foliage, or group two or three thinner plants to form a clump. You might even use a flowering vine such as morning glory (*Ipomoea* spp.), passionflower (*Passiflora* spp.), or mandevilla (*Mandevilla* spp.) for height in a container, supporting it on a stake, post, or bamboo tepee or even allowing it to wind its way up into the rafters of an overhead structure or a wall trellis. Tree forms (standards) may also be used for height, although they are often best grown as single specimens to show off their long, elegant legs, with only a simple low ground cover to soften the container's edges.

Filler plants are midsize plants, usually full and bushy in form. Use them to occupy the middle of your composition to create substance and weight below the taller, upright plant that gives the container garden its height. The filler plants can be bold- or fine-textured, or a combination of both, but it's their rounded to arching shape that is most important, since they are meant to take up most of the pot's volume. Choose one to three or more kinds of filler plants, depending on the container's size.

Lastly, soften the container's edge with cascading or weeping plants, such as green-and-white-variegated creeping fig (*Ficus pumila* 'Variegata') or the feathery-textured lotus vine (*Lotus berthelotii*). These drape outward and downward as a counterpoint to the tall plant in the center, occupying a different level. These edge plants also integrate all the plants in the container so that the whole arrangement brims vigorously over the container's edge. (For a listing of tropical plants for mixed containers, see pages 205–6.)

A mixed container creates a living bouquet of flowers and foliage and can be set right in a bed that lacks color or excitement.

Here are six suggestions for creating imaginative containers. Four are for sun and two for shade; all for 20- to 22-inch containers.

For sun

Fiery Color Combo   This hot color combination features glowing yellows and oranges made even more exciting by the textural contrasts between the bold canna leaves and the soft russelia foliage. Repetition plays a role, with leaf variegation painting both the tall canna and the trailing sunset plant, and bright orange defining the canna's and the cigar flower's blossoms. Pineapple lily creates an exclamation point.

Height	1 *Canna* × *generalis* 'Pretoria' (canna lily)
Filler	3 *Cuphea ignea* (cigar flower, firecracker plant)
	2 *Eucomis bicolor* (pineapple lily)
	4 *Oxalis vulcanicola* 'Copper Glow' (sorrel, shamrock)
Edge	2 *Russelia equisetiformis* (coral fountain, fountain plant)
	4 *Lysimachia congestiflora* (sunset plant)

Exotic Pastels   Soft shades of pink, purple, blue, and white define this design. The white in the passionflower blossoms is echoed in the rest of the planter by the cat whiskers' flowers and the silvery African daisy leaves. The soft dusty pink of the ruby grass's flower heads adds movement and complements the lantana's blossoms. The addition of purple heart vine, with its deep purple foliage, pulls the container together and enriches the color scheme.

Height	1 *Passiflora caerulea* (passionflower) (trained on a tripod)
Filler	3 *Orthosiphon stamenius* 'White' (cat whiskers)
	2 *Rhynchelytrum repens* (ruby grass, natal grass)
	3 *Arctotis* × *hybrida* 'Rosita' (African daisy)
Edge	3 *Lantana camara* 'Pink Caprice' (lantana)
	3 *Tradescantia pallida* 'Purple Heart' (purple heart vine)

Peach and Plum   The colors used in this container are reminiscent of ripe summer fruit, of Elberta peaches and Damson plums. Warm peachy hues paint the coleus leaves and the Cape fuchsia flowers, while the purple-brown of the New Zealand flax shows up again in the purple lip of the Cape fuchsia flowers, the plum hues of the coleus's stems and leaf undersides, the dark venation of the scented geranium foliage, and the iridescent leaf hairs of the purple velvet plant.

Height	1 *Phormium* 'Atropurpureum' (New Zealand flax, flax lily)
Filler	3 *Phygelius capensis* 'Trewidden Pink' (Cape fuchsia)
	3 *Coleus blumei* 'Aurora' (coleus)
	3 *Pelargonium quercifolium* 'Fair Ellen' (scented geranium)
Edge	4 *Gynura aurantiaca* (purple velvet plant)

Electric Neon Chartreuse and purple-black dominate this exotic planter, the two colors making a dramatic contrast. The black-marked leaves of the elephant's ears and the solid black leaves of the sweet potato vine intensify the chartreuse heat of the skyflower's and fancy-leaved geranium's leaves. Add magenta flowers from the geranium and the combination only becomes hotter. The centipede plant adds an exotic structure to the whole bouquet.

Height	1 *Colocasia esculenta* 'Illustris' (elephant's ear, taro, dasheen)
Filler	3 *Duranta erecta* 'Cuban Gold' (skyflower, pigeon berry)
	3 *Homalocladium platycladum* (centipede plant, ribbon bush)
	5 *Pelargonium* × *zonale* 'Persian Queen' (fancy-leaved geranium)
Edge	3 *Ipomoea batatas* 'Blackie' (sweet potato vine)

For shade

Sophisticated Variegation Eye-catching foliage patterns brighten this container, adding interest to a shady planter. At the top of the design, the green-and-white-variegated patterns of the flowering maple's leaves echo the pattern in the dainty, creeping fig's leaves, which spill over the bottom edge. The caladium's billowy, pink-and-white leaves add color and texture while echoing the fuchsia's pink flowers.

Height	1 *Abutilon* × 'Souvenir de Bonn' standard (flowering maple)
Filler	3 *Caladium bicolor* 'Pink Symphony' (angel wings, caladium)
	5 *Fuchsia* × *hybrida* 'Mrs. J. D. Fredericks' (fuchsia)
Edge	5 *Ficus pumila* 'Variegata' (creeping fig)

Tropical Shade This container evokes the shady atmosphere of a deep tropical rain forest. The flamingo flower and bromeliad bloom throughout the summer, bringing vivid red hues to the design. The rubber tree's rich burgundy repeats in the leaf undersides and stems of the rex-begonia vine, while the leafy green Boston fern softens and ties the group together. All the plants in this container make great houseplants, and you could actually leave them in their original pots and group them together in a large planter so they can be easily separated again and overwintered. Or you can unpot them and mingle them more closely, perhaps overwintering the planter in a bright spot indoors.

Height	1 *Ficus elastica* 'Burgundy Knight' (rubber tree)
Filler	1 *Anthurium andraeanum* (flamingo flower, red-flowered)
	1 *Neoregelia* spp. (bromeliad)
	3 *Nephrolepis exaltata* 'Bostoniensis' (Boston fern)
Edge	3 *Cissus discolor* (rex-begonia vine)

❖❖❖

Putting the pot together

Opposite: In this mixed container, *Phormium* 'Yellow Wave' makes a vertical accent, *Coleus* and *Ipomoea* 'Margarita' act as filler to create volume, and *Tradescantia* and licorice vine spill over the side.

Below: When a vine like this *Mandevilla* is planted in a container, it needs a support. Here, it climbs a stake then tumbles down to mingle with variegated *Miscanthus*.

Start planting from the center and work out, placing the tallest plant in the center, or a bit off-center to the rear if the planter is to be viewed from one side. Add the filler plants next, snuggling them up against the centerpiece. Then add cascading edge plants at intervals around the perimeter of the container, leaving some space in between to avoid creating a uniform collar around the pot.

Be sure to always rough up or tease out the roots from the root balls of the plants you're adding to the container. This important step lets the plants know they are no longer confined to their original pot and now have lots more root space to explore. If you don't do this, the roots may continue to grow in a tight compacted circle, sapping the plant of its vigor, because they cannot get enough moisture and nourishment to support its growth.

When sizing a pot, a good rule of thumb is to allow the root ball of a specimen plant, when freshly potted, only 2 to 3 inches of growing room on each side and no more, or it risks being waterlogged. In a mixed container, the plants can be pretty tightly packed in there, with only a few inches of growing room around the sides.

Ongoing grooming

Your living bouquet does just that—it lives and grows and changes, so you may need to make some alterations over the course of several months. Pinch and prune as needed to keep plants in form. Often one species grows more vigorously than another and has to be kept in check so it won't take over the entire planter. The edge plants in particular may need to be trimmed back if they trail too much. Deadhead spent flowers. You might even wish to ruthlessly pull out some plants if they aren't performing well—or if you want a change—and replace them with something else later in the season.

Positioning the pots

Containers make a high impact wherever you use them, and they can be used in so very many places. Try grouping containers on a patio or deck to create an intense but intimate tropical-looking setting. The pots can be rearranged and moved to change the effect—a plus in a small-space garden, where you might not have room for as much variety as you'd like.

Containers even work well placed among the permanent plants in a garden bed. You might pop a big, bouquetlike planter into the garden to cover a bare spot left behind when spring bulbs fade or place a dramatic single specimen on a pedestal to produce an instant focal point. Or set a pair of containers in the lawn on either side of the garden gate to point the way for visitors to go.

This huge specimen of *Phormium* New Zealand flax ('Yellow Wave') winters indoors in a conservatory but spends summers as a focal point amid a bed of flowering annuals and perennials.

Try clustering a number of single potted specimens together to create a gardenlike effect. Arrange them as you would design a mixed container planting (but with each plant in its own decorative pot) so you compose a pleasing grouping. Put the tallest ones in back and the lowest ones in front, but don't do this in a rigid way—play around with the arrangement so it makes an interesting combination of forms, colors, and textures. Shade-loving ferns and begonias, which are excellent and easy to winter over as houseplants, do fine when gathered together like this on a shady porch or deck.

Because they command so much attention, containers do an excellent job of framing a gate or front door, directing visitors to the home's or garden's entrance. Located on both sides of the door or gate, two symmetrically designed planters make a fairly formal statement, which is suitable for

You can easily train certain bushy tropical shrubs, such as fuchsia (*Fuchsia* spp.), scented geranium (*Pelargonium* spp.), hibiscus (*Hibiscus* spp.), coleus (*Coleus* spp.), African mallow (*Anisodontea* × *hypomandarum*), lantana (*Lantana* spp.), silver-dollar plant (*Eucalyptus cinerea*), and flowering maple (*Abutilon* spp.), into standards (tree-form shapes) with a single trunk and a beautiful round head of flowers or foliage. Fast growers take about six months to train; others may take a year or more. They'll only get more beautiful the older they become, so be sure you have a place for overwintering them.

The basic idea is to develop a single strong, woody stem or trunk, supported by a stake, and a rounded head of branches at the top, usually at a height of 3 to 4 feet, although smaller and larger standards can be grown. Follow these easy steps:

Trained to grow like a small round-headed tree, this *Solanum rantonnetii* (blue potato bush) sprouts from a tub of flowering annuals to make an effective vertical statement beside the front door.

1. Start with a plant that naturally has a single strong stem and is at least 1 to 2 feet tall.

2. Trim off the bottom two-thirds of the branches, cutting them as close to the trunk as possible. Keep the remaining side branches full and bushy for now because the leaves are needed to fuel the plant's growth.

3. Use a sturdy stake a foot longer than the height you want the plant to be. Plunge the stake all the way into the bottom of the pot alongside the main stem. Secure the trunk at intervals to the stake using plastic stretch-ties to avoid girdling the stem.

4. As the plant grows, continue to trim off the lower branches and to tie up the trunk. Once the plant has reached the desired height, pinch out the growing tip, cut off any excess stake, and cut back the side branches by two-thirds.

5. Keep pinching the tips of all new branches as they form at the top and sides of the plant's head. Pinch after one or two sets of leaves form. Continue pinching until the plant is the desired shape. Then pinch as needed to keep it looking neat.

❖❖❖

an entrance. Standards work beautifully beside an entrance, because their elegant tall shape and uniform crown make a welcoming living sculpture next to the door. If you want a more casual look, choose two different-size containers, but make them compatible by echoing colors and some plants from one to the other.

Pot choices

Sometimes it's difficult to decide what comes first, the pot or the plant. You might have a uniquely beautiful container that you want to put a plant in, or you might have a uniquely beautiful plant that you need a container for. Whichever way it works, one thing is sure: The container and the plants in it need to make a happy marriage for the combination to look good and complement your garden. So think it all through before you begin planting to make sure everything will work together.

The planters you add to your garden have a style all their own that influences the garden's appearance. For a tropical-style garden, you might pick something with an African or Asian flair. There's certainly a wide array of containers to choose among, from plain to highly decorative, from fairly inexpensive to shockingly exorbitant, but it's generally best to select a simple plain container for a mixed planting, especially if the leaf colors are tropically outrageous.

Hot-colored tropical foliage combines with the flowers of *Petunia* 'Purple Wave', *Fuchsia* 'Gartenmeister', and *Impatiens* 'New Guinea' to bring wildly wonderful colors to this waterside deck.

Pot materials

Containers come in a variety of materials: clay, plastic, ironstone, metal, concrete, wood, or fiberglass. Some gardeners even use found objects to hold their plants, such as old boots (although that's a bit passé by now), an abandoned kitchen sink or wheelbarrow, a stone cow trough, or an old copper washtub. Clay chimney flues come in a vast number of sizes and are relatively inexpensive at a brickyard; they make an unusual choice yet seem at the same time oddly familiar because of their color.

Clay pots possess earthy good looks that blend with almost any garden style and plant type, so the plainer ones among them make natural choices for tropical gardens. They aren't generally prohibitively expensive, although the fancier Italian terra-cotta ones can be pricey. Clay is porous, which is good for root health, because as water evaporates through the sides it cools the soil, preventing a container in full sun from suffering cooked roots. But the pot's porous nature means that the potting soil quickly dries out and that fertilizer salts can build up to ugly proportions on the outside of the pot. Neither ordinary clay nor most Italian terra cotta can be safely left outdoors where the temperature drops below freezing, because moisture in the clay freezes and expands, splintering and cracking the pot. Some Italian terra cotta can stay out all year, because the clay is of high quality and the pots are fired at a very high temperature. Clay pots can also be heavy, with large ones weighing in at 50 to 100 pounds.

If you like the look of clay but not the weight or the upkeep, select a plastic or fiberglass pot made to mimic the good looks of clay. Quality and style vary. Some of these containers look just like what they are—plastic trying to imitate clay—but others can't be distinguished from the real thing until you touch them. The latter, of course, cost more, but in the long run they may be worth it because you can leave them outdoors year-round in any climate, saving your back from those weighty moving chores.

Concrete and stone planters are available in lightweight imitation versions as well. The downside to the authentic versions is their high cost and extreme weight—both of which exceed that of clay pots. But these attractive containers are somewhat porous and possess a pleasing rough texture and a neutral color that blends with most garden styles. They are more durable than clay and can be left outdoors forever. When used in the shade, a stone container can become encrusted with moss and lichen, like an object abandoned to the jungle. Fake ones rarely acquire that great-looking patina, but you can age them with a light sponging of whitewash or add a hint of green to give them that been-here-forever look.

Some types of glazed Mexican or Thai pots bring bright colors to the garden, colors that can be echoed by leaves and flowers. Ironstone planters from Thailand are heavyweights, but they endure any kind of weather and have a beautiful earthy brown color that effectively shows off anything that's grown in them.

Wood is natural anywhere, and wooden containers can be built to any specifications. To extend the life of a wooden planter, fit it with a galvanized liner or line it with plastic. The type of wood dictates the cost and durability of a container. Redwood and cedar last longer than pine, but they also cost more.

The choice is endless, but keep in mind that whatever container you choose, it must have one or more drainage holes, and its size should fit the plants in it. Drainage holes are necessary so that excess water can flow through the soil and out the bottom to prevent waterlogging. If you find an interesting container that has no drainage hole, you can drill a hole in it, or you can set a potted plant inside the container but raise it up on a bed of gravel for drainage. Just be sure to carefully monitor the drainage water in this double-potted situation, and do not allow the inner pot to stand in water that collects in the bottom of the outer pot. The same holds true if you use a saucer under a plant—the saucer can easily fill up with drainage water or rainwater, which leaves the plant sitting in a puddle and ensures its demise.

Hanging containers

In a tropical-style garden, plants suspended in containers from tree branches and arbors or wall brackets add a layered look that brings a necessary, lovely lushness to the garden. Such containers are an intriguing place to grow vining plants, such as passionflower (*Passiflora* spp.) or potato vine (*Solanum jasminoides*), so that they cascade downward in a drapery of blossoms and foliage.

A moss basket makes a beautiful addition to a tropical-style garden. These baskets have a wire frame lined with sphagnum moss and then filled with potting mix. Install plants in the top of the basket and through its sides. Try designing a moss basket as a combination basket that contains several types of plants, using the same design strategies as for a terrestrial planter. This way you will get away from the flowering-ball effect and have an interesting hanging basket with a lot of depth and contrast.

Moss-lined baskets tend to dry out very fast. To slow down evaporation, place a sheet of black plastic (cut from a garbage bag) between the sphagnum and the potting mix. Be sure to poke a few holes in the plastic for drainage.

Other plants look good in decorative containers suspended at eye level or overhead if they have long cascading branches. The container doesn't need to have been originally designed for hanging—you can rig up wires or cords to hang real straw or rattan baskets and ceramic or clay pots. But please toss out the cheap white-plastic pots—these are much too eye-catching to be used anywhere in the garden, especially at eye level.

Vining tropicals suspended from an arbor or tree branch add to the layered jungly look. Three vividly colorful plants cascade from this container.

Weighty matters

Besides appearance and cost, there are other factors to consider when choosing a container, such as its weight. You'll want to use jumbo-size containers for those big tropicals, but you may not be able to move them once you plant them—in fact, you might have trouble moving even an empty container if it's sizable enough. So think ahead on this one.

Soil, when thoroughly moistened, weighs about 100 pounds per cubic foot, but the same amount of soilless mix used in most containers weighs only about 60 pounds. That's still a lot. Add to that the weight of the container and the plants and the whole thing can be mighty hefty. If you're planting a container and then going to move it into position, wait until it's moved to water it—that will cut significant pounds off the project.

One back-saving strategy is to use a handcart to roll containers from one place to another. Another strategy is to move the container to its permanent location first and then plant it. You'll of course need to unpot it there, too, if you plan to take tender plants in for the winter. And deep containers don't have to be filled entirely with potting medium unless they contain tall plants, because the roots won't ever get down that far. You can cheat and fill up the bottom third with Styrofoam peanuts before adding the soil mix.

Try double-potting large specimen plants, using a utilitarian lightweight plastic container to actually hold the root ball and then placing it inside a slightly larger, heavy, decorative container, but be sure water drains from both containers. When you want to move the specimen inside for the winter, transport the heavy container separately from the heavy plant, parceling out the weight you'd otherwise need to carry in one lift.

Soil, water, and fertilizer facts

Container-grown tropicals demand a bit more care and attention than those grown in the ground. Because they are confined to a pot, their need for moisture and nutrients is intense and their survival is all in your hands.

The soilless mix

Any plant grown in a container—and that includes tropicals—needs a nutritious growing medium that drains quickly but also retains moisture. Most horticulturists prefer using what's called a soilless potting mix based on peat moss and vermiculite and perlite, which are volcanic rocks that have been heated until they explode into airy little particles that absorb water like sponges. These mixes have no real soil in them. Unlike garden soil, soilless mixes are free of weed seeds, insects, and pathogens; are lightweight; and hold lots of water without getting soggy.

You can mix bagged topsoil or heavy potting soil with the soilless mix, at a rate of one part soil to two parts soilless mix, to make the potting medium a bit heavier and more water-retentive. Plants potted up in this mixture usually grow more vigorously than those in a completely soilless mix.

Attention to watering

Container-grown tropicals, except for the succulent sorts, need watering every few days—sometimes every day if they reside in a hot location or if a lot of thirsty plants are growing together in tight quarters. This holds especially true for plants in porous clay or concrete containers and moss baskets. Hanging baskets bask in so much air and wind that they dry out extremely quickly.

You can reduce the need to water quite so often by planning ahead. Line a porous container with plastic cut from a garbage bag before filling it with potting soil, and punch drainage holes in the plastic. This reduces moisture lost—and wasted—through the sides of the container. Be sure to tuck the plastic down so you don't see it protruding above the soil line like a slip hanging below a hem.

You can also incorporate a poly-acrylamide gel into the soilless mix before planting. This miraculous material works rather like gelatin—dump it from the package, add water, and presto, it expands tenfold, absorbing enormous quantities of water without altering soil drainage. It then slowly and happily releases the water to the soil as the soil dries. Just be sure to add this product to the potting medium sparingly, according to the package directions, because if

Many tropical foliage plants and some flowering ones perform well in light shade. Here, containers filled with tropicals summer outdoors, embellishing the front porch with lush greenery.

you overdo it you can create a quaking quagmire that expands and overflows the container. This gel holds so much water that where you might have had to water once a day you can water once or twice a week.

Don't water randomly just because you feel like it. Always check the pot first to see if it *needs* watering. Stick your finger into the soil and water if you discover that the top 1 to 2 inches of the soil is dry—this measure is pretty good for plants that like it evenly moist, as most do. For plants that like it drier, allow the soil to get dry a bit deeper down.

When you do water, add plenty—enough so that water flows out the bottom of the container. That way, you know that all the soil is thoroughly moist; this encourages roots to grow throughout the entire pot—and they usually need all the soil they can get. You can also set up a drip system of tubes and emitters to handle most of your pots, to simplify and automate the watering.

Fertilizer facts

Because soilless mixes are naturally nutrient-poor, you need to add fertilizer to keep your tropicals growing. Mix in a timed-released, balanced fertilizer at planting time. These products contain little pellets that slowly release nutrients over several months; three-, six-, and nine-month formulas, such as 14-14-14, are usually available. Use the nine-month version if you can find it. Foliage plants need a lot of nitrogen, so a formula such as 20-20-20 is perfect. For flowering plants, 10-20-20 is better.

But even with this magical fertilizer mixed into the potting medium, you'll need to supply additional nutrients because the water-soluble fertilizer leaches from the soil in the frequent waterings that a container demands. And when tropical plants are jam-packed into the crowded confines of a container, they have limited root space and need concentrated boosts of fertilizer to sustain them.

You can fertilize whenever you water by diluting powdered or liquid fertilizer into the watering can or with a hose-end fertilizer attachment. Use one-quarter the recommended strength with each watering if you feed each time you water. Or you can supply the liquid feed once every week or two and then pour it on at the full recommended strength.

Containers of tropicals bring concentrated jolts of color and excitement wherever you use them. And because they are so portable, you can rearrange them at will to suit your fancy, creating opportunities to grow exotic plants in places you never dreamed possible.

✦✦✦

CHAPTER FOUR

Hardy Plants
for a Tropical Look

When it comes to creating a splashy tropical-looking garden complete with big, bold plants and wildly colorful foliage in New York, Maryland, Illinois, Montana, or other places far from the tropics, you can approach the project in several ways. The first and most obvious—planting a vista of equatorial plants—is not totally practical in a temperate region. (Of course, who said this type of gardening was meant to be a practical endeavor anyway?) Alternatively, rather than relying exclusively on tender tropical plants, you can go the hardy-plant route. It's entirely possible to capture the look and mood of a tropical garden using mostly cold-hardy plants. The trick comes in choosing the right plants, those that possess the distinctive appearance of exotic species that hail from a warmer, lusher climate but by some quirk of nature survive winters in northern zones.

You can use these tropical-looking hardy beauties to create the framework for your garden and then splurge with swaths of true tropicals in key areas to create high impact. This way, you enjoy the tropical look from year to year with less planting effort each spring, and you also get to play with some very fascinating and unusual plants. Moreover, a garden so designed benefits from having a year-round structure of permanent plants, so that it still looks attractive even in winter.

Identifying the tropical look

A number of Temperate Zone plants have a tropical look about them owing to the size and shape of their leaves and flowers. The bigger and glossier or fernier the leaves, the lusher and more tropical their appearance; the larger and more intricate the flowers, the more exotic their looks. Also, brightly variegated versions of cold-hardy plants mimic the kaleidoscopic paint jobs that tropical garden plants are known for and do a pretty good imitation of a tropical plant when used in the right context.

Because large leaves and flowers are easily tattered in bad weather, lose a quantity of moisture during dry spells, and cost a plant a lot of energy to grow, most Temperate Zone plants have smaller leaves and flowers than do tropical-zone plants, which have fewer climatic challenges to endure. But

Seek out hardy plants that look tropical, like the *Cortaderia* 'Pumila' (dwarf pampas grass) and trumpet lilies shown opposite, and use them as the garden's permanent bone structure. Add tropicals like *Colocasia* 'Jet Black Wonder' as accents.

Magnolia grandiflora 'Edith Bogue', the hardiest southern magnolia, produces luscious flowers in zone 6.

Hibiscus coccineus grows to 10 feet in zone 6 and has immense red flowers.

there are exceptions to every rule, and there are, of course, a number of cold-hardy plants with enormous, bold, or ferny leaves and oversize flowers. Look for such tropicalistic plants among the trees, shrubs, and perennials that are hardy in your region. You'll be surprised at how many you find.

One place to start is among the cold-hardy species of genera or families comprising mostly tropical plants. Many such groups of plants have a few renegade members that stretch the limit of hardiness northward. These pioneers typically possess tropical-style good looks but take winters north of the equator—sometimes as far north as Canada—in stride.

The mallow family, to which tropical hibiscus (*Hibiscus rosa-sinensis*) belongs, is an outstanding example. One of the tropical species' cold-hardy cousins, the rose-of-Sharon (*H. syriacus*), is a summer- and fall-blooming shrub that flourishes in zones 5–9. Its pink, white, red, lavender, or blue flowers, which often have a contrasting darker eye in the center, bloom in quantity for several months, looking like small versions of the saucer-shaped blossoms of the tropical plant. Although the flowers are smaller—measuring 3 to 5 inches across, depending on the cultivar—their graceful shape and prominent column of eye-catching, yellow stamens leave no doubt about their kinship to tropical hibiscus. Neither do the jumbo-size flowers of two cold-hardy perennial cousins: rose mallow (*H. moscheutos,* zones 5–9) and red mallow (*H. coccineus,* zones 6–11).

Both of these perennials have woody bases and multiple, 8- to 10-foot-tall stems decked out with lobed leaves. However, it's their gargantuan flowers that grab your attention from midsummer into fall. Rose mallow blossoms grow to an extravagant 8 to 10 inches across and are usually red, pink, or white with a dark red eye, closely mimicking the tropical hibiscus with their dinner-plate proportions and crepe-paper texture. Red mallow is not quite as cold-hardy, but its palmately lobed leaves deliver a textural impact matched by the blossoms' wedge-shaped, rich red petals, which give the 6-inch-wide flowers an intriguing, snowflakelike silhouette.

Use any of the Temperate Zone *Hibiscus* in a garden to impart easy-care tropical flare. Rose-of-Sharon, being a woody shrub, offers a year-round presence from its stems and light brown bark, so use it as a specimen or as a background planting for screening. This old-fashioned shrub has a weedy reputation in some corners, because it tends to seed itself all over the garden. Newer cultivars, however, such as the rose-pink 'Aphrodite' and snow-white 'Diana', are sterile and don't self-seed. The perennial *Hibiscus* species die to the ground during the dormant season but shoot up to statuesque heights each summer, presenting their huge blossoms in such grand style and size that they demand a prime location in the border.

Seeking tropical-looking hardy plants ·

Palms, bananas, bamboos, and tree ferns symbolize the tropics, their very presence so evocative of an equatorial climate that they send out subliminal messages declaring "This is the tropics." You can play up these subtle signals by choosing cold-hardy plants that resemble in leaf shape and form these dramatic denizens of the rain forests and Caribbean isles, or seek out the hardiest species of these primarily tropical plants to grow as year-round residents of your garden. There are some bamboos, for instance, that are hardy even into zone 4, bananas that grow in zone 5 if protected during the coldest months, and palms that grow in zones 5, 6, and 7.

A magnificent stand of *Phyllostachys aureosulcata* (golden groove bamboo) is root hardy to zone 4. An underground barrier keeps the running bamboo in place.

Beautiful bamboos and grasses

Dense stands of bamboo, with their straight, jointed stems and fluttering leaves, soar to such great heights that they seem to touch the sky, stirring images of Asian and African jungles. But, in fact, there are bamboo species endemic to every continent, and some of them are extremely cold-hardy. Most species are evergreen, and cold-hardy types range in height from 20 or 30 feet to a foot or two, making them useful for all kinds of garden needs, from screening to ground covering. You can capitalize on the exotic look of these cold-hardy bamboos, which are actually woody grasses, by including a bamboo grove in your garden's permanent scenery.

A bamboo's new stems, called culms, emerge from the ground in spring and grow to their full height in a single season, forming a jointed cane that gets no taller or fatter during its lifetime—a decade or so. Canes can be sturdy and stout or slender and flexible, and be colored green, brown, gold, or black. During harsh winters, the canes of some hardy bamboos may die to the ground, but the plants send out new culms in spring and the canes grow to their full height within a month or two. Usually the culms are 10 degrees Fahrenheit hardier than the canes, so if a bamboo is rated as being hardy to 10°F, it will die to the ground but regrow from the roots if temperatures plunge to 0°F.

A few words of warning: Know and respect the difference between running and clumping bamboos. Running bamboos spread, sometimes slowly but normally quite vigorously, by sending out rhizomes that colonize new ground. The aggressive ones can be extremely invasive and almost impossible to get rid of once you let them into your garden. Nonetheless, they are beautiful plants and are worth the trouble it takes to manage them.

The best way to control a running type is to plant it within secure confines, such as corralled by a 3-foot-deep ring of sturdy fiberglass or polyethylene sheeting with nary a crack or peephole for the rhizomes to penetrate. The barrier should also rise 3 inches above the ground to prevent runners from leaping the top. Specialty bamboo growers sell everything you'll need to build a proper barrier and will offer specific advice.

Clump-forming bamboos grow gradually, forming ever larger stands, but they do not travel into new territory as do the running types. These well-behaved beauties make desirable additions to a tropical-style garden. Fountain bamboo (*Fargesia nitida*) and umbrella bamboo (*F. murielae*) are two graceful clump formers from China and are the most cold-hardy of any bamboo, remaining evergreen in winter temperatures down −25°F (zone 4b). These fine-textured bamboos look very similar to each other, both forming dense, 12-foot-tall clumps of narrow canes decorated with a cascade of delicate leaves. Fountain bamboo has blue-green stems, finer foliage, and a more weeping shape than the purple-stemmed umbrella bamboo, which is more drought-resistant.

Many cold-hardy ornamental grasses play a key design role in a tropical-style garden, where they offer their linear good looks, silvery flower plumes, and sometimes brightly colored or striped leaves. The biggest and most majestic grasses rule the tropical-style garden. They are especially important in dry or wet areas, where they can be massed to create the look of a tropical savanna or a marshy lagoon.

A really exotic looker is the giant reed grass (*Arundo donax*), which forms 10- to 25-foot-tall clumps of soaring, blue-gray stems and leaves. The plant rather resembles a coarse-textured bamboo or gigantic corn plant; indeed, the canes are used in the South like bamboo for building fences and other structures. The cultivar 'Variegata' sparkles with stripes of green and creamy white, adding the bonus of variegation to its huge size. The more moisture these grasses get, and the warmer the climate, the taller they grow. They spread rather invasively in the South and along the Gulf Coast, but they are better behaved—and more appreciated for their commanding architecture—in zones 6 and 7.

Above: Soaring 12 to 20 feet, *Arundo donax* (giant reed grass) creates a permanent tropical effect in zone 6.

Below: In zone 5, *Musa basjoo* (Japanese fiber banana) dies down in winter and regrows in spring.

Cultivars of maiden grasses (*Miscanthus* spp.) abound, ranging in height from 3 to 14 feet tall, but all offer a graceful vase of foliage and silvery plumes in summer and fall. The tallest among them is the giant Chinese silver grass (*M. giganteus*), which produces broad, arching green leaf blades on stems that tower to 10 to 14 feet tall and are topped by exotic, 2-foot-long, feathery silver flowers in late summer. Striped and variegated forms of *M. sinensis* bring extra color to the scene; choose 'Strictus' for its sturdy upright form and brightly banded, gold-and-green blades.

You can use grasses as specimens in the border or for contrast in a container. Mass them to create an exotic grassland that undulates and rustles in the breeze, or line up the big ones to serve as a screen to enclose your tropical-style garden. (For a listing of cold-hardy tropical-looking bamboos and ornamental grasses, see pages 209–10.)

Banana bonanza

Banana trees, with their stout trunks and umbrella of huge, paddle-shaped leaves, adorn gardens throughout the tropics, where they fill the role of edible landscaping because they also bear edible fruits. You can grow many beautiful banana species and cultivars outdoors in summer in almost any climate, but several species are durable enough to be left in the ground year-round in the North. Although these species act like perennials, dying to the ground during winter, they regrow in summer, getting larger and more startling each year as their corms become more massive. These cold-hardy bananas won't bear fruit, however, because the plants need twelve to fourteen months of warmth to flower and produce ripe fruits.

The hardiest banana, and one you might try growing year-round in Massachusetts or Pennsylvania, is the Japanese fiber banana (*Musa basjoo*). It endures winter temperatures down to just below 0°F (zone 6b) with no protection. Its bright green, 6-foot-long leaves remain evergreen all winter in zone 9, but the stems and leaves die to the ground when a hard freeze comes in fall and regrow in spring in zones 6–8. If you go to the effort of wrapping and insulating the banana's stem (see the sidebar "Banana Wars" on page 96) during winter in those zones, the banana starts off the growing season already 6 to 7 feet tall, so you end up with a magnificent specimen that can reach 12 to 16 feet tall. Imagine that—a 16-foot-tall banana tree growing in a Boston garden!

Another excellent candidate for pushing the limits is Chinese yellow banana (*Musella lasiocarpa*). This beautiful banana relative from China grows 4 to 5 feet tall and acts like a perennial in zones 7 and 8 if given some winter protection such as a heavy mulch. Left in the ground and protected in winter, this banana is more likely to produce its amazing starbursts of yellow flowers than if it spends the winter as a dormant root system in your basement.

One of the cold-hardiest palms, this small specimen of *Trachycarpus fortunei* (hardy windmill palm) will eventually reach 10 feet in a zone 7 garden.

Hardy-palm fan club

Palm trees line streets in Miami and Los Angeles, mark oases in the Sahara desert, and encircle beaches on Caribbean islands. But a palm tree growing in a Brooklyn garden? Doubtful, but possible. Several species of palm defy expectations and grow quite happily in zones 7 and 8, and if given winter protection (see chapter 5) can be kept in the ground year-round in zone 6. These hardy palms are not big palms—not the towering coconut palm or royal palm we all know and love—but smaller, more compact plants with low trunks and wonderful, fan-shaped leaves that, in some species, can get to be 6 feet across. (For a listing of cold-hardy palms, see page 207.)

The hardy windmill palm (*Trachycarpus fortunei*), a native of China, is the tallest and most popular of these hardy palms, eventually reaching 8 to 10 feet tall even in zone 7a gardens and 25 feet tall in warmer areas. Its 3-foot-wide, rounded leaves perch at the tips of 2-foot-long stalks and extend out at all angles from the top of a sturdy, rough, brown trunk, resembling a living imitation of a windmill waiting to catch the breeze.

The Kumaon fan palm (*T. takil*) from India looks like a bigger version of the windmill palm, and it is even a bit more cold-hardy. Unfortunately, this palm is a rare plant and difficult to find, although it is certainly worth seeking out from a specialty grower. Rarer still is the beautiful miniature Chusan palm (*T. wagnerianus*), which grows to 10 to 20 feet in height. Woolly white fibers decorate its $2^1/_2$-foot-wide leaves, which are very stiff and rigid. The leaves grow at jaunty angles, and because they are so inflexible, they are highly resistant to wind damage. Now extinct in its native Japan, this small palm is available only from specialty growers at a hefty price.

The needle palm (*Rhapidophyllum hystrix*) endures even colder winters than the hardy windmill palm, sending up its dark green, fan-shaped leaves in gardens as far north as Connecticut. But don't plant this one expecting to get a palm tree. It's nearly trunkless, even in the warmest parts of its range, although the big, palmately cut leaves can reach up to 3 to 5 feet from the ground. Needle palm is certainly not a palm tree, but it's nevertheless a plant whose architectural foliage can endow a garden with tropical style.

Dwarf palmetto (*Sabal minor*) is native to swampy areas of the southern United States and is one of the few palms that do well in wet soil. This low grower is a bushy plant that hardly ever forms a trunk but sends up rounded, greenish blue, fan-shaped leaves that are 3 to 6 feet wide. It's winter-hardy to −5°F. Give it a lightly shady spot underplanted with a contrasting ground cover and the beautiful fans will spell "tropical" all year in the North.

Saw palmetto (*Serenoa repens*) forms 10-foot-tall clumps of long-petioled leaves that are 3 feet wide and completely round, cut in palmate style. Leaf color varies from light green to blue-green, with the blue forms being truly exquisite. The multiple trunks spread outward and actually grow underground or just above the soil surface. This coastal native hails from the Deep South and performs well in full to partial sun, enduring winter temperatures down to about −5°F.

Many factors influence how much winter cold a hardy palm can endure. Older established palms and healthy plants take more cold in stride than do younger or unhealthy specimens. A hardy palm planted in a warm microclimate, such as against a south-facing wall, stays warmer all winter and may grow a bit farther north than expected, pushing the zone limits by several degrees. (See pages 97–98 for more about microclimates.) If it isn't protected by a layer of snow, a hardy palm's foliage may be burned by a severe winter storm that's accompanied by strong wind, making the palm unsightly. But as long as the growing point survives, new growth will replace the damaged leaves in spring.

A palm's origin may also influence its winter survival; that's why seed is usually collected from plants growing in the coldest parts of the plant's range in hopes of selecting a strain whose genetic makeup endows it with more cold hardiness. For instance, among the hardy windmill palms, the cultivars 'Norfolk', 'Charlotte', and 'Greensboro' were selected from seed collected from those cities in Virginia and North Carolina—the coldest limits of the palm's usual range. Choose these cultivars if you're trying to grow the palm in zone 7.

Fabulous ferns

Tree ferns like it cool and moist, which is understandable since they grow naturally at higher elevations in the rain forests of Central and South America, Australia, and New Zealand. The hardiest and perhaps most beautiful of these ancient plant species is the Tasmanian tree fern (*Dicksonia antarctica*). This fast-growing plant forms a rough-textured, stout trunk that can reach 6 to 20 feet tall and is topped with a crown of extremely lacy, 6- to 8-foot-long leaves. It's an amazing sight to see one of these ferns in a northern garden: it seems so inconceivably out of context but works so well at creating a prehistoric setting of luxurious greenery.

This primordial plant is cold-hardy in zone 8b, its leaves remaining evergreen even in the rare snowstorm. It grows successfully in gardens year-round in the cool coastal areas up and down the West Coast from Vancouver southward. Although it may suffer from the heat, try it along the Gulf Coast, in Florida, and in coastal areas of the Deep South—the exotic tree fern from down under just might do fine if you keep it in shade and protect it from drying wind.

While not even coming close to a tree fern's magnificent height and spread, several Temperate Zone ferns mimic the elegant, lacy look of a tree fern—a baby one, that is. The scaly brown crown of the thick-stemmed wood fern (*Dryopteris crassirhizoma*) measures about 4 to 6 inches across, and although it grows close to the ground, it resembles the growing point of a tree fern. From the crown's edges arises a spreading vase of 3-foot-long, evergreen or semievergreen, lacy fronds, the whole composition looking amazingly like a young Tasmanian tree fern. These ferns make wonderful sculptural specimens that can be sprinkled through a shady area to create a lush understory.

Other big ferns may not look exactly like tree ferns, but they create the primordial feel of a wet and humid jungle landscape when used in groups or masses. Cinnamon ferns (*Osmunda cinnamomea*) and regal ferns (*O. regalis*) can grow to 4 to 5 feet tall in very wet, almost swampy, areas. Where the soil is drier, but still moist, they may reach only 3 feet in height. These are great big ferns for creating dramatic texture. Cinnamon fern features rounded leaflets in tall, feather-shaped fronds, while regal fern displays a branched

The lush fronds and delicate greenery of most cold-hardy ferns, like this *Adiantum pedatum* (maidenhair fern), have a tropical look, especially when planted in quantity. It grows here in a Vermont garden with *Sasa veitchii* (dwarf bamboo).

arrangement of widely spaced, oval leaflets that give the plant an open, airy structure with a decidedly architectural air about it.

Most maidenhair fern species (*Adiantum* spp.) are tropical or subtropical plants, but several grow in cold northern climates and are surely the most beautiful and graceful ferns of the temperate woodlands. The northern maidenhair fern (*A. pedatum*) produces a fan-shaped arrangement of translucent, emerald green leaflets on shiny, ebony black stems that are so narrow that they seem to be made of wire. This gorgeous fern mimics the tropical species and is the perfect addition to a shade garden, where you can contrast its delicate texture with bold-leaved plants.

Practically any hardy fern, if planted in quantity in a shady garden, provides the lush look you're after when designing a tropical-style garden. Choose ferns first from the list on page 209, but don't be shy about experimenting and using whatever ferns you have available.

This primordial-looking specimen of *Dicksonia antarctica* (Tasmanian tree fern), the cold-hardiest species of tree fern, remains evergreen all year in this Seattle-area garden.

Tropical-looking trees and shrubs

Many of our fairly common deciduous and broad-leaved evergreen trees and shrubs have an exotic personality that you can capitalize on when designing a tropical-style garden. Look for big leaves, big flowers, and big colors. Summer bloomers are especially desirable because they display their flowers not in spring, when temperate gardens are showiest, but in summer, when tropical gardens expect to be showy.

Tall trees

Trees with large, glossy, rounded leaves, such as the many magnolias (*Magnolia* spp.), possess the lush look that helps them play a realistic role in a Temperate Zone tropical-style garden. The southern magnolia (*M. grandiflora*) dresses a garden with its polished, dark green, 10-inch-long, evergreen leaves and in summer adds dollops of white, dinner-plate-size flowers that emit a heady, lemony-sweet perfume. Several cold-hardy cultivars push the limits of this magnificent tree from zone 7 to zone 6—look for the most cold-hardy selections: 'Bracken's Brown Beauty', 'Edith Bogue', and 'Victoria'. Or for an even wilder look, select the less common, bigleaf magnolia (*M. macrophylla*) to capitalize on its 3-foot-long, paddle-shaped leaves and 12-inch-wide summer flowers. The enormous leaves of this deciduous tree, which is hardy in zones 6–9, create an instant jungle look.

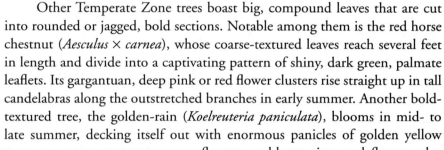

Other Temperate Zone trees boast big, compound leaves that are cut into rounded or jagged, bold sections. Notable among them is the red horse chestnut (*Aesculus* × *carnea*), whose coarse-textured leaves reach several feet in length and divide into a captivating pattern of shiny, dark green, palmate leaflets. Its gargantuan, deep pink or red flower clusters rise straight up in tall candelabras along the outstretched branches in early summer. Another bold-textured tree, the golden-rain (*Koelreuteria paniculata*), blooms in mid- to late summer, decking itself out with enormous panicles of golden yellow flowers—a bloom time and flower color rare among Temperate Zone trees. This dazzler grows into a rounded, open canopy of large, jagged leaflets that creates an emphatic tropical image.

Opposite: A tall, lacy-leafed *Albizia julibrissin* (silk tree) gives this zone 8 garden a year-round, tropical-looking structure. The fuzzy pink flowers *(below)* blanket the tree for weeks in late summer.

Another hot plant that no tropical-style garden can be without is Japanese angelica tree (*Aralia elata*). This gorgeous, coarse-textured tree grows into a pagoda shape with tiers of horizontal branches sporting 4-foot-long, compound leaves with pointed leaflets and large panicles of airy white flowers in summer. The best forms have an irregular pattern of variegation marking the leaf edges, which makes the tree even more eye-catching. 'Variegata' has creamy white leaf margins, while those of 'Aureo-variegata' are creamy yellow. Give these architectural plants a center-stage location—they'll look magnificent even when still young.

A few Temperate Zone trees belonging to the pea, or legume, family (Leguminosae), which contains a vast number of tropical trees, have fine-textured, compound leaves. Notable examples are silk tree (*Albizia julibrissin*),

black locust (*Robinia pseudoacacia*), and honey locust (*Gleditsia triacanthos*). These graceful trees cast the same lacy shadows and have the same outlines as their tropical relatives. Silk tree, with its beautiful fernlike leaves, profuse shocking pink powder puffs of flowers in July and August, and spreading umbrellas of zigzagging branches, looks more like it belongs in Kenya than in New Jersey, where it grows so well, although it is native to Asia and the Middle East. Use this fast-growing tree to create a tropical-looking canopy in your garden, but be sure to select improved disease-resistant cultivars, otherwise the tree will probably be short-lived.

Black locust and honey locust also produce gorgeous, rounded leaflets that cast a lightly dappled shade. Black locust tends to grow in various forms—some types are tall and narrow and others are spreading to irregular. But the tree always features fragrant, white flowers in small wisteria-like clusters in early summer. 'Frisia', a favorite cultivar, literally glows in the garden, its gleaming lacework of golden yellow leaves bringing hot highlights to the green tree canopy. By contrast, honey locust bears sweet-smelling, inconspicuous flowers in early summer but has a wonderful, wide-spreading, irregular branching pattern, which brings that African savanna look to a northern garden. You can cluster several of these trees together to make a high canopy for a lightly shaded garden. Gold-leaved cultivars of honey locust such as 'Sunburst' add a hot-hued touch.

These are just a few of the cold-hardy trees that bring a foreign flare to the garden. See the list on pages 206–7 for others to choose from. None are difficult to find or to grow, but when they are combined with true tropicals or other exotic-looking plants, their tropical-looking character blossoms.

Showy shrubs

Hardy, summer-blooming shrubs, especially those with large or lacy leaves, or shrubs with colored or shiny foliage possess flamboyant good looks that you can draw on when designing a tropical-looking garden. Use them as a year-round backdrop to true tropicals, or mix them with other hardy plants or with tropicals to paint an exotic garden picture.

Several species of hydrangea (*Hydrangea* spp.) deliver the goods when it comes to big and bold good looks. Bigleaf hydrangea (*H. macrophylla*), as

Top: When pruned in fall to keep a shrubby form, *Lagerstroemia indica* 'Hoppi' (crape myrtle) explodes with shocking pink flowers from July to September.

Above: The lacy summer blossoms and fernlike leaves of *Sorbaria kirlowii* seem to belong to a Pacific isle.

Sometimes using a rather common plant in a really different way makes it seem more exotic. If you hard-prune certain trees or shrubs by cutting them all the way back to the ground every spring (a technique called stooling), a big flush of tender growth shoots out from the stump. The new growth consists of several very tall, straight stems and extra-large leaves. If you hard-prune plants that already have big leaves, the result is even larger leaves that border on enormous.

This repeat, radical pruning produces a woody stump, or stool, near the ground after several years but doesn't kill the plant. All you do is cut the stems back to 6 inches from the ground every year in late winter or early spring. Make your cuts just above a bud or a pair of buds. Start with a young plant, one that is only a few years old. Stooled plants that bloom on old wood will not bloom if they are hard-pruned each year, but you're mainly after the foliage anyway.

The giant pentagonal leaves and soaring stems of this *Paulownia tomentosa* (empress tree) result from cutting it to the ground each year. The spectacular effect transforms a cold-hardy plant into a tropical-looking wonder.

Popular trees for stooling that can shoot up to 15 feet tall each season include empress tree (*Paulownia tomentosa*), which has big, fuzzy, pentagonal leaves; golden catalpa (*Catalpa bignonioides* 'Aurea'), which produces huge, golden, heart-shaped leaves; and tree-of-heaven (*Ailanthus altissima*), whose pinnate leaves are 4 feet long. Shrub candidates include purple smokebush (*Cotinus coggygria* 'Royal Purple'), which has luminescent, reddish purple leaves; and golden elderberry (*Sambucus canadensis* 'Aurea'), whose finely dissected leaves are golden yellow.

You can grow these glamorous stooled plants as specimens in a tropical-style border or plant them in groups to form a grove for a wilder-looking effect.

◆◆◆

its name implies, has large leaves, which are shiny and dark green and have a prominent pattern of veins. But it's the really big blossoms that draw the attention. The flower heads grow as 8-inch-diameter balls that are voluptuous by any measure, their intense shocking pink or rich blue color riveting the eyes. These flowers last until fall, going through several color changes as they age and ripen. The gangly oakleaf hydrangea (*H. quercifolia*) grows rapidly into a large shrub with truly magnificent leaves. Lobed like giant oak leaves with silvery undersides, they reach 8 to 10 inches long and almost as wide, with a shiny green top surface that turns rich reddish purple to bronze in autumn. In mid- and late summer, 10-inch-tall cones of snowy white flowers bloom, aging by fall to a charming pinkish tan rather like the color of a paper bag.

Sometimes a cultivar of a common shrub offers an unusual leaf color or variegation pattern, which suddenly makes that common plant unique and interesting. For instance, forsythia (*Forsythia × intermedia*) is common enough to be boring, but select 'Goldleaf', a dwarf, shade-loving cultivar, as a ground cover and you have an exotic-looking rarity that can bring a carpet of hot color to the garden. Purple smokebush (*Cotinus coggygria* 'Notcutt's Variety') paints its leaves a beautiful wine red that glows with an inner light when struck by the angled rays of the sun, much like the many purple- and bronze-leaved versions of tropical plants.

Broad-leaved evergreen shrubs feature shiny leaves that resemble the glossy foliage of rain-forest plants. And when you go for the variegated forms, the effect intensifies. Japanese acuba (*Acuba japonica*) is one such plant that comes into its own in a tropical-style garden. Cultivars with the characteristic very shiny, smooth-edged leaves are readily available in gold-spotted versions. These can be so brightly variegated that the plants resemble crotons. The boldly variegated *Euonymus fortuneii* 'Emerald 'n Gold' often looks gaudy and unattractive in traditional gardens but glows when paired up with hot-colored plants in a tropical-style garden.

These are just a few of the hardy shrubs that will work for you in an exotic-looking garden. More are listed on pages 207–8, and you can also search out many others that will grow in your region that have characteristics seemingly more exotic than native.

Perennials and bulbs for flowers and foliage

Some of our most traditional and beloved perennials and bulbs transform themselves into exotic wonders when combined in designs that emphasize their bright colors or enormous stature. Again, it's the oversize blossoms or leaves, vivid colors, and bold textures that make these commonplace plants suddenly seem uncommon.

Leafy giants

Some hardy perennials—mostly ones that grow in shade or in wet soil conditions—possess big, luscious-looking leaves that mimic the foliage of equatorial plants. And some of these extraordinary foliage plants paint themselves with beautiful variegations that relieve the tedium of green. You can take advantage of these big, leafy plants to create a permanent tropical ambiance in your garden scene. Although they wouldn't win a look-alike contest, many of these showy perennials evoke the image of the lush, glossy leaves of tropical plants such as elephant's ears, bananas, and cannas.

The largest types of *Hosta*, like this golden 'Sum and Substance', have lush rounded leaves that give a northern garden a jungly look.

Among the most sumptuous of these leafy giants are the biggest forms of hosta (*Hosta* spp.), whose leaves can measure 1 to 1½ feet across and grow into magnificent clumps 5 feet or more high and wide. Use these grand-size hostas—not midsize or small versions—for creating a tropical look, and choose green, gold, blue, or variegated forms to enhance your chosen color scheme. Notable cultivars include 'Sum and Substance', which has glossy, puckered, chartreuse leaves; 'Blue Mammoth', which puts out huge, corrugated, blue leaves; 'Sun Power', whose twisted, upright leaves are a lovely gold; 'Krossa Regal', which holds its upright, powdery blue leaves in a vase-shaped clump; *H. montana* 'Aureo-marginata', whose leaves have a gray-green center and a wide creamy edge; 'Colossal', which produces truly massive green leaves; 'Great Expectations', the leaves of which display a big, creamy yellow center and irregular blue-green margins; and 'Northern Exposure', which has corrugated, blue-gray leaf centers and contrasting wide, creamy yellow edges.

Other winners in the big-foliage contest are not quite as universally known as hostas. The giant Japanese butterbur (*Petasites japonicus* 'Giganteus') thrives in damp soil, spreading rapidly to cover large areas with its enormous, wavy-edged, rounded to kidney-shaped leaves, which can reach 2 to 3 feet across and as tall. Similar-looking but less aggressive is the umbrella plant (*Darmera peltata*), which also flourishes in moist shade. Its toothed, umbrella-shaped, dark green leaves get to be 2 feet across and grow on 2- to 4-foot-tall stems. Both of these plants are very cold-hardy and can bring the tropical look on a permanent basis to gardens as far north as New England. Not as cold-hardy but growing to extreme proportions is gunnera (*Gunnera manicata*), a Brazilian plant whose spiny, 6- to 10-foot-tall leaf stems rise directly from the ground and are topped with kidney-shaped, coarsely toothed, lobed leaves that can attain 6 feet in width if the plant has wet feet. So coveted is this astonishing perennial that plant-crazy gardeners have been known to protect it with heating cables during winter so it will grow as far north as Vermont. Choose the hardy yuccas (*Yucca* spp.) to mimic the tufts of sword-shaped leaves exhibited by the tender aloes (*Aloe* spp.) and century plants (*Agave* spp.) of the arid tropics. *Y. filamentosa* 'Gold Band' is a good hardy substitute for *Phormium* 'Yellow Wave', both catching the eye with brightly striped, sword-shaped leaves. Other arid-region look-alikes boast spine-covered leaves, such as sea holly (*Eryngium* spp.) and spiny bear's breeches (*Acanthus mollis*).

For glossy, beautifully lobed leaves, nothing beats the hellebores (*Helleborus* spp.) as a ground cover in light shade. For foliage color, incorporate the purple hues of purple-leaved beardtongue (*Penstemon digitalis* 'Husker Red') and purple-leaved coralbells (*Heuchera micrantha* 'Palace Purple') and similar cultivars. The foliage of golden ray (*Ligularia stenocephala*) often has rusty or bronze casts to it, as well as enchanting bold shapes. And rodgersias (*Rodgersia* spp.) offer rough leaf textures and bold shapes that contrast dramatically with the linear leaves of irises (*Iris* spp.) and torch lilies (*Kniphofia uvaria*).

Floral fantasy

Some foliage plants, such as hostas, also bring beautiful flowers to the garden. And if they are large and trumpet-shaped, as so many tropical blossoms are, or simply big and outrageously weird, the blossoms of many hardy perennials and bulbs will fit right into a tropical-looking design.

Plume poppy (*Macleaya cordata*), a vigorous spreader, is one of the tallest flowering perennials you can grow. This stunner tops out at about 8 feet tall when its feathery white blossoms open up in late summer. The clumps of upright stems feature magnificent, 10-inch-long, lobed, blue-gray leaves. Other statuesque stunners include goatsbeard (*Aruncus dioicus*), another feathery bloomer but an early-summer one. This can reach 6 feet in height and has coarsely divided, bold leaves. Queen-of-the-prairie (*Filipendula rubra*) blooms for weeks in midsum-

This exotic-looking Washington garden layers cold-hardy, tropical-looking trees, shrubs, ornamental grasses, and flowers from top to bottom.

Perennials with orange or scarlet flowers, like this *Crocosmia* 'Lucifer', which blooms in mid- to late summer, heat up a border to sizzling temperatures.

mer, producing hot pink plumes above boldly cut leaves on 4-foot-tall stems.

Hot orange, red, or gold blossoms are mighty welcome in an exotic-looking garden, adding sparks of lava to sizzle up the color scheme. Choose torch lily (*Kniphofia uvaria*), Peruvian lily (*Alstroemeria aurantiaca*), montbretia (*Crocosmia* × *crocosmiiflora*), and golden ray (*Ligularia stenocephala*) for their molten-hued flowers.

These are just a few of the exciting perennials and bulbs that you can add to the garden to give it an exotic appearance. See the lists on pages 208 and 210 for other hot choices.

Creating a hardy backbone

Once you've selected the most tropical-looking hardy trees and shrubs that do well in your region, you can begin to use them to build your garden's backbone of permanent plants. These woody plants remain throughout the year and give the garden an enduring structure that you can decorate with tropical-looking perennials or with true tropicals. By fleshing out the garden with tropicals, such as cannas, gingers, flowering maples, coleus, bananas, and elephant's ears, you can redecorate the garden each year, following whatever whim strikes your fancy.

Tropical-looking combinations

When making combinations of hardy plants, keep in mind all the guidelines given in chapter 2 about using contrasting shapes, textures, and colors to jazz up your design. Hardy plants with the same characteristics as tropical plants should be used the very same way to make emphatic compositions. Contrast big, bold leaves with ferny, finely cut ones; hot orange flowers with cool blue ones; and tall, upright stems with cascading ones.

Layering the garden

You'll want to start off putting the garden together by planting the chosen hardy plants in layers, starting from the tallest and working down. Select a few trees and space them out as specimens or in groves, always keeping their ultimate size in mind. (If you already have mature tall trees, you may not need to plant more, but you can choose small understory trees to go beneath or off to the sides of the existing tall trees.) Beneath the trees plant groups of shrubs, leaving spaces in between the shrub groupings for adding perennials or tropicals. Keep the tallest shrubs to the rear if you're planting a border, or

in the center if you're planting a bed that will be viewed from all sides. Lastly, plant ground covers beneath the shrubs to weave the whole design together.

The garden's backbone does not necessarily have to be a structure of shrubs or trees that may take several years to become established—it could be constructed from fast-growing perennials and ornamental grasses to give you an almost instant effect. Although they may not afford year-round structure, they'll provide winter relief while the woody plants are getting established. Big grasses and perennials can shoot up to 6 to 10 feet tall in a relatively short time, and give the appearance of a substantial and mature planting the year after they are planted. Start a tropical-looking border of hardy plants in spring and it will look quite good the first year and become magnificent the next.

An easy tropical-looking design of hardy plants might begin with groups of three to five plants of ravenna grass (*Erianthus ravennae*) or maiden grass (*Miscanthus sinensis*) planted on 3-foot centers in the back of the border. Include groups of joe-pye weed (*Eupatorium maculatum* 'Atropurpureum') in between the groups of grasses, where its 4- to 5-foot-tall, purple-spotted stems and large, dome-shaped, purple flower heads will contrast in color and form with the lines of the grasses. Underplant it all with the sun-tolerant, quick-spreading, hay-scented fern (*Dennstaedtia punctilobula*), whose light green, 2-foot-tall, arching fronds will grow into a fine-textured swath of ground cover. You might also add groups of exotic-looking, heavily scented 'Golden Splendor' trumpet lilies (*Lilium*). These elegant lilies grow 6 feet tall and bloom in midsummer, before the late-summer blossoms of joe-pye weed, producing 10-inch-long, maroon flower buds that open into huge, golden trumpets. Add a couple of patches of blue lilyturf (*Liriope muscari* 'Big Blue'), mixing its very dark green tufts of grasslike leaves and spikes of summer-blooming blue flowers among the ferns for a sharp contrast of foliage texture and color.

Vines add a faintly mysterious touch to a garden when they are allowed to grow unrestrained to tangle with tree and shrub branches, creating the impression of an impenetrable maze. In a temperate garden, a few hardy vines work better in simulating that wild, layered jungle look than do tropical vines, because their woody trunks and main branches form gnarled ropes that mimic the huge, strangling lianas of the rain forest. Choose one or more hardy vines that can grow to massive proportions, such as a purple-flowered wisteria

(*Wisteria floribunda*), orange-flowered trumpet vine (*Campsis radicans*), or large-leaved Dutchman's pipe (*Aristolochia durior*), to bring a sense of strength and permanence to your garden. (For a listing of cold-hardy tropical-looking vines, see page 209.)

If you wish, encourage tropical vines, which you can treat as annuals, to wind their way up and into the hardy vine for an extra dollop of tropical splendor. Spring-flowering hardy vines, such as anemone-flowered clematis (*Clematis montana*), a particularly robust clematis species, and Carolina jessamine (*Gelsemium jasminoides*), make perfect candidates for using as ladders for summer-blooming tropical vines. Long after the hardy vine has finished blooming, a passionflower (*Passiflora* spp.) or morning glory (*Ipomoea* spp.) will be dishing out its flowers in the same spot.

The tropical plunge

Once you've established a backdrop of hardy plants, it's easy to put a tropical twist to the garden. To this basic structure you can add decorative containers planted with tropical plants, or plunge as many tropicals as you wish right into the garden bed wherever you find space. You can plan for as much or as little room for additional big or small tropical or perennial plants as you desire.

You might use the dramatically exotic-looking elephant's ears (*Colocasia* spp. and *Alocasia* spp.) to make a bold leaf contrast with ferns and ornamental grasses. Add a tall overwintered banana, a palm or two, and a colorful swath of coleus to your backbone of hardy trees and shrubs and you've got yourself a garden of such horticultural opulence that you might expect to see Dr. Livingstone setting up camp.

Lush foliage surrounds a small round pond with contrasting textures. All cold hardy, the plants include cutleaf red and green Japanese maples, sweet reed grass, umbrella plant, and ostrich fern.

CHAPTER FIVE

Winter **S**urvival **T**echniques

The large windows in this northern Connecticut conservatory make the garden outside part of the elegant indoor setting and provide plenty of light for overwintering tropicals.

Most tropical plants are perennials in their native habitats, thriving in mild, year-round temperatures. But when grown outdoors in a temperate garden, they're one-timers that quickly succumb to frigid winter temperatures unless you take measures to get them through. Most horticulturally inclined people typically have a nurturing gene and enjoy saving their tropical plants and growing them from one year to the next. After a while these plants become like old friends that you look forward to seeing in your garden each year.

Overwintered tropicals generally get better and better over the years, because they achieve impressive sizes with a lot of character. Being able to start out the season with a fully grown specimen that can make an immediate impact is reward enough for the effort involved in overwintering a good-size plant.

Having an overwintered plant on hand come spring can be a real time- and cost-saver. Instead of shopping around trying to find the perfect plant for a specific area, you can haul out an overwintered houseplant, bring a dormant containerized plant back to life, or plant out stored roots and tubers in the garden.

Many tropicals, whether you acquire them as young plants or as tubers or bulbs, are costly. The rarer species, because of their scarcity, can be even more expensive and are not easy to come by. Once a rare specimen comes into your possession—whether as a costly purchase, a gift from a special friend, or through your collecting endeavors—you'll surely want to carry it through many winters so you can savor its delights year after year.

Often a tropical plant that you've been growing outdoors for the summer is still growing vigorously and looks wonderful in early fall just before a frost. If this is a plant that will flourish as a houseplant, all the more reason to bring it indoors and continue enjoying it while it's in its prime.

The measures you take to overwinter a tropical plant in a temperate climate depend largely on the particular plants you want to save. The general idea is to mimic the way the plant rests during its natural dormancy period—if it has one—without allowing it to freeze. In a tropical climate, where daylength and temperatures vary only slightly throughout the year,

Winter Survival Techniques **89**

seasonal dry periods normally induce dormancy in which plants may actually drop their leaves for a month or longer or enter a period of slowed growth. But unusual cool spells may also slow a tropical plant down without killing it.

You have five basic choices when it comes to carrying tropical plants through the winter in a cold climate: overwintering the tropical as a growing houseplant, storing it as a dormant plant or tuber, collecting seed to start again in the spring, taking cuttings to root over the winter, or leaving it outside but protected from the elements. Some plants adapt to several different techniques, and you can pick and choose whatever methods work best for you. By all means, if you have a specific way of overwintering a plant that works well for you, then don't change a thing.

Below: This garden room features subfloor heating and large windows, doors, and skylights, making it ideal for plants and people. The brick floor isn't harmed by spilled water. *Bottom:* A second-floor glass-enclosed balcony offers a sunny winter retreat for tender plants.

Houseplant haven

Many tropical and subtropical plants that spend spring through fall outdoors in your garden adapt readily to wintering indoors as houseplants. Specimens used in containers on a porch or patio are easy to move in and out. Some mixed planters keep on growing happily indoors, too, so you can enjoy them as living bouquets in your living room or front hall. You can unearth tropicals that you plunged into a bed or border and plant them in decorative containers for their indoor sojourn. And if a specimen has gotten too large to fit into your house or greenhouse, consider radically pruning it to control its size or taking cuttings to carry it over as small youngsters and tossing out the overly large parent plant.

Many tropicals perform well as houseplants, but only if they get enough light and humidity. Sunlight levels in the North are low in winter, and a sunny south-facing window in January offers a lot less light than a sunny garden location in July. A plant that you've grown in shade in the garden might need a full-sun location indoors. If there isn't enough natural light in your house from windows and skylights, consider using grow lights to boost your houseplants' health.

Since heated indoor air is exceedingly dry, tropicals, especially the rain-forest dwellers, can be unduly stressed by low humidity levels. Try to counter this by growing sensitive plants in a humid location such as the kitchen or bathroom, or run a humidifier during the winter—the extra humidity will be good for you, too. Grouping plants together raises the humidity in their vicinity, as does using water-filled pebble trays under the pots. Also, try turning down the thermostat—cooler air seems less dry, and most tropicals will enjoy day and night temperatures in the 60s without complaint.

Sunporches and plant rooms

A sunny living room or kitchen will do as a place for tropicals to spend the winter, but better still is a solarium, sunporch, or conservatory—or even a greenhouse. A sun-drenched solarium or heated winterized porch designed as an extension of your indoor living space—with French doors or floor-to-ceiling windows on two or three sides and perhaps a skylight or two—offers the right light and humidity levels for nurturing growing tropicals through the winter. If it has a stone or brick floor, you won't need to worry about water spilling from the plants and damaging the flooring. You can turn a solarium into a garden room all dressed up with wonderful plants, and happily spend the winter there yourself basking among the greenery.

This homemade greenhouse attached to the side of a garage features a fiberglass roof and a small heater.

Unlike a solarium, a greenhouse is designed for plants first and people second. A greenhouse is glazed all over with glass or fiberglass and maintains much higher humidity levels than a conservatory. It should have a concrete or gravel floor with a drain, so you can splash and spill water at will. You don't really need a greenhouse unless you're into overwintering and propagating tropicals in a big way, although plant hobbyists will get a lot of pleasure from having a greenhouse where they can really putter.

Gradual reintroduction

Any tropical that you've overwintered as a houseplant or conservatory plant must be gradually reintroduced to the great outdoors so that it can readjust to outdoor sun levels. Too much sun too soon will burn the new growth, and if it doesn't kill the plant outright, it will set it back significantly. Placing a houseplant outside in full sun in May is rather like you going to the beach on the first day of summer and lying in the sun all day without applying any sunscreen. Both you and the plant will surely burn.

The best way to begin reintroducing a plant to higher light levels is to take it outside on a cloudy spring day and place it beneath the shade of a dense tree. Leave it there for a few days and then move it to a slightly brighter but still shady location. Give it forays into the full sun for an hour or two either very early or very late in the day for several more days—but never at midday. Finally, after a few weeks of acclimatizing it, move the plant to its permanent sunny location, but make the move on a cloudy day.

If your garden offers little shade, then you can try wrapping your plants in some type of protective shade cloth, such as several layers of sheer white curtain or cheesecloth. Every few days, remove a layer. It's best to do this unwrapping on cloudy days, too. Another option is to build a temporary overhead structure and cover it with shade cloth—the kind used in greenhouses—to keep off the sun.

Overwintering bulbs, tubers, and corms

Many tropical and subtropical plants, such as elephant's ears (*Alocasia* spp. and *Colocasia* spp.), fancy-leaved caladium (*Caladium bicolor*), canna lily (*Canna* spp.), sweet potato vine (*Ipomoea batatas*), and pineapple lily (*Eucomis bicolor*), form bulbs, tubers, or corms (commonly all referred to as "bulbs"). These underground storage structures contain nutrients and have growing points from which new stems and leaves can emerge. Such plants normally die down to the ground during dry spells or cool periods and survive underground as this dormant storage structure, remaining at rest for from two to three months to over a year until rain or warm temperatures induce them to send up new top growth. While it's dormant, the bulb remains dry and cool, and it is, of course, away from sunlight and freezing temperatures. In a temperate garden, usually cool or frosty autumn weather induces a bulbous tropical to go dormant, or you can bring on dormancy by withholding water. Once the plant has died back, carry it through the winter months by digging the bulb and storing it in a cool (but not freezing), dry, dark place. A root cellar, basement, garage, winterized porch, or even the back of a closet can make a good resting place.

Dig *Canna* and other tender tubers or bulbs in autumn after the first frost kills the top growth. Start digging far enough away from the stems to avoid damaging the tuber. Be sure to label the plant when you dig it up.

Steps to storage

The best time to dig up or harvest bulbs, tubers, and corms is in autumn right after the first frost has turned the plant tops black or brown and crisp. The plant will have then gone naturally dormant, having stored much-needed energy inside the bulb. It is in a state of suspended animation, needing no sunlight, water, fertilizer, high humidity, or heat, and sometimes not even soil, to survive until desirable growing conditions return.

After frost has killed the top growth, you can cut the stems back to 6 inches from the ground, so you have enough of a stem to use as a handle. Then use a spade or garden fork to carefully dig a circle around the outer edge of the plant. Thrust the fork under the root ball and gently push down on the tool's handle to lift the mass of bulbs from the ground. Be sure to label each plant when you dig it, because it's easy to mix the plants up and not know what you have once they're out of the ground.

There are several methods for storing dormant tropical bulbs. None is really all that much better than another; it's more a matter of what is easiest for you. If you have your own technique for storing tender bulbs, tubers, and corms such as gladioli or dahlias, then that's the way to go with your tropical plants, too. If you don't already have a favorite procedure, then the following methods will guide you.

The best way may be to wash all the soil from the bulbs and then allow them to air-dry for a few hours. By washing off the soil, you remove insects and fungal spores that may be in the soil, and you can examine the bulbs for rot or damage and cut away any diseased portions. Once they're dry, it's a good idea, although not necessary, to coat them with an antidesiccant spray to help reduce moisture loss and ward off fungal attack. (These sprays contain a biodegradable, waxy substance and are available at most garden centers.) Then wrap each bulb loosely in newspaper and store it in an opaque plastic garbage bag.

Some people favor digging, washing, and then packing the bulbs in peat moss, small bark chips, or sawdust. Others prefer to leave the soil intact around the dug-up bulbs and store them piled in cardboard boxes or milk crates covered by a sheet of plastic. Still others dry the clump upside down in the sun, shake or brush off the dry soil, apply a fungicide powder, and then store the bulbs in plastic bags or sawdust.

No matter whether you leave the soil on or wash it off, wrap the bulbs in plastic or bury them in peat moss, they need the right storage climate to make it until spring. Keep the dormant bulbs in a dark place, such as a basement, garage, cellar, or unheated sunporch, where the temperature hovers around 40° to 45°F, although a range of 35° to 50°F will not be lethal. Examine the roots every month or so to check for signs of rot or decay or excessive shrinking. Discard diseased bulbs and spray a bit of water on shriveled ones to rehydrate them.

Storing dormant tender plants or bulbs over the winter allows you to get an early start on spring. You can resurrect the dormant tropicals by potting them up, bringing them into a sunny room or setting them on a radiator to provide bottom heat, and starting to water them much sooner than you can if you plant them directly outside. This jump on the season means that you can enjoy larger, fuller plants in your tropical-style garden much earlier in the summer. For example, a canna tuber planted in the ground

Top to bottom: Cut off the tops and remove excess soil and long roots. After washing and spraying with antidesiccant, wrap dry tubers in paper. Place the labeled tubers in a plastic bag and keep them in a cool, dark place.

after the last frost date in your area will be weeks behind one started earlier in a pot indoors.

The great divide

Many tropical and subtropical plants that grow from bulbs, tubers, and corms can be propagated easily by division. This way, you can increase your stock for additional plantings, or use the bulbs to barter or trade with.

During the growing season, these plants put out a lot of growth and the underground storage structures increase in size. In fall, you can dig up the bulbs, store them intact, and then divide them in spring into several separate plants before you replant them. Or, if you wash and store them in newspaper or peat moss for the winter, you can divide them in fall. The choice is yours.

Usually bulbs and corms separate easily into individual structures when you dig them in fall. But to divide a tuber or a tuberous root, you may have to cut it apart. Be sure that each piece contains an "eye," or growing point.

Storing dormant tropical shrubs

Replacing the traditional doors to this cellar with glass doors turned them into skylights, transforming the basement steps into a perfect out-of-the-way winter storage area for tender plants.

You can induce many tropical plants and tender perennials—even ones that grow as shrubs and trees—into dormancy and keep them in that state for the winter. Even plants that normally grow year-round in the tropics and never experience a natural dormancy can be forced to go dormant in temperate regions if water is withheld and they are kept in a cool, dark place.

This is a very good method of overwintering tropical plants that you have no room for as houseplants but that you want to overwinter as large specimens for spring planting. Instead of keeping them as big plants in your living room while winter rages outside, you can store them out of the way as dormant plants in a basement, garage, or unheated porch. As long as the temperature stays above 35°F, many tropical plants just drop their leaves and rest until the growing conditions improve.

Steps to storage

Cut back the tops of herbaceous tropicals such as angelonia (*Angelonia angustifolia*), fountain grass (*Pennisetum setaceum*), sword fern (*Nephrolepis acutifolia*), and sunset plant (*Lysimachia congestiflora*) after frost has withered their tops. Then dig up the root ball and plant it in an appropriate-size pot in a soilless mix. If the plant is already in a container, you can leave it in its current pot for winter.

Bring woody tropical plants inside for storage just before a frost is expected. Don't cut back or prune woody plants in fall.

Just dig them up from the ground and plant them in a container of soilless mix, or wrap the soil-encased root ball tightly in plastic sheeting, a plastic bag, or a piece of burlap to keep it intact and then stuff it into a bucket, tub, or cardboard box. If the plant still has leaves, they will gradually yellow and probably drop off. New leaves will grow when you return the stored plant to light and warmth in spring. That's the time to prune the plant to shape it and control its size, if you wish, and to remove any dead wood or damaged branches.

Keep these dormant plants on the dry side, but not so parched that the soil shrinks away from the sides of the pot or becomes powdery dry. Check the soil moisture every two weeks or so, and if it is dry down to 2 to 3 inches, add a small amount of water. If the storage temperatures are cool, you will probably have to water only every two to four weeks.

Once spring arrives, the stored plants may sense it and begin to grow. Bring them out to the light and warmth, gradually reintroducing them to full sun as described earlier in this chapter.

In this cool, dark basement, potted hibiscus, angel's trumpet, ginger, banana, and elephant's ear have gone dormant and await spring's return.

One of the most fun—and easiest—tropicals to overwinter is a banana. This is because it is so exotic-looking and because if you overwinter it, it becomes larger and even more exotic. There are several methods to choose from.

Method one For a container-grown banana, chop the pseudostem (false stem) right off at pot level when frosty temperatures start to wither the foliage. Then store the container in a cool, dark place until spring, watering it occasionally. In spring, when new shoots begin to push up from the sides or from the central stem and form new plants, return the banana to the great outdoors.

Method two If the container and banana are too heavy to transport, or if you grow the plant right in the ground, dig it up before the first frost. Leave most of the soil around the roots and wrap them in a plastic bag. Store the plant in a dark, frost-free place until spring planting time. When storing a banana this way, don't remove the leaves or cut the stem; let them dry and brown naturally.

Method three If you have space in the house or in a conservatory, you don't have to force the banana into dormancy but can grow it as a houseplant, where it will remind you of summery weather even in February—and you may even get blossoms and fruit!

Method four In regions one or two zones colder than the banana's hardiness rating, you can protect the plant and leave it in the ground all winter. In fall just after first frost, cut off the blackened leaves at their bases, leaving the trunklike pseudostem. Pile mulch around the base of the plant. Then tie sheaves of straw around the stem with garden twine, add a layer of black plastic or tarpaper, tack the edges down, and wrap the whole thing up with burlap. Unwrap the banana in early spring when nighttime temperatures rise into the 40s and the last frost date has passed.

All wrapped up snug as bugs for winter, these *Musa basjoo* (Japanese fiber banana) survive temperatures as much as 20 degrees colder than they could without protection.

Defying winter

Ever since people started gardening, they've tried to grow the impossible, testing the limits of their zone and growing plants foreign to their region. Palm trees in Rhode Island? Bananas in Michigan? Why not? By learning a few survival tricks and techniques, you can get many tropical plants to live outdoors year-round in your garden, no matter where you live. Cajoling tropical plants to survive outdoors in winters colder than their hardiness limit provides a challenge and an intriguing hobby for many gardeners.

Many factors influence a plant's winter hardiness. Winter temperature is the most obvious one, but soil drainage, wind direction, sun exposure, duration of freezing temperatures, and even a plant's origin also affect its winter survival. When stretching a plant's hardiness limit out of its natural zone, you need to take all these factors into consideration. Techniques for overwintering tender plants outdoors in a harsh climate vary from a simple burlap covering to an elaborate underground heating-cable system. You can try all the methods described below and perhaps experiment with others on your own.

Young specimens of *Trachycarpus fortunei* (windmill palm) are nursed through the winter with protective wrapping.

It's usually possible to push a plant's zone limit by only one or two zones. Subtropicals hardy into zone 9 or 8 are the most likely candidates for surviving a winter in zone 7 or 6, if well protected. True tropicals, which are hardy only in totally frost-free conditions, cannot survive those zones even if protected, but they may be able to get through the winter in zones 9 and 8 with the proper measures. (For a listing of tropicals to overwinter outdoors, see page 210.)

If you live in colder zones than these, such as zone 5 or 4, you may not be able to push the limits of tropical plants, but you can with tropical-looking species that are hardy only into zone 7 or 6. Thus in Vermont, while you cannot get *Musa velutina* (zone 8b) through the winter even with protection, you can get *M. basjoo* (zone 6b) to grow year-round in the ground by wrapping it with insulation.

Thoughtful plant siting is probably the most important element for stretching a plant's limit by a zone or two. Every yard has microclimates, places in the garden that are colder or warmer than other areas. You want to seek out the warm spots and avoid the cold ones.

Warm and cold microclimates

A south-facing wall absorbs heat from the sun during the day and slowly radiates it back during the night, creating a location that's warmer during both the day and the night than the area would be without the wall there. An enclosed courtyard benefits from absorbed and radiated heat, as does a spot against a brick chimney or along a black asphalt driveway. Even a location near a clothes-dryer vent is warmer because the soil absorbs the vented heat. Sites protected from the wind by a wall, fence, tall hedge, or windbreak planting, such as a stand of tall evergreens, remain warmer in winter than unprotected areas.

Locations facing north and east are open to northerly gusts and winter storms and are colder than protected spots. Cold air flows downhill and settles in low spots on a property. Frost is likely to form first in these low areas, which are called frost pockets. Avoid these cold microclimates as sites for overwintering tender plants.

Protective wrapping

Depending on a plant's hardiness and how far out of its zone you're attempting to overwinter it, you may need only a light wrap of burlap or a really heavy insulation made up of several warm layers. You may want to experiment with a few "extra" plants you have around until you've figured out a method that works best for you, or to talk to other gardeners in your area.

Wait until cold temperatures or a light frost zaps the plant's foliage, which encourages tropicals and subtropicals to enter dormancy and actually become more cold-tolerant. Then wrap it up with as much protection as you think it needs.

For maximum protection, layer first with straw. Peel the straw off in sheets from the bale, packing it around the plant to build up a 1-foot-thick layer from top to bottom. The straw allows the plant to breathe and prevents condensation from forming on its stems and branches. Encircle the straw with garden twine or wire to hold it in place. Then cover the straw with opaque plastic sheeting, either white or black, secured with twine. The plastic keeps the straw dry and precludes water from settling in the plant's crown, a necessary step to prevent winter rot, and also makes an excellent wind block.

To keep the protective wrapping from taking off in the wind, secure it to the ground with U-shaped pins made from wire coat hangers. You can also mound mulch up and over the edge of the wrapping to hold it down.

You could stop here, but a plastic-wrapped plant residing in the garden all winter is rather unsightly, resembling a big discarded garbage bag. Turn the wrapped palm or fig into a garden gnome by adding a layer of burlap, cut evergreen boughs, or even a feather boa to camouflage the plastic.

If you are trying only to protect a borderline hardy plant from light frost or from desiccating wind, all you'll need is a wrapping of burlap. On mild sunny winter days, remove the wrap for a short time so the plant doesn't cook.

When nighttime temperatures remain consistently above freezing in spring, take off the wrapping. Remove all the insulating straw and plastic layers, but put the burlap back on for a few days to gradually accustom the tropical plant to the cold and to prevent sunscald from the sudden exposure to the light. Keep the plant covered lightly with burlap for a few days, uncover it for half a day for a few more days, and then remove the covering altogether on a cloudy or rainy day.

After all this effort, don't let a surprise late frost or snowstorm freeze your overwintered tropical. It's a good idea to keep the burlap wrap, and plastic, and maybe even the packing material, handy for a late-season freeze or snowstorm. Just in case.

Much-needed mulch

To protect tender perennials and tender bulbs left in the ground in a cold climate, try piling up a deep layer of mulch over the ground to insulate them. Place 6 to 12 inches of shredded wood chips or rotted compost on top of the soil. In areas where the ground normally freezes only a few inches down, this deep layer of mulch prevents the soil from freezing and protects tender roots and bulbs sufficiently to bring them through the winter.

Tender plants can be overwintered right in the ground by burying them in very deep mulch to protect the roots from freezing. Remove the mulch in spring.

Miniature greenhouses

In the Deep South or in subtropical areas where frost can occur, you can build a wooden frame covered with clear polyethylene sheeting or fiberglass panels to create a miniature portable greenhouse to enclose a tropical plant or two during the winter. Ventilation is important to avoid cooking the plants on sunny days. Make the sides from heavy-duty sheets of polyethylene, so you can roll them up or down, depending on the weather. Be sure, too, that you secure the structure to the ground so it won't blow away during a storm.

In colder areas, you can pack the frame with dry leaves—oak leaves work well because they don't compact. In late winter or early spring, depending on the temperature and the type of plant you're protecting, lift the frame off to allow for air circulation and to prevent warm temperatures from triggering the plant into growing. On cold nights, replace the frame or wrap the plant as need be.

Such a frame, even if it is not stuffed with insulation, can get some plants through a winter they would not normally survive, because it keeps them warmer, but also because it keeps water from settling into the plants'

A vented mini-greenhouse, *left*, provides winter protection for a tender fan palm that grows outdoors all year at the Brooklyn Botanic Garden, effectively pushing its hardiness limits. After the palm's winter wraps are removed, *right*, it feels at home in a New York summer's heat and humidity.

crowns and causing them to rot. This is especially true for yuccas (*Yucca* spp.), century plants (*Agave* spp.), tree ferns (*Dicksonia* spp.), and some palms.

Artificial heat sources

Besides locating them in a warm microclimate or protecting them with insulation, you can also keep tender plants toasty outside in winter by providing them with artificial heat. Gardeners who have attempted to push the limits of their zones have tried many methods. Here are some that have been surprisingly successful.

- Wrap strings of Christmas lights fairly densely around a plant's limbs and leave them turned on night and day as needed during freezing weather.

- Install a 100-watt light bulb inside a polyethylene tent covering the plant and turn it on every night. Ventilate the tent during the day if needed.

- Bury low-wattage heating cables (available at most hardware stores for preventing frozen pipes) in the ground over a tender plant's roots.

- Twine a low-wattage heating cable inside the insulating material of a plant wrapped with protective plastic and straw.

- For a more sophisticated, permanent system, run hot-water pipes underground. These are sometimes used in commercial greenhouses and also as snow and ice melters under sidewalks and driveways.

*H*ave fun experimenting with these and any other overwintering methods you can dream up, and be sure to enjoy the challenge. No matter how you get your tropicals through the winter, they are sure to reward your efforts with a blaze of glory in summer.

Encyclopedia
of Plants

Abelmoschus manihot (Hibiscus manihot)

(ai-bill-MOW-schuss MAN-eh-hot)

Yellow Musk Mallow

Tender perennial treated as an annual; grows 4 to 6 ft tall in one season. Hardy in zones 9–11.

Big and dramatic yet extremely graceful, this fast grower looks terrific planted in groups among perennials and grasses, and it can be used for height in a grand-size container. Arrange it with lower plants in front to cover up its occasionally bare knees, but allow its sprays of pale yellow, hibiscus-like flowers to tower undeterred to head height. Sheer like crepe paper, the blossoms have maroon eyes, and the large, green leaves are deeply lobed like those of most hibiscus. If started early from seed indoors and set outside as soon as danger of frost has passed, yellow musk mallow blooms from mid- or late spring until a heavy frost. You can use the dried seedpods in arrangements.

Cultivation

Grow in full sun in average garden soil. Plants bloom best and are most vigorous if the soil is not allowed to dry out and fertilizer is applied monthly. Deadhead faded flowers and then cut off spent flower stalks just below the last blossom to encourage branching and continuous bloom. Let the seedpods mature at the end of summer to use in dried arrangements or for collecting seed. Don't try to overwinter this one—treat it as an annual.

Cultivars and Similar Species

A. manihot 'Cream Cup': This desirable cultivar blooms profusely, producing larger flowers in a clear, creamy yellow with small, deep burgundy eyes.

A. moschatus (Hibiscus abelmoschus) (musk mallow, silkflower): This tropical-looking, tender perennial can grow to a shrubby 5 ft tall, but some of its popular cultivars, such as 'Mischief' and 'Pacific Light Pink', are much lower and more compact, reaching only 18 in. high. Flowers are cup-shaped and pink or red, often with white eyes. When this species is grown in full sun, the foliage takes on a red burnish. ✦✦

Abelmochus manihot 'Cream Cup'

Abutilon (ah-BOO-tih-lon)

Flowering Maple, Chinese Lantern

Upright or weeping shrub, to 1 to 10 ft tall and 3 ft wide, depending on the species; grows 1 to 3 ft in one season. Hardy in zones 8–10; some to zone 7.

Aptly named for their showy, maplelike leaves and for their eye-catching bell- or bowl-shaped blossoms, flowering maples grow into slender weeping shrubs or small trees in a single season. Even if they didn't bloom, these plants would offer plenty of exciting color and texture just from their foliage, which is often variegated with yellow or white. However, bloom they do—almost nonstop. Blossoms dangle along the lengths of the stems, their sheer, crepe-paper-like texture catching the sun. Use bush types as fillers in a container or border; weeping types look best in an overhead hanging basket, where you can look right into the depths of their downward-facing blossoms. Although flowering diminishes during summer's worst heat, cool autumn nights encourage profuse rebloom. Flowering maples fortify the fall garden with flowers and foliage, because they continue undaunted by light frost.

Cultivation

Abutilons thrive outdoors in partly shady to mostly sunny locations where the soil is evenly moist, but they suffer in hot, dry, windy spots. They need heavy fertilization; apply slow-release fertilizer when planting and then liquid fertilizer weekly during active growth. You can train or prune these shrubs into almost any shape, so don't be afraid to cut a large one back severely if it gets too big. Flowering maples can be overwintered as houseplants as long as you can provide an indoor location with strong light and cool temperatures. If you don't have space indoors for a large plant, take semi-ripe cuttings from the stem tips in late summer and root them to carry over during winter as small houseplants.

Species and Cultivars

Numerous cultivars are available with yellow, gold, orange, pink, red, burgundy, or white flowers and with solid green or gold- or white-variegated leaves. Some of the best performers are listed below.

Upright Types

A. pictum 'Thompsonii': Probably the best-known flowering maple, this old-fashioned tropical houseplant has bell-shaped, salmon flowers and mottled green-and-yellow leaves.

Abutilon pictum 'Thompsonii'

A. × 'Marion Stewart': Combine this cultivar with gold-variegated plants for a hot color scheme; its blossoms are bold orange with deep red veins, creating a vivid effect. The green leaves, though narrow, are still lobed like a maple's. This is one of the most cold-hardy types, surviving winters in zone 7.

A. × 'Snowbell': With a simple but beautiful green-and-white color scheme, 'Snowbell' enhances white-variegated plants such as *Canna* 'Stuttgart' or silver-foliaged plants such as *Plectranthus argentatus.* Yellow stamens adorn the pure snowy white bells, which stand out against the solid green, lobed leaves.

A. × 'Souvenir de Bonn': Everyone loves this cultivar's flowers, which are large salmon bells with darker veins. But most gardeners grow it for its maple-shaped green leaves, which measure up to 6 in. wide and feature bright white margins, lending a crisp effect.

Cascading Types

A. megapotamicum 'Variegata' (variegated weeping Chinese lantern): An arresting plant for the daring gardener, this weeper features long, drooping flowers that seem like a red-and-yellow cousin of fuchsia. A red, balloonlike calyx forms the base of the flower and from it protrude a twist of yellow petals and several long black anthers. These striking flowers echo the raw colors

of the heavily marbled, green-and-yellow, lance-shaped leaves.

Mounding Types

A. × 'Apricot Glow': Pastel blossoms in a delicate apricot-pink make a gentle accent against the green leaves. This cultivar combines well with orange- or pink-variegated *Coleus,* the burnished leaves of copperleaf (*Acalypha* spp.), the various leaf colors of *Ipomoea batatas,* and almost any floral shade of nasturtium.

A. × 'Moonchimes': You can't go wrong with 'Moonchimes'—its green leaves and soft-spoken, yellow blossoms blend well with almost any color in the garden.

A. × 'Pink Blush': This cultivar grows into a mound of green leaves and delicate pink, bowl-shaped flowers with pale yellow centers. The color scheme makes it a good companion for plants that lend themselves to a gentler, pastel look, such as *Plumbago, Helichrysum, Felicia,* ferns, and the small-flowered fuchsias and begonias.

A. × 'Tiber's Red': Use this cultivar, which has green leaves and bright red flowers, to drip over the edge of a container, where it will look splendid echoing red- and purple-toned leaves of nearby foliage plants such as *Coleus* 'Stormy Weather', *Alternanthera* (bloodleaf), or even an interesting green or green-and-white cultivar of ivy. ◆◆◆

Acalypha (ak-ah-LYE-fah)
Chenille Plant, Copperleaf Plant

Tender woody subshrub to use as a trailing ground cover or as a large shrub to 12 to 15 ft; grows 2 to 3 ft in one season. Hardy to zone 10.

Acalypha repens 'Strawberry Firetail'

Several colorful species of this tropical genus make popular choices for adventurous gardeners. Two are grown for their flowers and two for their foliage. *A. hispida,* admired for its bizarre-looking, long, dangling flowers that resemble velvety tails made of chenille, commands attention as a very large oddity. Its more subdued cousin, *A. repens,* forms a smaller, trailing plant of more delicate proportions. *A. wilkesiana,* grown for its shiny leaves, which are patterned like colorful marble and bunched together in fanlike clusters, becomes much larger than *A. godseffiana* 'Heterophylla', which has slender, but equally colorful, leaves. Use these attention-getting plants as focal points or specimens in a border or container, where they can be combined with green plants or ones with more subdued flowers and foliage that echo copperleaf's palette of rusty red, olive, pink, and burgundy foliage or chenille plant's exotic flowers.

Cultivation

All grow best with full sun in rich, well-drained soil, although *A. hispida* performs pretty well in half a day of sun. Try to keep the soil evenly moist, because these plants lose their leaves if the soil dries too much. Fertilize twice monthly during the growing season. These plants respond well to pruning, so don't be afraid to cut them back to maintain a desirable size and shape.

You can easily overwinter containerized copperleaf or chenille plants as houseplants in a highlight situation. Be sure to bring them indoors before nights drop into the 40s, and keep them well watered in the dry indoor conditions. If plants grow too large, cut them back severely or take semihardwood cuttings in summer and fall to propagate new plants.

Species and Cultivars

A. godseffiana 'Heterophylla' (**lance copperleaf**): Unlike chenille plant, lance copperleaf is a colorful foliage plant grown for its lance-shaped, 2- to 3-in.-long leaves, which are rusty orange with splashes of olive green and gold. Insignificant, reddish bronze, fuzzy catkins hide behind the leaves. This small, showy shrub grows 18 to 24 in. in a season but doesn't get much taller than 3 feet.

A. hispida (**chenille plant**): One of the odder-looking plants you can grow in northern climates, chenille plant produces 18-in.-long, dangling red, pink, or rose catkins in clusters along the branches. 'Alba' has creamy white catkins. Plants grow rapidly: a small one set out in early summer can grow to 3 to 4 ft tall by summer's end. If left unpruned and overwintered indoors, this shrubby, upright plant can reach 12 to 15 ft in height, but you'll probably want to treat it as an annual.

A. repens (A. pendula) (**strawberry firetail**): Resembling a miniature chenille plant, strawberry firetail has bright rose-red, bushy catkins that are only 2 to 4 in. long. These bloom prolifically all season on trailing stems. This species looks wonderful in a hanging basket or as a trailer at the edge of a container.

A. wilkesiana (**copperleaf**): Another plant with exceptionally colorful leaf patterns and shapes, this one also bears somewhat showy flowers in the form of 2- to 3-in. upright catkins, which vary in color. 'Ceylon' has rounded leaves in copper-maroon with cream to pink leaf margins. 'Kilavea' (miniature fire dragon) is a dwarf form with red, pink, and cream spindle-shaped leaves. 'Macrophylla' (giant heart copperleaf) has 12-in.-wide, heart-shaped leaves variegated with red, copper, and green. Copperleaf is a large upright shrub that can grow to 12 to 15 ft tall if unpruned; a small plant set out in early summer can grow to 3 to 4 ft during its first season.

◆◆◆

Acidanthera bicolor var. murieliae

(Gladiolus callianthus)

(ass-ih-DAN-ther-uh BYE-kul-or mew-ree-el-LEE)

Abyssinian Gladiolus, Peacock Orchid

Tender bulb (corm), to 3 to 4 ft tall;
grows to mature size the first season.
Hardy in zones 9–11; to zone 8 with winter protection.

Acidanthera bicolor **var.** *murieliae*

Use this elegant plant for its sword-shaped leaves and tall flower sprays in a mixed container, where it won't be missed at summer's end when it must be cut back. Or plant it in a border among lower plants. However you grow it, be sure to locate Abyssinian gladiolus where you can enjoy the fine fragrance. This bulb actually originates from Mozambique in southeastern Africa—thousands of miles from Abyssinia (Ethiopia).

Cultivation

Purchase corms and start them indoors in pots for an early-summer show, or plant them in groups of three or more corms in garden beds after the danger of frost has passed. Plant corms 4 to 6 in. deep and 6 to 12 in. apart. To ensure summer-long blossoms, plant a succession of corms, as you would with hybrid gladioli, every two weeks. Plants grow best in full sun but perform well in half a day of sun. They need well-drained soil that dries between waterings and flourish in average to heavy soil. Fertilize monthly.

For best appearance, deadhead individual blossoms. When blooming stops and the foliage becomes unattractive, cut it back. In cold climates, dig up the corms after frost and overwinter them in a cool, dry place; leave them in the ground where they are hardy. Parent corms will have doubled in size and will bloom prolifically the following year. Grow the small baby corms (cormels) in containers or a nursery bed for a season until they reach blooming size. ✦✦

Resembling a tall clump of graceful, gray-green iris leaves, this summer-blooming subtropical "bulb" bears arching sprays of long-stalked, 4-in.-wide, white flowers with maroon starbursts in their throats. The blossoms emit an exotic, sweet fragrance. Individual flowers last only a few days, but the sprays keep on producing more of them over several weeks and make excellent cut flowers. As one flower stalk finally ceases blooming, new stalks may grow from younger corms if the plant is growing vigorously. Eventually blooming stops altogether and the leaves begin to decline as the plant goes dormant.

Agapanthus (ag-uh-PAN-thus)
African Lily, Lily-of-the-Nile

Fleshy-rooted perennial, to 1½ to 3 ft tall; reaches mature height the first season. Most types hardy in zones 9–11; some hardy in zones 6–11.

Big, round clusters of blue, funnel-shaped flowers swaying at the tops of 3-ft-tall, bare flower stalks give African lily a bold elegance that evokes the lushness of the tropics. When planted in groups in a border or a container, these tender bulbs bring drama to the garden. Most cultivars bloom more profusely in early summer, then continue blooming more lightly throughout the growing season. Leaves are glossy dark green and strap-shaped, forming dense basal clumps. Several species of this amaryllis-family member hail from coastal or mountainous regions of South Africa and bloom prolifically in mild climates. To create a tropical look with cold-hardy plants, choose one of the many new hybrids, which can be left in the ground with a heavy winter mulch in moderate climates.

Agapanthus africanus 'Peter Pan'

Cultivation

African lilies thrive in full sun or part shade and humus-rich, moist soil. Fertilize them once in spring and once in summer. Cut off faded flower stalks. Container-grown plants bloom most lavishly if pot-bound, so don't be too eager to repot them. You can overwinter containerized plants as house-plants in a sunny location, where they'll keep growing and blooming with regular water and fertilizer. If you don't have a suitable place indoors to grow the plant over winter, you might try storing the container in a cool, dark place and allowing the soil to go dry and the plant to go dormant. If you're growing African lilies directly in the ground, leave the cold-hardy cultivars in place and mulch heavily in fall. Dig up roots of tender types and store them as you would dahlias.

Species and Cultivars

A. africanus: This species has narrow leaves and 1½- to 2-ft-tall flower stalks that are topped with rounded heads of pale blue, tubular flowers. Flower heads may contain 20 to 50 flowers per cluster. Individual blossoms are darker along the edges of the petals and in the center. 'Albus' is an elegant, white-flowered form with shorter stems; hardy to zone 7 with winter protection. 'Baby Blue' has pale blue flowers on 18-in. stalks. 'New Blue' bears 2-ft-tall stalks of sky blue blossoms in late summer.

A. praecox ssp. *orientalis* (*A. orientalis*): Glossy and bold, the arching leaves of this species are wider than those of *A. africanus* and are about 2 ft long. Flower stalks grow taller, to 3 to 4 ft. Flowers are various shades of blue, are held in rounded clusters 6 to 12 in. across, and contain up to 100 individual, trumpet-shaped flowers. 'Albidus' bears white flowers in dense clusters. 'Aureovittatus' has yellow-and-green-striped leaves and blue blossoms. 'Blue Moon' features a large head of deep blue flowers on strong, 3-ft stems in late summer; hardy to zone 8. 'Variegatus' has white-and-green-striped leaves.

Hybrids

'Bressingham Blue': Very dark blue flowers on compact plants with thin, strap-shaped leaves characterize this cold-hardy cultivar. Flower stalks reach 2 ft tall. Hardy to zone 5.

Headbourne Hybrids: The flower color of this group of cold-hardy, 3-ft-tall hybrids varies from pale blue to deep purple. All grow into tall, sturdy plants and will overwinter in zone 7, or perhaps 6, with a heavy winter mulch.

'Midnight Blue': This strong grower with large flower heads bears dark blue-violet flowers on 3-ft stems. Hardy to zone 7.

'Peter Pan': This cold-hardy, dwarf form reaches 1½ to 2 ft tall and produces numerous rounded clusters of medium blue blossoms for several weeks in early summer. Hardy to zone 7.

'Petite Blue': Delicate light blue flowers in small rounded umbels make this an ideal container plant. Leaves are narrow and reach 1 ft tall. Hardy to zone 8.

'Tinkerbell': This dainty, compact grower forms small clumps of cream-and-green-variegated leaves and blue flowers. Hardy to zone 8.

'Wavy Navy': This striking cultivar is a medium grower with broad leaves and dark blue flower clusters on 2-ft-tall stalks. Hardy to zone 9.

❖❖❖

Agave (ah-GAH-vay)
Century Plant

Slow-growing, evergreen, succulent perennial, from 1 to 10 ft tall.
Hardy in zones 9–11, some types to zone 7 or 6.

You either love or hate these denizens of tropical and sub-tropical North and Central America, but either way you cannot ignore them, because century plants stand out wherever they grow, evoking images of hot, thirsty surroundings and beating sun. Sculptural in appearance, their thick, succulent leaves grow in stemless whorls to form a rosette of armored foliage—often side shoots (pups) grow at their bases, forming clusters of several rosettes. Some kinds throw out long-reaching, swordlike leaves, while others tightly bundle their leaves into neat symmetry. All arm themselves with vicious spines at their leaf tips and usually along the leaf margins. Flowering is not common. Although some species bloom when 4 to 5 years old, others, such as *A. americana,* reputedly do not bloom until they are 100 years old, thus the name "century plant." The flowers grow on a tall, leafless wand or candelabrum, and once they set seed, the parent plant dies, allowing the pups to carry on. Century plants look best used as specimens in large decorative containers on a patio or deck, where other plants won't compete with their dramatic outlines. You might also include one in an arid border or a xeriscape garden.

Cultivation

Give agaves full sun and well-drained, sandy soil, to mimic their natural habitat. If necessary, amend

Agave americana 'Glauca'

the soil with gravel or coarse sand. Fertilize only sparingly, if at all, at the beginning of the growing season. Allow the soil to dry out between waterings, and keep plants very dry in winter. Specimen plants in containers will do well over the winter as houseplants or conservatory plants if you provide a very sunny place and do not overwater them. Where plants are cold-hardy, winter survival often depends on soil moisture; plants suffer from root rot in wet winter soil.

Species and Cultivars

A. americana (**American century plant**): In its natural habitat, this species reaches monstrous proportions—10 ft tall and wide with 25-ft-tall flower stalks. Even in captivity, this dweller of the American Southwest becomes enormous

when grown in a container, its far-flung and downward-curving, big, fat leaves reaching several feet long. Leaves vary from dusky green to blue-gray to striped and have hooked thorns along the margins and a long vicious thorn at each tip. The species grows year-round in zones 9–10 and in warmer parts of zone 8 under dry conditions. 'Glauca' looks quite thirsty and offers bright steel blue leaves. 'Marginata' has gray-green leaves with yellow or white leaf edges. The leaves of 'Mediopicta' are green with a wide central yellow band. The cultivars are not as cold-hardy as the species.

A. macroacantha: Blue-gray, 1-ft-long leaves form an urn-shaped rosette about 2 ft tall. The small, curved spines growing along the leaf margins are fairly harmless, but watch out for the vicious black thorns at the tips. Hardy in zones 10–11; marginal in zone 9b.

A. parryi (**mescal**): In contrast to American century plant, mescal forms a neat, self-contained, dense rosette of foliage. The beautiful leaves are almost rounded, are blue-gray with dark contrasting spines, and form a rosette 2 to 3 ft across. Tall spikes of creamy flowers may appear in summer on mature plants. Native to the mountains of Arizona, New Mexico, and Mexico, this is one of the most cold-hardy species of *Agave,* surviving into zone 5 if winter conditions are dry.

A. parviflora: Forming a looser, 1-ft-tall rosette of narrower leaves, this odd-looking, smaller agave is as striking in its own way as is mescal. The green leaves have white margins decorated with curling white fibers, instead of thorns, and a single sharp spine at each tip. Yellowish green flowers may bloom on 5-ft-tall stalks. Hardy in zones 7–10.

A. stricta: Resembling a big green or blue-green porcupine, this agave grows to 3 ft tall and 4 ft wide. Rounded in outline and very fine-textured, the plant has a refined architectural appeal. Its 3-ft-long, skewerlike, green leaves grow in a symmetrical rosette and have spines only at their tips. Flowers are red to purple. Hardy in zones 8–10.

❖❖❖

Allamanda cathartica
(al-ul-MAN-duh kuh-THAR-tih-kuh)
Golden Trumpet, Bush Allamanda
Tropical vine or shrub, to 10 ft; grows 3 to 4 ft a year.
Hardy in zones 10–11.

Allamanda cathartica 'Hendersonii'

This fast-growing South American vine leaps across an overhead arbor, cloaking it in short order with dripping branches of foliage and bunches of sunny blossoms right up until an autumn frost. The 3- to 5-in.-long, bright yellow blossoms bloom almost nonstop and are well complemented by whorls of glossy, green leaves. In its native jungle habitat, golden trumpet can reach 50 ft, but in a temperate-garden setting it grows with more restraint. Because this vine clambers rather than twines, you'll need to tie it in place on a tree trunk, arbor, or wall trellis. And because it responds well to pruning, you can train the vine to form a bushy, open shrub or a standard with a rounded head full of golden flowers. Combine golden trumpet with bright-leaved plants such as *Alternanthera, Coleus,* and *Strobilanthes,* or echo the yellow flowers with yellow-variegated foliage plants such as *Canna* 'Pretoria' or *Sanchezia.* Flowering plants such as *Plumbago, Lantana, Verbena, Heliotrope,* and *Duranta* also make excellent companions.

Cultivation

Grow golden trumpet in full sun in almost any well-drained soil, from fertile to sandy. Keep it fairly moist when it's blooming and drier when it's not actively growing. Fertilize containerized plants weekly with half-strength liquid fertilizer. If you plan to overwinter the containerized plant in a sunroom, greenhouse, or conservatory, locate it where it has plenty of room to grow. To control its size, prune back in spring before taking the vine outside. Exercise caution when pruning, because the milky sap can cause skin irritation and all plant parts are poisonous if ingested.

Cultivars and Similar Species

A. blanchetii (A. violacea) (**purple allamanda**): This bushy vine blooms during summer, producing 3-in.-long, purplish pink trumpets with darker throats. It is not as vigorous a grower as golden trumpet.

A. cathartica 'Hendersonii': This vigorous selection has 6-in.-long, golden yellow flowers with brown throats and bronze-tinged flower buds, creating a rich look.

❖❖❖

Alocasia (al-oh-KAY-see-uh)
Elephant's Ear, Taro, African Mask
Herbaceous perennial, to 1 to 10 ft tall;
can grow to mature height in first year.
Hardy in zones 9–11; some to zones 7b–8.

Their often giant, shield-shaped leaves evoke the eerie lushness of the jungle like few other plants can, making elephant's ears a must for any tropical-looking garden. These tropical and subtropical foliage plants adapt readily to temperate climates, flourishing during summer's heat, humidity, and plentiful rain showers. Their big, flashy leaves rise from very short stems that grow from underground rhizomes or tubers. New leaves continue to develop throughout the summer, and side shoots create full clumps of exotic foliage. The plants can reach their full height over the course of a single growing season, forming bigger and bigger clumps over the years. Large species work well planted right in the garden to make a bold focal point among lower or finer-textured plants, or planted in a container to create an eye-catching specimen plant. Smaller species look less dramatic but no less tropical—arrange them in groups in a border or use them in combination with smaller flowering plants in containers.

Cultivation

Elephant's ears thrive in humus-rich, moist soil. Most do best in part shade, but some need full sun. To prevent the leaves from wilting and turning yellow, provide plentiful water and do not allow the soil to dry out. Fertilize the large species weekly, especially those in containers; smaller species, every other week. You can divide mature plants easily by digging them up and gently pulling off and replanting the small side shoots. Containerized plants can be overwintered as houseplants provided you can maintain high humidity—a sunny bathroom is ideal. Otherwise, allow the plants to go dormant and store them in their containers over winter. Dig tubers from plants growing in the ground after the leaves have died back and store the roots in a cool, dry place until spring planting time.

Species and Cultivars

A. × *amazonica* 'African Mask': Eerily reminiscent of a ritual tribal mask, the narrow, arrow-shaped leaves of this striking plant are a glossy, deep dark green with silver-white markings outlining the scalloped edges and painting a facelike pattern of veins in the center. It grows 2 to 3 ft tall. This cultivar cannot withstand even a chill; don't bring it outdoors until daytime temperatures are above 70°F. You can overwinter it as a houseplant in a warm, humid location out of direct sun.

A. 'Black Velvet': A small type, to about 1 ft tall, this pretty plant features velvety, heart-shaped leaves colored so deep a green that they look almost black. A contrasting pattern of silver veins radiates from the leaf centers, making this a real beauty. Grow this variety in shade. It also makes a good houseplant. Hardy to zone 10.

A. 'Hilo Beauty': Small for an alocasia, this hybrid forms 1½-ft-tall clumps. Arrow-shaped and less than 1 ft long, the leaves have an apple green background delicately spotted with cream, white, and light green. Hardy to zone 9.

A. macrorrhiza (giant elephant's ear, giant taro): Glossy green with pale green veins, the leaf blades of this gigantic plant are 3 to 4 ft long and are borne on 4-ft-long leaf stalks, creating a plant that becomes 8 to 10 ft tall and wide. The leaves grow upright at first, pointing toward the sky, hence their other common name: upright elephant's ear. This Asian tropical needs plenty of moisture and grows readily in boggy soil, in sun or shade. It is cold-hardy in zones 8–10 and can overwinter outdoors in zone 7b with a heavy

Alocasia × *amazonica* 'African Mask'

mulch. The leaves of 'Variegata' are patterned with creamy white, gray-green, and dark green blotches, but the plant reaches only to 3 ft in height and is less cold-hardy.

A. plumbea: The 2- to 3-ft-long, shield-shaped leaves of this highly ornamental, medium-size species are metallic, reddish green on top and have deep reddish plum undersides, veins, and stems. The new leaves are borne pointing up at an angle like those of *A. macrorrhiza.* This species makes a poor houseplant; overwinter it as a dormant tuber stored in slightly moist soil. Hardy in zones 9–11; marginal in zone 8b.

For additional elephant's ears, see Colocasia *and* Xanthosoma *entries.*

❖❖❖

A*loe* (AL-oh)
Aloe

Slow-growing, succulent, shrubby or treelike perennial,
from 1 to 10 ft tall.
Hardy in zones 9–11; some types to zone 8.

Most aloes grow as ground-hugging rosettes of succulent green, gray, or blue-gray leaves armed with sharp teeth along their edges; some, however, have trunks and branches in a candelabrum shape, with spiny leaves bunched in rosettes at the branch tips. These desert dwellers are similar in habit to agaves, to which they are related and with which they are often confused, but unlike the New World agaves, these lily-family members hail from Africa and their fleshy leaves exude slimy juice when cut—agaves have a stringy, fibrous interior. Flowers form freely in many species, blooming in eye-catching clusters on tall, bare stems in winter and spring. The large species look most impressive in large ceramic or earth-toned containers; the smaller species can be massed in a decorative, low container. Both sizes can be put in the ground in a xeriscape garden, but they may suffer in areas of high rainfall or in heavy soil.

Cultivation

Grow aloes in full or almost full sun in sandy, very well drained soil. Fertilize and water sparingly. They make excellent houseplants during the winter if given a sunny window. Water when the leaves begin to show signs of shriveling. Water winter bloomers more often and fertilize them once a month.

Aloe striata

Species and Cultivars

A. **arborescens:** When young and grown in a 10- to 12-in. pot, this aloe forms an impressive rosette of narrow, curved, spiny, gray or blue-green leaves. Eventually, however, the plant starts to grow a trunk and branches, which looks beautiful but makes it difficult to locate and to handle. Flowers are spikes of tubular, scarlet or yellow blossoms with green tips. Hardy in zones 10–11; marginal in zone 9.

A. **plicatilis** (**fan aloe**): Lacking spines, this succulent forms a dramatic, one-sided, fanlike arrangement of 1-ft-long, fleshy, gray-green leaves. With age, the plant grows a trunk and branches with leaf fans at the branch tips. Red to orange flowers bloom in spring on 2-ft-high spikes that emerge from the leaf fans.

A. **striata** (**coral aloe**): Closely resembling an agave, this aloe produces thick, silver-gray leaves that have thornless edges with a narrow white or red margin, giving it a lovely color scheme. Plants grow into 3-ft-wide, stemless rosettes that send up a tall, branched spike of coral-red blossoms in spring.

♦♦♦

A*lternanthera* (all-ter-NAN-thur-uh)
Calico Plant, Bloodleaf,
Christmas Clover, Joseph's Coat

Sprawling, tender herbaceous perennial; grows to 1 ft tall in a season.
Hardy in zones 8–11.

The delicate texture of these foliage plants is offset by their attention-grabbing color schemes. Calico plants distinguish themselves as the perfect filler in a tropical garden, where their fine-textured leaves weave like a tapestry around the feet of gingers and bananas in beds and borders or spill like a wave of color over the edge of a container. The oval or lance-shaped leaves vary from ½ to 3 in. long. Plants range in habit from low and sprawling to tidy and mounding; the latter types are easily pruned into little hedges for annual knot-garden displays, as was a popular use for them during Victorian times. Because the plants offer a variety of color choices, you can get creative and combine the painted leaves with an assortment of bold-colored flowering plants to generate some real excitement in your garden. Although these plants are not grown for their flowers, the small, white, cloverlike blossoms add a pretty note when they bloom in late fall and winter. Don't confuse *Alternanthera* with two other closely related tropicals that go by the same common names. *Amarathus tricolor,* also called Joseph's coat, looks rather like an *Alternanthera* on steroids: it grows upright to 3 ft tall and has large, wildly colored leaves. *Iresine lindenii,* also called bloodleaf, grows upright to 1 to 2 ft tall and features narrow reddish purple, pink, or magenta leaves.

Cultivation

Although calico plants grow well in part shade, their colors are brighter in full sun. Provide rich, well-drained soil. All types need plentiful moisture, but *A. dentata* suffers most if allowed to dry out. These plants are not heavy feeders; fertilize them once a month during the growing season. The more vigorous species may need to be cut back once or twice during summer to keep them in bounds, but the smaller, compact ones will not. All types make good houseplants, and you can overwinter specimens indoors on a sunny windowsill, where they will bloom during winter. Treat mass-planted calico plants as annuals, since they are easy to come by and reach full size in a single season. You can also carry them over the winter by taking cuttings in late summer or early fall before they set buds.

Alternanthera dentata 'Tricolor'

Species and Cultivars

Sprawling Ground-cover Types

A. dentata 'Rubiginosa' (bloodleaf): This sprawler from the West Indies forms a 1-ft-tall, 3-ft-wide, spreading mound of 2- to 3-in.-long, deep burgundy, lanceshaped, highly glossy leaves. It's a vigorous grower that may walk all over other plants in a combination planter or window box if you don't keep pinching it back.

A. d. 'Tricolor': Similar in growth habit to 'Rubiginosa', this cultivar is more wildly colored—the glowing burgundy leaves are splashed with bright magenta and hints of lime green.

A. polygonoides 'Purple Select': Forming a dense, spreading mound to 10 to 12 in. high and wide, this selection displays lanceshaped, 1½-in.-long leaves that are coppery purple—not as deep a purple as those of 'Rubiginosa' but a useful metallic color nevertheless, especially because the plants are less vigorous and do not require cutting back or pinching.

Compact Mounding Types

A. ficoidea var. *amoena* (parrot leaf): This compact grower, 6 to 12 in. tall, offers leaf colors that include green, yellow, red, magenta, and burgundy in almost any combination. 'Krinkle' features small, wavy, rounded leaves in dark rust splashed with green and yellow. 'Yellow Wide Leaf' glows bright golden yellow. 'Yellow Fine Leaf' is the same color, but its foliage is almost threadlike.

◆◆◆

Angelonia angustifolia

(an-jel-OH-nee-uh an-gus-tif-FOH-lee-uh)

Angelonia

Tender perennial, to 2 ft tall; reaches mature height in first season.
Hardy in zones 9–10.

Delicate spires of small, twolipped, snapdragon-like violet, pink, purple, white, or bicolored flowers give angelonia a delicate grace that makes it a great little plant for filling in between bolder plants in tropical beds or containers. It's also a good spike-formed annual in a flower border and a long-lasting cut flower. While the foliage of this tropical from Central and South America is unremarkable (green, lance-shaped, 2-in.-long leaves), the plant's overall effect is lovely because it blooms constantly. Blossoming begins in early summer, continuing well into fall until a cruel frost cuts down the plants.

Cultivation

Angelonia performs best in full sun in average garden soil that is kept evenly moist. Fertilize monthly during active growth. Cut off faded flower stalks to encourage repeat blooming. This tropical does poorly as a houseplant, so don't bother bringing it indoors to grow on a windowsill. You can, however, cut containerized plants back to soil level and store them over winter in a cool, dark, frost-free area to force dormancy. In spring, bring the plants out into the warmth and light and they will break dormancy.

Angelonia angustifolia 'Hilo Princess'

Cultivars

'Alba': An ethereal charmer, 'Alba' features white flowers and bright green leaves.

'Blue Pacific': The purplish-blue-and-white flowers have the color scheme of a whitecapped ocean. Combine with white dahlias or other bold, white flowers.

'Hilo Princess': This cultivar forms a nice compact plant, to 16 in. tall, with numerous, deep purple-blue blossoms that contrast well with yellow foliage plants.

'Pink': The color of these flowers is pure pink without a hint of lavender. They make a pretty statement in a container arrangement with silver-leaved *Plectranthus argentatus* or *Helichrysum petiolare* and a dash of heliotrope for purple flowers and fragrance. ✦✦✦

Anisodontea × hypomandarum

(an-eh-so-DON-tee-uh hi-poe-MAN-dare-um)

African Mallow

Slender subshrub, to 8 to 10 ft tall; grows 3 to 5 ft in the first season. Hardy in zones 9–11; marginal in zone 8.

Where a large, fine-textured plant is called for, African mallow might be just the answer. This fast grower makes a slender form cloaked with small, three-lobed leaves and delicate pink, ½-in.-wide, shallow-cupped flowers prettily netted with dark veins. Because it grows so fast, you can grow this tropical as a shrub or train it as a standard. It readily makes a nice, rounded head when pruned. Blossoms appear profusely in spring and fall and more sparsely during summer's heat. 'Julii' is a more open shrub, which if left unpruned grows over 10 ft tall, adding 3 to 4 ft. in a season. The light to medium

Anisodontea × hypomandarum

pink flowers are much larger, 2 to 3 in. across. The maplelike, 3- to 5-in.-wide leaves are gray and fuzzy when young, maturing to green. Plant in the background of a mixed border.

Cultivation

African mallow needs full to part sun. Provide well-drained soil and be careful not to overwater; allow the soil to dry somewhat between waterings. Fertilize twice monthly, especially if you're growing this hybrid species in a container. If you want a bushier plant than the typical narrow, upright shape, you can prune out the leader to encourage branching and a fuller figure. African mallow does poorly as a houseplant, so toss it out at the end of the summer, or propagate it by taking tip cuttings.

Anthurium (an-THUR-ee-um)
Flamingo Flower, Anthurium

Terrestrial or epiphytic tropical perennial;
grows to 2 ft tall in a single season.
Hardy in zones 10–11.

Anthurium 'Venus'

A garden in bloom with anthurium flowers invites comparisons with Hawaiian gardens resplendent with dripping vines and screeching parrots. The long-stemmed inflorescence is actually a complex structure consisting of a wandlike, flower-packed spadix rising from an outstretched, puckery, heart-shaped spathe, or bract. Spathes vary from red to white, with all shades in between, and have a finish so glossy that the plant is sometimes called the patent leather flower. Thriving plants bloom almost constantly, offering you homegrown versions of the expensive florists' flower. While all anthuriums bloom, some types are extraordinary foliage plants with large, velvety leaves and pronounced veins. These shade-loving tropicals work best as specimens in large containers or baskets on a porch or terrace. You might also try tucking a potted one into the branches of a tree for a lush equatorial look.

Cultivation

Denizens of tropical rain forests, anthuriums grow best with lots of moisture in humid conditions. Grow them in full to light shade. Use an epiphytic orchid mix for potting and keep this constantly moist. Fertilize lightly once a month when plants are in bloom. Anthuriums flourish as houseplants if kept out of direct sun and where the humidity is high, such as in a bathroom or greenhouse, or resting on a bed of gravel and water, which raises the humidity.

Species and Cultivars

A. andraeanum (**flamingo flower**): This is the showiest of the anthuriums, bearing heart-shaped flowers varying in size from 2 to 8 in. across in an array of colors. Many named cultivars are available. The long-stemmed, 2-ft-long leaves are oval to heart-shaped and arise from the crown of the plant, forming a large clump.

A. crystallinum (**strap flower**): Satiny, deep green with silvery white veins, the leaves of this species are oval to heart-shaped and 2 ft long and 1 ft wide, creating a foliage sensation. Blossoms rise above the leaves and consist of a long, drooping, yellow spadix with a strap-shaped white spathe. This one thrives in low light and high humidity.

◆◆◆

Arctotis × hybrida
(arc-TOE-tis hi-BRIH-duh)
African Daisy

Tender perennial; grows to 1 ft tall the first season.
Hardy to zone 9; sometimes to zone 8.

A prolific bloomer, African daisy covers itself with long-stemmed, 2- to 3-in.-wide, daisy-shaped blossoms from spring until a hard freeze finishes it off in fall. The popular cultivars are hybrids of two species native to South Africa, *A. venusta* and *A. fastuosa*, and have fine-textured, silvery gray foliage that forms a basal rosette from which arise 12-in. stems of solitary flowers. The flowers come in an array of colors, including white, yellow, red, rust, copper,

Arctotis × hybrida

taller tropicals in a border, or in a mixed planter. Since these plants thrive on heat, they do well on a sunny patio.

Cultivation

Provide a warm, full-sun location with well-drained soil for best blooming. Plants may rot in wet conditions, so allow the soil to dry between waterings. Fertilize once at planting time. Plants are easily propagated from seeds or cuttings that can then be carried over the winter, but it's best to treat the African daisy as an annual and not try to overwinter it.

Cultivars

'African Sunrise': This dwarf, compact plant produces orange blossoms with dark centers. It combines well with many other plants that tolerate a hot, sunny

site, such as the yellow or orange blossoms of *Lantana* and the soft feathery plumes of *Stipa tenuissima* (Mexican feather grass).

'Bacchus': This plant's sexy, purple flowers are a bit larger than those of other cultivars and contrast well with their silver leaves, inviting combinations with white, pink, or lavender blossoms.

'Rosita': Very silvery foliage and pale, dusty pink blossoms with purplish black centers make this cultivar a great companion for purple-leaved plants such as *Tradescantia pallida* 'Purple Heart'.

'Torch': This cultivar's salmon-orange, 3-in. blossoms with black centers look great in the dry garden or scree bed with other plants that enjoy well-drained soil, such as *Agave, Aloe, Yucca,* and various cacti.

❖❖❖

pink, and purple, and there may even be a contrasting ring of color near the center for a bicolored effect. Centers may be yellow or black. Use African daisy as an easy-care annual for massing in front of

Aristolochia (air-is-tow-LOCK-ee-uh)
Dutchman's Pipe, Calico Flower, Pelican Flower

Tropical vine; climbs to 6 to 20 ft high in a single season.
Hardy in zones 9–11.

Cousins to the cold-hardy *A. macrophylla* (zones 5–11), which has similar leaves and less showy flowers, the fast-growing tender vines listed here fortify a tropical-looking garden with dramatic, heart-shaped leaves and bizarre-looking blossoms. Reddish brown with creamy speckles and shaped like a curved pipe with a wide-flaring bowl, the dangling flowers look quirky and weird, inviting comments from beholders. It's not advisable to sniff these blossoms—they sometimes emit a foul odor, which serves to attract

Aristolochia elegans

the flies that pollinate them. Because the vines climb by twining, plant them at the base of a post, stake, or arbor or alongside a fence, so they can wrap themselves around something solid and hoist themselves skyward to display their blossoms. For a very jungly look, plant one or two vines to climb over shrubs or twist into a tree, where they'll bloom for months.

Cultivation

Provide full sun to part shade and average soil. Although the vines tolerate soil on the dry side, growth is most rapid—and jungly—with plenty of water. Growth and blooming will also be most prolific if you fertilize weekly. Containerized plants can be overwintered on a sunporch or in a greenhouse; otherwise treat plants as annuals. They grow easily from seeds or cuttings.

Species

A. elegans (A. littoralis) (calico flower): This fast-growing vine is the daintiest of the species, growing from seed to 8 ft long in a single season. Its pipe-shaped flowers are white with maroon marbling, measure 4 to 5 in. across, and are, luckily, odorless. The dark green leaves have the typical heart shape and grow to be 4 to 6 in. across. Frost kills the vines, but the dried stems and seedpods are decorative all winter.

A. grandiflora (pelican flower): Truly weird-looking, the gigantic blossoms of this species may be 1 to 1½ ft across and have a 3-ft-long tail. Unopened buds resemble a pelican with a pouchlike beak, hence the common name. This botanical curiosity comes with a disadvantage: the blossoms truly reek, but only during the first day they open. Leaves measure up to 8 in. across. Hardy in zones 10–11.

◆◆◆

Begonia (buh-GOH-nee-uh)
Begonia

Tropical or subtropical perennial or subshrub, from 1 to 4 ft tall;
reaches mature size the first season.
Hardy in zones 9–11; some types to zone 6.

Begonia × tuberhybrida

This diverse genus of hardy tropical plants offers gardeners an overwhelming choice for creating lush color effects in a semishady setting. Some types boast vividly variegated leaves; others bear gorgeous waxy blossoms in brilliant, jewel-like colors; and still others astonish with both striking flowers and foliage. All begonias produce two kinds of flowers: large, usually showy, male flowers with yellow stamens and smaller female flowers that eventually produce seed. Use begonias as eye-catching specimens in containers and hanging baskets, or plant them in the garden with shade-loving, delicate-flowered plants such as fuchsia, abutilon, and *Globba winitti* 'Mauve Dancing Ladies'.

Cultivation

Plant begonias in light, dappled shade—most do not tolerate full sun—and warm conditions. They need a rich, moist but well-drained soil. Fertilize with liquid fertilizer twice a month while they are actively growing. Fibrous-rooted and rex begonias make excellent houseplants or greenhouse plants and can be overwintered in bright, but not direct, light.

For the best results with tuberous begonias, start them growing in March by embedding them hollow side up in moist peat; keep the plants warm and evenly moist, in a draft-free place, until leafy shoots form. Then move them into decorative containers or plant them in the garden, making sure the soil is warm and all danger of frost has passed. Dig up the tubers before the first frost and allow them to dry naturally before storing them in damp peat moss at 45°F. Check them occasionally during storage to cull out the ones that show symptoms of dry rot, and sprinkle the peat with water so the tubers don't shrivel and dry up.

Species and Cultivars

More than 1,000 species and hundreds of named cultivars characterize the genus *Begonia*. Here are several main groups that work well in tropical-style gardens.

Cane or angel-wing begonias: Both their flowers and their foliage make these fibrous-rooted plants unparalleled performers in tropical settings. Tall and exotic, these begonias delicately color their jagged, green leaves with contrasting spots or streaks of silver. Their tall, bamboo-like canes can reach 3 to 4 ft tall. Airy sprays of delicate pink or white flowers bloom in spring or summer, standing above the clusters of leaves like soft clouds. Plants need a protected location and perhaps staking for best performance, and they can be cut back severely if they become leafless at the bottom. Bring indoors in early fall when temperatures begin to cool.

Rex or rhizomatous begonias (B. × rex): Their exceptionally beautiful leaves make the rex begonias the king of foliage plants. They form large, low clumps of evergreen leaves that can vary from long and pointed to small and round, often with crinkled or undulating margins. Washes, streaks, or stripes of silver, pink, or burgundy mark the upper leaf surfaces, which can be metallic or velvety, while the undersides are often burgundy or pink. Pale pink flowers are borne in panicles just above the foliage during much of the summer.

Tuberous begonias (B. tuberhybrida): These fleshy-stemmed plants have large, stiff, succulent, pointed, green leaves and amazingly showy rose- or peony-shaped male flowers. They grow from underground storage tubers and reach 1 to 2 ft tall in a season. Numerous cultivars are available—both upright and cascading types—with exquisite male flowers, flanked by two smaller female flowers, in pastel or deep shades of red, pink, white, yellow, and orange. Flower size varies from 3 to 8 in. across—the large ones look gloriously gaudy, perfect for a tropical setting. Pinch off the female flower buds to keep the male flowers attractive longer.

◆◆◆

Bougainvillea (boo-gan-VEAL-lee-uh)
Bougainvillea, Paper Flower

Sprawling or vining tropical shrub, 6 to 20 ft high;
grows 4 to 6 ft the first year.
Evergreen in zones 10–11; root-hardy in zone 9b.

Bougainvillea 'Lavender Queen'

Creating a visual extravaganza of vibrant blossoms, bougainvillea "vines" tumble all over fences and arbors in California and the Caribbean islands. You can mimic this exotic effect during summer in colder climates by growing one in a container and training the canes to a support, where it will bloom its head off all summer. In full sun and warm temperatures, blooming commences in spring, continuing on new growth until cold weather arrives. Individual flowers are composed of a tiny, white center of floral parts surrounded by three large, petal-like, papery bracts—in almost any color imaginable, including some truly outlandish shades of magenta. These inflorescences form large, showy clusters that remain colorful for months because even after the actual flower passes, the bracts retain their vibrancy. Bougainvilleas aren't actually vines but have long, pliable canes that sprawl rather than twine. You can hoist the canes overhead by tying them to a support, but watch out when you're working among them, as they bear sharp thorns. The heart-shaped green leaves of these plants may be reddish or bronze when young. Most bougainvilleas used in gardens are complex hybrids between three Brazilian species.

Cultivation

A bougainvillea possesses a very brittle, sparse root system that does not hold soil well, so it is difficult to dig up and transplant. Because of this, keep it in a plastic container that can be sunk into the ground or incorporated into a larger decorative container of mixed plants. That way, if you choose to overwinter the plant, you can move it easily without root damage. Do not repot, but every spring remove some soil from the top of the pot and replace it with good compost. Provide full sun and well-drained soil. Water when the soil begins to dry. Fertilize once a month, or less. Prune as needed.

You can overwinter a growing plant in a conservatory or greenhouse, where it will continue to bloom if given full sun, warmth, and humidity. If you cannot provide these conditions, try cutting the canes back to about 6 in. and storing the plant in a cool (40° to 45°F), dark place. Plants forced into dormancy this way initiate rapid growth when returned to sun and warmth in spring and make excellent specimens in a temperate garden.

Cultivars

'California Gold' (**'Golden Glow'**): The golden to pale yellow blossoms of this cultivar combine well with plants that have gold- or yellow-variegated leaves or yellow, orange, or warm red blossoms.

'La Jolla': Use the vivid red flowers on this compact grower to call attention to container plantings.

'Lavender Queen': Easy to combine with pink or purple blossoms, this cultivar features heavy crops of large, pinkish lavender flowers.

'Manilla Red': These vibrant blossoms pretty much define the color magenta. Use with the bright yellow-green leaves of *Ipomoea* 'Margarita' or *Xanthosoma* 'Chartreuse Giant', or grow with the tropical-looking bird-of-paradise (*Strelitzia reginae*) for an eye-popping combination.

'Orange King': These bronzy orange blossoms look great with foliage plants in rich, deep colors, such as *Phormium tenax* 'Atropurpureum' and *Acalypha wilkesiana* 'Macrophylla'. 'Orange King' is open and rangy, so it makes a good specimen for training to an arbor or post.

'Raspberry Ice' (**'Hawaii'**): Dense clusters of cerise flowers and leaves variegated with green and creamy white make this one of the most colorful of all bougainvilleas. Use this compact grower as a specimen in a container, where it will form a colorful mound up to 4 ft tall and wide. ✦✦✦

Breynia disticha 'Roseapicta'
(bray-knee-ah dis-ti-kah)
(Breynia nivosa)
Hawaiian Snowbush

Tropical shrub, to 3 to 8 ft tall and half as wide; grows 3 to 4 ft the first season. Hardy in zones 9b–11.

New growth on the Hawaiian snowbush starts out almost pure white and becomes blotched with pink, deep red, and green, creating a light, bright—but never gaudy—effect. Zigzagging dark red branches hold the oval leaves in a horizontal plane, enhancing the plant's intricate texture and detail. Don't expect a floral show—the flowers are so small that you might not even notice their pale little presence hidden among the leaves. Although Hawaiian snowbush grows rapidly during the growing season, the plant makes an exceptional show if it's carried over the winter so it can grow to full size. Overwinter a containerized plant, if you can, so it can mature into a 3- to 5-ft-tall specimen. (If you don't prune it, it might even grow to 8 ft tall.) Then plunge the container directly in the garden. This shrub's red and pink hues make lovely color echoes and texture contrasts with big, blowzy red, pink, or white dahlia blossoms, the large, dark purple leaves of *Canna* 'Intrigue', or the dusky linear leaves of *Phormium tenax* 'Atropurpureum'.

Cultivation

Hawaiian snowbush grows well in part shade to full sun, although the best color develops in sun and on new growth. Provide moderately rich soil and keep it evenly moist. Feed monthly during spring and summer. Prune occasionally to encourage vigorous new stems and more colorful leaves.

To overwinter, relegate plants to a cool sunporch, conservatory,

Breynia disticha 'Roseapicta'

or greenhouse. They do not fare well as houseplants because their leaves tend to drop if the humidity is low. If left in the ground over winter in zone 9, this shrub may be killed to the ground, but it will regrow. You can propagate plants from semi-ripewood stem cuttings or root cuttings.

Cultivars

B. disticha: The straight, unimproved species is adorned with green-and-white-variegated leaves with red stems.

B. d. ssp. *nana* (**dwarf snowbush**): A dwarf type, this one is a low-growing plant that reaches only 2 ft tall. The new growth is pure white on red stems, so it benefits by having protection from the afternoon sun.

B. d. '**Thimma**': This yellow-and-green-variegated cultivar is pretty with yellow-flowered plants.

◆◆◆

Bromeliaceae (bro-mill-ee-AY-see-ee)
Bromelia or Pineapple Family
Vase Plant, Urn Plant, Pineapple, Spanish Moss, Air Plant

Epiphytic or terrestrial tropical perennials, to 2 to 6 ft tall. Hardy in zones 9–11; a few are marginally hardy in zone 8.

These denizens of New World rain forests and tropical woodlands usually grow overhead as epiphytes attached to tree branches or clinging to crevices along the trunks. There, rainfall collects in their vaselike whorl of thick, green or variegated leaves, providing their primary source of water, since their root systems are designed more for anchoring than for absorbing. Terrestrial species are fewer, and their leaves are often grassier. Both types produce bright, multicolored spikes or candelabra of otherworldly-looking flowers that remain showy for months. In some species a bright flush of color appears in the center of the leaf rosette, signaling the onset of flowering. Pups, or offsets, typically form at the base of a bromeliad, increasing it from a single plant to a small colony. You can exploit their junglelike charac-

Guzmania 'Ice Cream'

ter in your garden by mounting several bromeliads on tree trunks and branches overhanging the garden or terrace. For an exotic effect, you can also attach bromeliads to a cut dried branch and plunge the branch into a container with other plants. Try planting terrestrial types in a pot or in the ground; some epiphytes do well in the ground, too, so long as the soil is well drained. Bromeliads have a rough-and-tough appearance that is enhanced when they're combined with gentler-looking ferns and other fine-textured plants.

Cultivation

Most bromeliads do best in bright light or dappled shade well out of direct sunlight, although a few need sun. Those with slender, hairy, leathery leaves tolerate the most sun. If you plan to overwinter epiphytes and terrestrials as houseplants, grow them as specimens in containers of bark mix designed for orchids; otherwise, plant them in potting soil combined with other plants. The growing medium should be allowed to dry out between waterings. You can wire epiphytes to a slab of tree bark, tucking some sphagnum moss around their roots, and then tie them to tree branches or an arbor. Both types can be grown in the ground as long as the soil is amended with gravel or sand and they are not overwatered, which quickly causes rotting. Keep water standing in the "vases" of those types that have them. Fertilize monthly with half-strength liquid fertilizer.

Bromeliads make excellent houseplants. They can be wintered in a sunny window provided the humidity is high. Divide mature plants with pups, if desired.

Species and Cultivars

There are 45 genera of bromeliads and more than 2,000 species. Here are just a few of the popular, easy-to-grow ones for tropical-looking gardens.

Aechmea fasciata (**silver vase plant**): This colorful Brazilian epiphyte has 2-ft-long, pale green leaves with silver, horizontal bands that form a tall, flaring vase. A short flower stalk produces an odd but attractive, clublike cluster of starburst blossoms composed of bright pink bracts and violet flowers. Forms with other variegation patterns are available.

Ananas bracteatus (**red pineapple**): One of the few bromeliads that prefer full sun, this relative of the edible pineapple makes a highly attractive ornamental, especially in its variegated forms. The long, narrow leaves can reach 3 ft in length, are dark green or green striped with silver, and have sharp teeth arming the margins. They form an open, vaselike clump that looks similar to *Cordyline indivisa*. A flower stalk grows from the middle of the clump, producing a red-tinged, sticklike structure with small red leaves and a red flower at the very tip. The flower ripens into a miniature, scarlet-hued pineapple. 'Albomarginata' is a beautiful form with white stripes along the leaf edges. 'Striatus' has linear white stripes throughout the leaves. 'Tricolor' is the most gorgeous of all, with green-, yellow-, and red-striped leaves.

Billbergia nutans (**queen's tears**): This epiphytic species forms a funnel-like rosette of strap-shaped, gray-green leaves with finely toothed margins. A prolific bloomer, it produces gracefully arching sprays of flowers with blue-edged, pink bracts and apple green petals. This is one of the easiest bromeliads to grow, and it forms large, impressive clumps of many rosettes about 18 in. tall. Locate it outdoors for the summer in part sun.

Guzmania **spp.** (**guzmania**): Most of the species in this genus are epiphytes hailing from the rain forests of the Andes mountains. Leaves are glossy green and lance-shaped, but showier, variegated forms can be had. In summer, small white or yellow flowers surrounded by a large, blossomlike arrangement of pointed yellow, red, or orange bracts bloom on thick stalks. Provide shady, moist, humid conditions.

Neoregelia **spp.**: These glossy-leaved, green or striped bromeliads form a low, wide rosette that becomes quite colorful when they are about to flower. The innermost leaves take on striking colors: hot pink, magenta, red, or orange. Although the flowers themselves are brightly colored, they nestle low in the rosette and are not held aloft like those of most other bromeliads. Plant these bromeliads directly in the ground.

Tillandsia **spp.** (**air plant**): The linear to almost threadlike leaves of these small ephiphytes can be silvery gray-green or highly colored. Flowers on short stalks develop colorful bracts and bloom in spring or fall. These tough little plants get all the moisture they need from the air and thrive where there is plenty of humidity. You can wire them directly to palm trunks or tree branches without putting any soil or sphagnum moss around their roots. ✦✦✦

Brugmansia 'Jamaican Yellow'

Brugmansia (brugh-MAN-zee-uh)
Angel's Trumpet

Subtropical shrub or tree, to 12 to 30 ft tall;
grows 5 to 6 ft the first year.
Hardy in zones 9–10; marginal in zone 8.

A large specimen of angel's trumpet puts on a splendid flower show, a show so magnificent that a plant in full bloom evokes cries of awe from its beholders. Huge, trumpet-shaped blossoms dangle from the branches in clusters, each opening from a beautiful, pleated bud that unfurls slowly and gracefully over several days. Open flowers remain fresh for only several days before they wilt and fall off, but new blossoms unfold to take their place. These glorious flushes of bloom happen periodically, every four to six weeks, sometimes cycling with the full moon. A mature, shrub-size

Brugmansia 'Jamaican Yellow'

plant can produce several hundred gorgeous blossoms in each cycle. To add to the excitement, the flowers often scent the air with a sweet, intoxicating perfume that is most noticeable during the evening. Angel's trumpets form woody stems and have coarse, green leaves. All plant parts are poisonous. Be sure to include at least one angel's trumpet in your tropical-style garden, locating it near a frequently used patio or bench, where its luscious scent can be thoroughly enjoyed. You might even wish to spotlight the plant at night because the luminescent blossoms literally glow like a lantern when struck by soft light. Keep this large plant in a container as a specimen, or sink the container in a garden bed and surround with low-growing or ground-covering companions.

Cultivation

Brugmansias need full sun and rich, well-drained soil. Keep them well watered but not soggy. Since blossoms form on new growth, your goal should be to keep the plants growing vigorously by adding a slow-release fertilizer and compost at planting time. Then fertilize every two weeks with liquid fertilizer to stimulate growth. Because large plants look the most stunning, overwinter your angel's trumpet so it can grow into an imposing specimen. A greenhouse or conservatory is best. Lacking that, force the containerized plant into dormancy by keeping it at 35° to 40°F. In spring, root-prune overwintered mature plants, repotting them in fresh soil in the same size pot.

Species and Cultivars

Most brugmansias grown in tropical gardens are hybrids. They derive from *B. arborea,* which bears 6-in.-long, flaring white flowers; *B. aurea,* which has 10-in.-long, deep golden yellow to white, widely flaring blossoms; *B. suaveolens,* which offers white or occasionally yellow or pink, narrow, 1-ft-long trumpets; or *B. versicolor,* which produces 1-ft-long, white blossoms that age to apricot. These plants are closely related to *Datura,* which has upward- or outward-facing, trumpet- or bell-shaped flowers, and were once classified in that genus.

B. × *candida:* This hybrid group is widely grown and features vigorous plants with gorgeous gold or pure white blossoms. 'Double White' is a heavy bloomer that produces 6- to 8-in.-long, night-scented, hose-in-hose, creamy white blossoms.

B. 'Charles Grimaldi': Flowers are a rich salmon-pink; form wide, pendent trumpets to 10 in. long; and emit a luscious fragrance at night. The flower color works well with a warm color scheme.

B. 'Ecuador Pink': With flowers tinted a delicate, shell pink and forming recurving, fluted trumpets, this hybrid is possibly one of the loveliest of all the angel's trumpets. It's also one of the largest, the pendent blossoms measuring 12 to 16 in. long.

B. × *insignis:* The bell-shaped flowers of this hybrid between *B. suaveolens* and *B. versicolor* are 1 ft in length and may be pink or white; they give off a heady fragrance. The leaves are also 1 ft long and have toothed margins.

B. 'Jamaican Yellow': This floriferous plant produces heavily scented, trumpet-shaped, creamy yellow blossoms that measure 8 to 10 in. long and age to a deep golden yellow.

◆◆◆

Caladium bicolor (ka-LAY-dee-um BYE-kul-or)
(*Caladium* × *hortulanum*)
Angel Wings, Fancy-leaved Caladium
Tuberous perennial, to 8 to 30 in. tall;
reaches mature height the first season.
Hardy in zones 9–10.

These fancy-leaved beauties defy the shade, putting on a fabulously colorful show of foliage even in dim light. The leaves, which resemble those of elephant's-ear plants in size and shape, differ from them greatly in color and texture. They are almost paper-thin and translucent, seeming as crisp as paper, and come in

Caladium 'Pink Beauty'

variously mottled and speckled patterns in combinations of red, pink, and white with a minimum of green. Often the veins are brightly colored and create a network that contrasts handsomely with the background. Newer forms have strap-shaped leaves and do well in part to full sun. Caladium tubers are affordable enough to be planted in large masses of a single type. Combine these plants with other shade lovers such as begonias, fuchsias, ferns, and flowering maples (*Abutilon* spp.) to electrify difficult, dark areas of a shade garden. They'll remain showy until nights get cool in early fall. Their big, colorful leaves also work well in mixed containers to make a bright focal point.

Cultivation

In early summer, after all danger of frost is past, plant the tubers directly in the garden in rich, moist but well-drained soil, or, for best results, start them in pots indoors in March, keeping the pots at 70°F. Bury the tubers 1 in. deep in the garden and just beneath the soil surface for pot culture, so there's plenty of room for root growth. Most types need at least light, filtered shade to prevent the leaves from burning and perform well in deep shade. Strap-leaved types tolerate sun if they are never allowed to dry out. Keep the soil evenly moist; in shady areas under thirsty tree roots, water frequently. Fertilize weekly with liquid fertilizer once the plants are growing. Remove the flowers when they form—they are not attractive, and flowering encourages the tubers to go dormant. Dig up the tubers when they go dormant in fall or after the tops are killed by frost and store them over winter in slightly moist peat or sawdust. Caladiums grown in containers need not be dug up; store the containers in a cool, dark place over the winter.

Cultivars

Types with Heart-shaped Leaves

'**Little Miss Muffet**': This cutie is a miniature, growing to only 8 in. tall. The color patterns are a dainty combination of a creamy lime green background flushed with pink in the center and along the veins and speckled all over with wine red. It makes an excellent edger or foreground plant.

'**Pink Beauty**': This exotic looker features large, pink leaves with deep rose-pink veins and a wide, green-and-white, marbled border. Combine it with white or pink impatiens, ferns, or *Abutilon* 'Snowbell' or 'Pink Blush'.

'**Postman Joyner**': The large, deep red leaves of this old-fashioned favorite are marked with bright red veins and a generous, dark green border. Combine it with green foliage plants or dark red impatiens.

'**White Christmas**': The chalky white leaves are marked with contrasting green veins for a very crisp effect. Plants reach 18 to 24 in. tall. This foliage plant looks especially nice combined with maidenhair ferns (*Adiantum* spp.) to create a texture contrast and a green color echo.

Types with Strap-shaped Leaves

'**Florida Sweetheart**': A pastel charmer, this one has a light pink background marked with dark pink veins and mint green margins. It performs well in sun.

'**Pink Symphony**': This form has narrow pink leaves with green veins and margins. It makes a lovely color combination with the large, billowy flowers of white tuberous begonias. This cultivar grows 10 to 16 in. tall.

'**Red Frill**': A dark green ruffle decorates the borders of the long, narrow, bright red leaves. Combine this sun-tolerant plant with a tropical grass for a pleasing juxtaposition of foliage shapes and texture.

◆◆◆

Canna × generalis (KAN-uh × jen-err-AL-iss)
Canna Lily, Indian Shot

Rhizomatous perennial, to 3 to 14 ft tall;
grows quickly to mature height the first season.
Hardy in zones 8–11; to zone 7 with winter protection.

If one plant were chosen to epitomize a tropical garden, canna lily would be it. Its sometimes gaudy foliage, stately posture, soaring height, and flamboyant blossoms spell "tropical" in anyone's book. Canna lilies bloom all summer, producing stalk after stalk of gladiolus-like flowers in 2-ft-tall spikes at the tops of the plants. The huge, paddle-shaped leaves are reminiscent of a banana plant's, but rather than green they are often striped in bright patterns or flushed with maroon. Most cannas grown in today's gardens are complex hybrids between many South American and Asian species, but where a more elegant, but still tropical, look is desired, you might choose one of the species. These have more delicate-looking blossoms, suggestive of a wild gladiolus or orchid.

Use cannas in clusters of three to five plants in the midground or background of a border, and contrast them with finer-textured plants to create an instant tropical effect. Because of their great size, they combine well with tall perennials and shrubs, such as boltonia, joe-pye weed (*Eupatorium* spp.), butterfly bush (*Buddleia* spp.), and ornamental grasses, and they sustain the perennial garden with foliage and flowers right up until frost. You can also use these dramatic plants in large-scale containers for height, and some flourish as aquatics in the boggy soil or low water along a pond. Almost any cultivar will grow well in standing water if the tubers are started in water; those with narrow leaves adapt best, however. Be careful when choosing planting companions, because the color combinations of the variegated leaves and their flowers are sometimes rather wild. Nevertheless, if used with imagination, cannas create wonderful color contrasts and echoes.

Cultivation

Plant the rhizomes 6 in. deep in the garden when all danger of frost has passed, spacing them 1 to 2 ft apart. Or start them indoors in containers in March. Grow in full sun for the heaviest blooming and the brightest foliage color. To spur on these vigorous tropicals, provide humus-rich, moist soil and

Canna 'Garbo'

add additional compost or rotted manure as a side-dressing during the growing season. Fertilize monthly with liquid plant food. Give them plenty of water and avoid letting the soil dry out. Remove faded flower petals from each flower cluster as they wilt, to keep the plants tidy, but leave behind the ovaries to ripen into attractive seedpods if you wish. For the most blossoms, however, cut back each flower stalk when it finishes blooming to encourage a new flush of flowers.

Dig up the tubers after the tops are blackened by frost. Divide them into sections, each with at least one eye, and store them wrapped in newspaper in a plastic bag in a cool (35° to 40°F), dark place.

Cultivars and Similar Species

Tall Types 5 to 14 Ft Tall

'Intrigue': A splendid plant for dramatic foliage color, this cultivar produces lance-shaped, stormy purple leaves and small, orange flowers. This one grows 6 to 10 ft tall.

'Panache': Tall and elegant like a lady dressed for a ball, this canna has narrow, graceful, gray-green leaves on 6- to 8-ft-tall stalks. The flowers are creamy apricot, orchid-like concoctions flushed with pink.

'Pretoria' ('Striata', 'Bengal Tiger'): Even when not in bloom, this popular canna is a standout in the garden because its glossy green leaves are heavily striped with narrow, gold bands. The bodacious flowers glow brilliant, light golden orange. A reliable performer, it grows to 5 to 9 ft tall.

'Red King Humbert': This readily available canna grows to a towering 7 ft, its orange-red flowers making a grand statement against its bronzy red to dark green leaves.

'Stuttgart': Canna lovers suffer heart pangs over a well-grown specimen of 'Stuttgart', for it's a bit temperamental. Maturing at 6 to 8 ft tall, this is a majestic plant with narrow leaves that are variegated with large, blocky sections of white, with lesser patterns of gray-green, silver, and darker green. The delicate-textured flowers color themselves a soothing salmon-pink. You'll be most successful with this one if you grow it in shade and provide plenty of moisture and fertilizer to prevent the leaves from burning.

'Wyoming': This readily available cultivar produces bright orange blossoms and dark burgundy leaves—a deliciously outrageous color combination. It's a fast grower that reaches 5 to 6 ft tall.

C. grande: A grand canna at 10 to 14 ft in height, this species—with its very wide, elliptical, deep green leaves that have a narrow red border and deep burgundy stems—looks very much like a banana plant until it blooms. Then it shows off its unmistakable, small, orange flowers.

C. iridiflora 'Ehemanni': Big and exotic, this canna has huge, banana-like, medium green leaves and grows to 8 to 10 ft tall. Its late-blooming, trumpet-shaped blossoms drape like orchids on graceful, pendulous stems but strike a hot note with their vivid cerise petals.

Short to Medium Types 3 to 5 Ft Tall

'Durban': The new leaves of this hot-colored canna emerge deep red with orange stripes radiating from the central, green midrib. As they fully mature the leaves become splashed with gold, red, olive, violet, and rose. Blossoms are a brilliant vermilion. This cultivar grows to 4 to 5 ft tall.

'Garbo': The large, salmon-pink blossoms of this 3- to 4-footer stand out against the coppery purple leaves, painting a sophisticated picture.

'Pink Sunburst': This cultivar's very shiny, multicolored leaves have an overall pink tint and audacious yellow, orange, and green striations. The blossoms are quite large and are colored soft pink. It grows 3 to 4 ft tall.

'Tropicana' ('Phasion'): This relatively new cultivar is similar to 'Durban', but its leaves are painted a more vivid, glowing red-orange and are striped with olive green and purple. The flowers glow a compatible bright orange. ✦✦✦

Cestrum (CESS-trum)
Jessamine, Night-blooming Jessamine

Tropical or subtropical, spreading or vining shrub, to 3 to 10 ft tall; grows 2 to 3 ft in one season.
Hardy in zones 9–11; to zone 8 with winter protection.

These easy-to-grow tropicals cycle in and out of bloom from spring through fall, producing clusters of pretty, tubular flowers, but their most rewarding aspect is the intense fragrance that some species emit in the evening. The blossoms' perfume smells so strong and sweet that it literally permeates the air, filling the entire garden with an exotic scent. Include these bushy plants in beds and borders or grow them in containers. Container culture allows you to move the plant closer—or farther away—from your outdoor sitting area to intensify or lessen the fragrance, as you prefer.

Cultivation
Provide full sun and well-drained, average to humus-rich soil. Keep evenly moist and fertilize weekly for best blooming. Pinch or prune back as needed to shape the plants. *Cestrum* makes a good houseplant if you can overwinter it in a sunny location.

Species and Cultivars
C. elegans (red cestrum): This handsome jessamine forms an arching mound of slightly fuzzy, matte green leaves and sprays of colorful, tubular flowers. Blossoms may be pink, red, or purple, and

Cestrum elegans var. *smithii*

shades in between, and ripen into purple berries. *C. e.* var. *smithii* bears beautiful, salmon-pink flowers. *C. e.* 'Newillii' has cranberry red flowers.

C. nocturnum (night-blooming jessamine): The terminal clusters of 1-in.-long, creamy or greenish yellow, tubular blossoms aren't particularly showy, but their powerful fragrance is impossible to ignore. It intoxicates the entire garden, especially on a hot summer's night. Leaves are glossy green, are 2 to 3 in. long, and cloak the bushy, 3- to 4-ft-tall plant.

C. parqui (willow-leaved jessamine): The powerfully scented, yellowish green flowers bloom in showy, star-shaped clusters throughout summer and fall. The narrow, willowlike leaves offer a fine texture, but the plant can be rangy and needs pruning to shape it.

Cissus discolor (CISS-sus DIS-kull-or)
Rex-Begonia Vine
Tropical vine, climbing to 10 to 30 ft high;
grows 3 to 4 ft a season.
Hardy in zones 10–11.

Climbing with delicate tendrils, this exotic vine hoists itself up a trellis or into a small tree or shrub, where it will display its colorful leaves and stems like ornaments hung for display. Named for its close resemblance to the rex-begonia plant, this vine actually belongs to the grape family, but its 6-in.-long, toothed, oblong leaves do indeed mimic a rex begonia's striking leaf pattern. Stems and leaf undersides are deep burgundy, and the dark green top surfaces are quilted and velvety to the touch and are painted generously in the middle with silver and pink markings that radiate from the midribs. This plant's flowers are insignificant, but who needs them with foliage like this? Use this colorful vine to climb up a trellis on a shaded porch or in a hanging basket, where it will trail beautifully over the sides to create a curtain of variegated leaves. In beds and borders, encourage it to scramble over a green shrub—it isn't aggressive enough to smother shrubbery. Its showy but gentle color scheme makes a good companion for purple sugarcane (*Saccharum officinarum* 'Violaceum') and purple fountain grass (*Pennisetum setaceum* 'Rubrum'), as well as for flowers in cool hues of lavender, pink, and purple.

Cultivation
Grow this vine in light shade or in half a day's morning sun with shade in the afternoon to prevent the leaves from burning. It needs moist soil amended with lots of organic matter. Water generously without overwatering; leaves may drop if the plant is either over- or underwatered. Fertilize monthly with liquid fertilizer when it's actively growing. Rex-begonia vine makes a good houseplant and may be overwintered indoors. If you don't have room for a large plant, take cuttings in fall and grow them over the winter.

Similar Species
C. antarctica (kangaroo vine): Not colorfully patterned, but a neutral glossy green, the toothed, oblong, 3-in.-long leaves of kangaroo vine make a good filler in a tropical border or container. It grows rapidly to 4 to 6 ft long—use it to cascade from a container or to trail like a ground cover in a border.

❖❖❖

Cissus discolor

Clerodendrum (klear-oh-DEN-drum)
Glory Bower, Bleeding Heart Vine, Butterfly Bush

Tropical vine or sprawling shrub, to 4 to 15 ft high;
grows 4 to 6 ft in height the first season.
Hardy in zones 9–11.

These vining tropicals from Africa constantly decorate themselves with bouquets of intricate blossoms, providing color at eye level and overhead. Unlike many tropical vines, these are well behaved and grow slowly enough that they won't take over the garden if you turn your back. By the end of the season they will have grown 4 to 6 ft. Because their performance gets better the bigger they are, you may find it worth the effort to overwinter these vines to obtain large specimens. The species described below make excellent container plants and can serve as the tall element in a mixed container if you train them to climb up a stake. You can also position the container next to an arbor so the vines can grow up the posts and across the overhead beams to drip their pretty bouquets downward, or you might try planting them in the garden to scramble over shrubs and trees. Because these plants do not have tendrils but climb by twining or wrapping around their supports, tie the stems in place to secure them against wind and to encourage them to grow where you want them.

Cultivation

The *Clerodendrum* species listed below do well in full sun or part shade if given rich, well-drained, slightly acid soil. Enrich the soil at planting time with organic matter, and fertilize with liquid fertilizer

Clerodendrum ugandense 'Blue Wings'

twice a month. Keep the soil evenly moist for best blooming. You can grow them in a conservatory or sunny room over the winter, as long as you can provide plenty of space. If not, allow potted plants to go dry to bring on dormancy, then store the containers in a dark place at about 45°F for the winter months. These vines are easily propagated from stem cuttings.

Species and Cultivars

C. × speciosum (**glory bean**): Flowers of this hybrid of *C. splendens* and *C. thomsoniae* resemble those of the latter except for their wild color scheme: bright purplish red sepals and red petals. Combine the vine with purple foliage plants for luscious effects.

C. thomsoniae (**bleeding heart vine, glory bower**): Decked out in

traditional Christmas colors, this vine twines its way up a support or into a shrub, where it produces 8- to 10-in.-wide clusters of white-and-red flowers set off against dark green, oval leaves. The odd-looking blossoms consist of a balloon-shaped arrangement of long-lasting, papery white sepals, from which drip a burst of bright red petals resembling drops of blood. 'Variegata' has green leaves with creamy white markings, adding sparkle to a planting even when the vine is not blooming.

Clerodendrum × speciosum

C. ugandense (**butterfly bush**): Sometimes called butterfly bush because its delicate blossoms resemble little blue butterflies, this tropical is more shrubby than vining, at least when young. Grow it in a container or in a border as a 3- to 4-ft-tall bush, its flowers appearing in spires at the stem tips. Each butterfly-like blossom consists of a single, dark blue petal flanked by four light blue petals that are swept back like wings and topped with long, curling, antennae-like stamens. If you overwinter the plant, it begins to vine as it grows taller, and it can twine to great heights in a conservatory or greenhouse. 'Blue Wings' has bicolored blossoms of navy and powder blue.

◆◆◆

Clivia miniata (KLEE-vee-uh min-ee-ATE-uh)
Kaffir Lily
Fleshy-rooted evergreen perennial, to 2 ft tall.
Hardy in zones 9–11.

Clivia miniata

When planted in a moist, shady garden in a warm climate, this African perennial multiplies into a thick ground cover, but in northern climates you're best off growing it in a decorative container as a specimen plant, because it blooms best when potbound. In winter, spring, and summer, this easy-to-grow plant rewards gardeners with 2-ft-tall stalks of 3-in.-long, trumpet-shaped, electric orange blossoms with yellow throats. These are arranged in whorls at the tops of the stalks, which emerge directly from the base of the plant. When out of bloom the plants still look attractive, although certainly more low-keyed, featuring very thick ribbons of glossy green leaves arranged in flat fans on the stemless plants. 'Citrina' is a very rare form with pale yellow flowers that is quite the collector's item, sometimes selling for hundreds of dollars at rare-plant auctions or in mail-order catalogs. Other yellow-flowered forms, listed under the name 'Aurea', may be buttery yellow or orange-yellow and are less rare, but still not common.

Cultivation
Plant the roots with their tops barely protruding in a pot not much larger than the root system. Use well-drained soil. Kaffir lily does best in light shade or morning sun with afternoon shade. Allow the soil to dry slightly between waterings. Fertilize with liquid plant food once a month when the plant is actively growing and when it's entering the bloom cycle. If it does not bloom its first season, be patient; once the plant is mature enough to bloom, it will produce several cycles of blossoms each year. Divide plants in spring, but only when they are severely potbound and have been growing in their pots for many years, perhaps waiting until they get so crowded that they crack their pots. Kaffir lily makes an excellent houseplant or conservatory plant. Let the outdoor plant become drier and remain in the garden in fall until night temperatures plunge into the low 40s or high 30s—this encourages bud set and winter blooming. Then move it indoors for the winter and back to a shaded patio for the summer.

❖❖❖

Codiaeum variegatum var. *pictum*
(koh-DIE-ee-um var-ee-uh-GOT-um PICK-tum)
Croton
Tropical shrub, to 8 to 12 ft tall; grows 2 to 3 ft in a season.
Hardy in zones 10–11.

Codiaeum variegatum var. *pictum*

Unrivaled among tropical plants for foliage drama, this flamboyant shrub is so ubiquitous in gardens in the tropics that by including one in your garden, you can create a sense of place that clearly says "Tropical setting!" Highly polished, the big leathery leaves vary from oval to linear and may be lobed, twisted into spirals, or wavy-edged. Leaf colors sizzle at the hot end of the spectrum: gold, yellow, orange, red, green, and even almost black, in dizzying patterns that include stripes, dots, and blotches. Young leaves may start out green and quickly develop flashier hues. Because of their bold colors, use crotons as focal points in the garden or in a container among more subdued, green-leaved plants, echoing the crotons' leaf colors with complementary flowers.

Cultivation

For the most vivid leaf colors, provide full sun. The soil should be well drained and evenly moist, although a bit on the dry side is acceptable. Fertilize weekly with liquid fertilizer during spring and summer. Crotons resent being moved around and may drop their leaves if their roots are disturbed too much—when transplanting, handle the root ball carefully. They

are also susceptible to cold, so if you plan to overwinter them, bring the plants inside well before frost, when night temperatures dip into the 50s. They perform well as houseplants in a sunny location or in a conservatory.

Cultivars

'Andreanum': One of the more subdued cultivars (everything is relative), this shrub's oval leaves feature a green background painted with copper and yellow along the veins and golden yellow along the margins. Older leaves develop a coppery burnish all over.

'Big Dipper': Unusual colors make this a conversation piece—

the broad leaves are painted blue-black with orange and green blotches.

'Carrieri': New leaves emerge lime green, then mature to dark green with a wide red rib running down their centers.

'Fascination': The very narrow leaves give this croton a finer texture than most, but it is nevertheless boldly colored with yellow stripes over a red-flushed background.

'Reidii': Oblong with upward-curving edges, the bowl-shaped leaves of this variety are suffused with red and overlaid with a creamy pattern of bold veins.

◆◆◆

Coleus blumei (KOAL-ee-us BLUE-mee-eye)
(*Solenostemon scutellarioides*)
Coleus, Painted Nettle
Tropical perennial or shrub, to 1 to 3 ft tall;
grows to mature height in one season.
Hardy in zones 10–11;
dies to the ground but regrows from the roots in zone 9.

Coleus 'Aurora'

Well known since Victorian times as a shade-loving garden annual with colorful leaves, coleus recently sparked a resurgence of plant mania across the country, due partly to the availability of named, cutting-propagated plants. Until recently all coleus were grown from seed, resulting in a mix of plants in different colors and patterns—these look fine as long as you can plant them in groups of a single color, but to do this you have to pick and choose among the seedlings. Now a few seed-grown cultivars that produce uniform seedlings are available, but these are far surpassed by the brilliant new cut-

ting-grown coleus. These cutting-grown types represent the very best colors and wildest combinations their breeders could select, and some even tolerate sun. And they are available in quantity, allowing you to plant identical plants in all-of-a-kind groups for startling effects. Unrivaled among tropicals for its amazingly colorful foliage, coleus comes in a kaleidoscope of colors and patterns—every hue imaginable, and then some. And these are certainly rare colors for leaves: shocking pink, electric orange, deep purple-black, and scarlet, to name but a few. These wild colors mix into bicolored, tri-colored, and multicolored, mar-

bled patterns. Coleus leaf shapes vary from broadly oval, to lobed like an oak leaf, to almost thread-like, some with modestly toothed edges and others with frilly, ruffled edges. Size varies from less than 2 in. to 8 in. long. The popular group called "ducksfoot coleus," which have been grown since Victorian times, form neat mounds of small, lobed, ¾-in. leaves.

Use groups of coleus in beds

and borders for season-long color, placing each cultivar where its ultimate height can be accommodated and carefully considering how the leaf colors look with nearby plants. Some of the most useful coleus, however, are not the flamboyantly variegated forms but those with leaves in solid colors such as chartreuse or burgundy, perhaps marked with a modest stripe or two of a contrasting color. You can use these subtler forms to provide bold color without a fear of gaudiness, while making terrific color echoes. Multicolored cultivars are gorgeous but take skill to combine well with other plants; however, when they are used carefully—matching leaf color to a neighboring flower, for instance—the effect is earth-shaking.

Cultivation

Part shade is best for most types of coleus. Although some perform well in full shade, the most vibrant leaf colors develop with some sun.

Coleus 'Magenta Frill'

Many new cultivars have been bred to tolerate even full sun. The soil should be rich and moisture-retentive; improve it with compost if necessary before planting. Water regularly to keep the soil evenly moist. Coleus wilts easily in dry soil, and even plants that have ample water may wilt in midday heat if exposed to a lot of sun. Incorporate fertilizer into the soil at planting time, and apply liquid fertilizer once every two weeks thereafter. Pinch out flower spikes as they develop, to keep the plants growing vigorously—the flowers are not very attractive on most forms anyway. For types that are not self-branching, pinch every few weeks to keep them bushy. Pinching also encourages flushes of bright new leaves.

Coleus makes a good houseplant, and plants grown outdoors can be dug up and overwintered in a well-lit location. They can also be readily propagated from cuttings—which root even in water—so you might consider taking cuttings of your favorite cultivars in autumn to grow over the winter.

Cultivars

Hundreds of coleus cultivars are now available at local nurseries and from specialty growers, making selection a challenge. To complicate matters, the same plant may go by different cultivar names from one catalog or grower to another, because when growers across the country hopped on the coleus bandwagon, they began selecting and naming plants without realizing that other growers already offered an identical plant under another name. Here's a small selection of the best and

brightest coleus varieties that are widely available.

Ducksfoot Types with Tiny Lobed Leaves and Forming Compact Mounds

'India Frills': This easy-to-use variety features small, frilly pink leaves with yellow-green edges. Use it to spill over the edge of a container, or plant it in masses in the foreground of a border.

'Mars': Forming a more upright mound of dense, lobed leaves, this old-fashioned cultivar is colored an unusual deep salmon, rather like old bricks, and has a velvety finish.

'Thumbelina': Brightly colored in lime green with burgundy zones, 'Thumbelina' is perfect for filling in little spaces between plants in a combination planter.

Tall Types with Big, Bold Leaves

'Aurora': Painted like the northern lights, this has a creamy center, pink veins, and a light green scalloped edge.

'Indo 5': Marbled with salmon-pink and bright pink and a little olive green thrown in for good measure, this one is a sturdy grower that makes a beautiful mass planting.

'Lemon Twist': The solidly colored leaves of this cultivar, in bright, light green with a pretty scalloped margin, act as a useful foil to more wildly colored plants, while still making a color statement of their own.

'Magenta Frill': This is an in-your-face plant—the big leaves are a glowing magenta and have an extremely serrated edge marked with small splashes of light green and ivory. Contrast it with dark burgundy or green foliage, or match it with the similarly colored flowers of *Mandevilla* 'Red Riding Hood'.

'Penny': The leaves are coppery yellow with a green patina and are marked with bright pink veins. The stems and leaf undersides are also bright pink, creating a marvelous glow that works wonders with pink-flowered neighbors.

'Pineapple Beauty' ('Lime Queen'): The centers of these oval leaves are burgundy and the wide margins are golden yellow, the whole concoction marked with a network of burgundy veins. Both stems and leaf undersides are also burgundy, creating an outstanding, two-tone effect. Combine this cultivar with plants that have solid burgundy leaves or purple flowers.

'The Line': Colorful yet elegant, this cultivar has bright yellow, oval leaves marked with a thin, but prominent, dark purple central vein. Combine it with purple foliage and flowers for a colorful contrast.

Medium Types with Small Leaves

'Inky Fingers': This compact grower features deep burgundy, almost black, leaves with a bright, lime green margin marking the deeply scalloped edges. It looks beautiful with yellow-green hostas and blue and purple flowers.

'Kiwi Fern': Deeply cut, fern-like leaves give this compact grower a fine texture. Its color is easy to use in the garden, too—burgundy with a creamy margin edged with a narrow strip of bright green.

'Sunset': "Spectacular" describes these leaves, which paint themselves the deep, salmon-orange hue of the setting sun. A thin gold edge outlines the leaf margins. For a hot color combination, pair this variety with gold foliage and flowers. Or try a pastel shade of salmon-pink.

'Zap Gnarley': Twisted and curled, the leaves of this unusual form mix a marbling of purplish black, bright green, and creamy white.

◆ ◆ ◆

Colocasia esculenta
(Koal-oh-KAY-see-uh ess-kyou-LENT-uh)
Elephant's Ear, Taro, Dasheen
Tropical and subtropical tuberous perennial, to 4 to 6 ft tall;
grows to mature height in a season.
Evergreen in zones 10–11;
dies to the ground but regrows from the roots in zones 8–9
and perhaps in zone 7b with winter protection.

*I*ncorporate a few of these magnificent plants anywhere in your garden to create an instant tropical effect. The huge, heart-shaped leaves resemble elephant's ears in size and shape as well as in the way they droop downward from off the tops of their tall stems. The leaf stems arise directly from the ground to form impressive clumps of lush foliage. Leaves of the species are bright apple green, but there are cultivars available that have foliage marked with burgundy or purplish black patterns or painted black all over adding to the exotic look of these plants.

Colocasia lends a dramatic touch to tropical-style gardens when combined with other bold plants such as *Canna* and *Senna*. They can be planted in the ground or used in containers placed between hardy shrubs such as oakleaf hydrangea (*Hydrangea quercifolia*), bamboo (*Fargesia* spp.), and butterfly bush (*Buddleia* spp.). Where they are cold-hardy the plants spread by their underground root systems to cover a lot of ground, and they've naturalized throughout the South and in most of the world's tropical areas. Flourishing in moist garden soil, they'll thrive

Colocasia 'Jet Black Wonder'

at the edge of a natural pond or submerged in containers in a pond or garden pool. Their edible roots, called dasheen in the Caribbean, are a major food staple in many parts of the world, but they must be properly cooked to remove toxins.

Cultivation

These plants like full sun to part shade and rich, moist to boggy soil. Elephant's ear is a heavy feeder, so improve the soil with compost or manure when planting and fertilize weekly with high-nitrogen, liquid fertilizer during the growing season. Containerized plants need a large container and do best with a timed-release fertilizer. For best growth, provide generous amounts of water, never allowing the soil to dry out. The leaves can be tattered by the wind, so locate the plants in a protected location. Overwinter them in cold climates by allowing a hard frost to kill the tops and then digging and storing the roots at 40° to 45°F. Do not dig up containerized plants; you can store them right in their pots in a cool basement. Propagate the plants by dividing the tubers of large ones.

Cultivars

'Illustris': The leaves of this cultivar feature a light green background that is generously marked with iridescent, blue-black to brown in a softly irregular pattern down their centers and along their edges. Heart-shaped, the leaves measure 1¹/₂ ft wide and 2 to almost 3 ft long. Plants grow 3 to 4 ft tall. This is the most cold-hardy form, surviving short periods in the ground at 0°F. It is worth trying to winter this cultivar outdoors in a protected warm microclimate in zone 7 or perhaps zone 6.

'Jet Black Wonder' ('Black Magic'): Smoky and exotic-looking, this unusual plant displays magnificent leaves that are the purple-black hue of an eggplant; the undersides are a lighter purple. The deepest, most velvety color develops on plants grown in full sun. This cultivar grows 5 to 6 ft tall.

For additional elephant's ears, see Alocasia *and* Xanthosoma *entries.*

❖❖❖

Cordyline (kord-uh-line)
Cabbage Palm, Ti Plant, Dracaena

Tropical shrub or tree, to 5 to 25 ft tall; grows 2 to 3 ft in a season.
Hardy in zones 9–11.

Another group of popular, tropical houseplants that successfully find a place in temperate gardens, these species offer their architectural drama to help turn an ordinary garden into an exotic setting. Young plants are nearly trunkless and have a symmetrical whorl of very long, linear leaves. Leaf width and color varies with the species—some offer subdued hues and others are brightly colored. Older plants develop slender, canelike trunks from which the rosette sprouts from the top like a yucca, with which they are sometimes confused. Some types eventually form multiple or branched trunks with spiky rosettes at each stem tip. Mature plants that are eight or more years old may bloom, producing long spikes of fragrant flowers. Use these plants as focal points in containers sunk into the garden, where they will look perfect combined with *Mandevilla, Plectranthus, Lantana,* and *Pelargonium.* To emphasize their structure, allow a fine-textured vine, such as cardinal climber (*Ipomoea* spp.), to climb over them.

Cultivation

Grow these plants in full sun to part shade in fertile, well-drained soil. The soil should be evenly moist during the growing season, but it is better to allow the soil to dry out between waterings if you're overwintering these species as houseplants or conservatory plants. If leaf tips begin to brown, water more frequently. Feed every

Cordyline australis 'Atropurpurea'

two weeks from spring through fall; do not fertilize in winter.

Species and Cultivars

C. australis (**cabbage palm, giant dracaena**): Admired for its strap-shaped, grayish green leaves, this New Zealand native matures into a single- or multiple-stemmed, palm- or yucca-like tree. The pointed leaves, which are slenderer than a yucca's, can be 1 to 3 ft long and only a few inches wide, forming a dense, rounded tuft at the top of the trunk. 'Albertii' is boldly colored, featuring green leaves with red midribs, cream stripes, and pink margins. 'Atropurpurea' is a beauty with purple-flushed leaves; combine it with deep red dahlias and coleus. 'Variegata' has glowing, yellow-striped leaves. All three grow slowly to 15 ft tall.

C. indivisa (Dracaena indivisa): Leaves of this spiky-leaved plant are 3 to 6 ft long and are arranged in a stiff, open rosette, creating an ethereal, starburst effect. The species features medium green leaves that sometimes have reddish overtones. 'Purpurea' is a smoky bronze-purple. These plants are often used to create a spiky effect in a container.

C. terminalis (C. fruticosa, Dracaena terminalis) (ti plant, Hawaiian ti, Hawaiian good luck plant): The species grows to 12 ft tall or more over many years and has pale green, strap-shaped, oblong leaves that are 2 to 3 ft long and are used for hula skirts. The more commonly grown colorful cultivars are gaudily made up to look like psychedelic palm trees. 'Calypso Queen' is a compact grower with deep bronze-red leaves with purplish centers. 'Firebrand' (red dracaena) is a fairly compact form with slender, recurving leaves that are deep red with crimson midribs when young and mature to satiny purplish red. 'Tricolor' is striped and streaked with red, cream, and pink.

◆ ◆ ◆

Crinum (KRY-num)
Crinum Lily, Spider Lily, Swamp Lily

Bulbous perennial, to 5 ft tall; grows to mature height in a season. Hardy in zones 9–11; some to zone 8 or colder with winter protection.

Like its amaryllis relatives, crinum lily produces a rosette of glossy green, strap-shaped, 4-ft-long leaves, but unlike the leaves of amaryllis these fan out from the top of a 1¹/₂- to 2-ft-tall stalk with a thickened base that resembles a leek. This bizarre arrangement makes for a really interesting foliage plant. But more spectacular still are the fragrant flowers. In summer and fall, 2- to 3-ft-tall flower stalks develop from in between the leaves and are topped with whorls of tubular or trumpet-shaped blossoms. Large and sweetly scented, the flowers are usually white but may be pink or rose-red. Use these plants in tubs sunk into the garden near a sitting area so you can enjoy their wonderful fragrance. They look especially exotic when grown amid a low ground-covering tropical such as *Trades-cantia* 'Purple Heart' or *Lantana* 'Lavender Cascade' so their odd-looking fleshy stems can be admired. You can cut the flower stalks for indoor arrangements—they last a week or more and scent an entire room.

Cultivation

This bulb needs full sun to part shade and well-drained, rich soil. Plant in the ground or in large containers, leaving the neck of the bulb protruding above the soil by a few inches. Space individual bulbs 2 ft or more apart. Keep the soil moist during the growing season and allow it to dry out during dormancy. Fertilize monthly from spring through summer. You can overwinter crinum lily as a house-plant in a cool, bright location—the bulb will rest but won't lose its leaves. Or leave it outside until

Crinum asiaticum

frost kills the tops and then store the bulb as you would for a dahlia. These plants form larger clumps from year to year, and crowded bulbs can easily be separated and divided.

Species and Cultivars

C. americanum (Florida swamp lily): This native American subtropical begins blooming in spring and keeps on sending out flushes of flowers all summer. The flower heads contain about six fragrant, white, 6-in.-long, trumpet-shaped blossoms. Cultivars with pink or red flowers are available. Provide very moist, even boggy conditions, or grow in a water garden.

C. asiaticum (spider lily, poison bulb): Hailing from Southeast Asia, this big, bold tropical produces towering stalks of fragrant flowers sporadically through the summer. Each flower head may consist of as many as 30 spiderypetaled, white blossoms, creating a dramatic yet fine-textured appearance. *C.a.* var. *procerum* has gorgeous wine red leaves and the undersides of the white petals are flushed wine red.

C. moorei (Cape coast lily): This giant from South Africa grows to 4 ft tall and features white or pale pink, trumpet-shaped blossoms in late summer and fall. Leaves are about 4 in. wide and can be 4 ft long, forming an arching clump. Provide afternoon shade; plants do best with light shade. Hardy in zones 8–10.

× *Amarcrinum* 'Fred Howard': This cold-hardy, pink-flowered bulb is a hybrid between *Amaryllis belladonna* and *Crinum moorei*. Lovely pink trumpets top 2-ft-tall flowering stems beginning in midsummer and continuing into fall. Hardy in zones 8–11. ◆◆◆

Cuphea ignea (KYOU-fee-uh IG-knee-uh)
Cigar Flower, Firecracker Plant

Tender perennial, to 2½ ft tall; reaches mature height in a season.
Hardy in zones 10–11;
dies to the ground but regrows from the roots in zone 9.

Often literally smothered with blossoms, cigar flower makes up for the small size of its individual blooms by producing them in dazzling quantity. Each orangered, tubular flower is about 1 in. long and has a slightly flared lip that ends in a grayish ring tipped with a glowing white-and-yellow band; the whole concoction resembles a tiny cigar with glowing ash at its tip, hence the common name. Blooming commences in spring or early summer and continues until a hard frost, making this plant a wonderful season extender. A bushy plant with tidy green leaves that make a great background for the hot-colored flowers, cigar flower enhances other plants that feature orange, red, gold, or yellow foliage or flowers, to create a truly sizzling

Cuphea ignea 'David Verity'

display. Use it in a border or in a container. Because the plant tolerates cool temperatures, you can set it outside earlier in spring than you can many other tropicals.

Cultivation

Provide full sun and well-drained, average soil. Evenly moist soil is best, but the plant won't suffer if the soil dries a bit between waterings. Fertilize weekly with liquid fertilizer to support the heavy blossoming. If plants grow too tall or leggy, cut them back; they will readily branch and be back in bloom in no time at all. Cigar plant is best treated as an annual, but it can be overwintered as a blooming houseplant in a cool, sunny window. Alternatively, cut it back to just a few inches tall and allow the plant to rest by keeping it in a cool, dark place, withholding water so that it stays very dry until you can take it outside again.

Cultivars and Similar Species

'David Verity': The most commonly available form, this cultivar closely resembles the species but is even more floriferous, if that's possible.

'Variegata': Variegated with bright yellow patches, the leaves on this cultivar echo the smoldering tip of the flower, creating an exciting color combination.

C. hyssopifolia (Mexican heather): Closely resembling heather in size, form, and texture, this species features needlelike, ½-in.-long, green leaves that cover the 1- to 1½-ft-tall shrublet. The ¼-in., lavender or purple flowers are made up of six little petals, and plants can have hundreds of flowers. They make good houseplants. ◆◆◆

Cycas (SIGH-kass)
Sago Palm, Cycad

Tropical or subtropical, palmlike tree, from 3 to 8 ft tall or more;
grows only a few inches in height each year.
Hardy in zones 9–11; marginal in zone 8b.

Cycas revoluta

These exotic-looking, palmlike plants are among the most primitive plant forms inhabiting the earth today. You can exploit their prehistoric appearance to create a jungly effect in your garden by using several sago palms in strategic places. The plant consists of a short, stout, rough-barked trunk crowned with a whorl of very stiff, 2- to 8-ft-long leaves that are cut into stiff leaflets. The plant's growing point forms a fuzzy tan dome in the center of the symmetrical leaves, drawing the eye to its lovely form. Usually only one set of leaves grows each year, adding to the layers of older leaves below. Eventually the oldest leaves yellow and fall off, leaving behind leaf scars that give the trunk its attractive rough texture. The new leaves unfold dramatically, staging a beautiful performance, because they stand upright as they unfurl,

eventually arching downward to fill in the ring of foliage below.

Cycads grow very slowly, so even though they may reach a great height, you can enjoy them for many years as low plants—it may take fifteen years for the trunk to reach 2 to 3 ft tall. Plant your cycad in a plastic tub that you can easily place in a decorative container on a patio or, better yet, sink into the garden. Situate the plant where you can appreciate its wonderful texture and symmetry, and underplant it with a uniform sea of contrasting low plants or ground covers to act as a foil. Good choices are *Coleus, Verbena, Tradescantia, Wedelia tribolata,* and *Lysimachia nummularia* 'Aurea'.

Cultivation

Cycads grow well in full to half sun. They need well-drained but evenly moist soil, except during

winter, when the soil should be allowed to dry out somewhat between waterings. Fertilize only twice a year, once in spring before the new foliage develops and again in midsummer. Cycads are easy to grow and make excellent houseplants. Because their beauty increases with age, overwinter them in the house, greenhouse, or conservatory. If offsets form at the base of the plant, you can remove and root them or leave them in place so the plant forms a clump.

Species and Cultivars

C. circinalis (queen sago): More graceful and finer-textured than *C. revoluta* (see below), this cycad resembles a tree fern more than a palm. It sends its bright green, 8-ft-long leaves out at a higher angle, forming an open dome of foliage. It's taller, too, maturing after many years at 12 ft tall, and it often forms clumps. Hardy in zones 10–11; marginal in zone 9b.

C. revoluta (sago palm): This is the most common and easiest of the cycads to grow. It is a short species that grows slowly—only a few inches a year—but with time can reach 10 to 12 ft tall. A whorl of very stiff, very dark green, leathery leaves that are held out almost horizontally tops the trunk. Use this sago palm for its bold, rough texture. It's the most cold-hardy species, surviving outdoors in a protected site in zone 8b. Dwarf and variegated forms may be available from specialty growers.

Dioon edule: A cycad relative, this Mexican native grows slowly and survives winter in zones 8–11, and even into zone 7 with winter protection or siting in a warm microclimate. The 2- to 3-ft-long leaves are shaped like those of

C. revoluta but are a little less rigid-looking. Leaf color varies from deep green to gray-blue—the bluish forms are the most coveted. Plants reach 3 to 4 ft tall and about as wide. Plant in very well drained soil in part shade.

Zamia fischeri: This small cycad relative is noted for its whorl of leathery, light green leaves boldly cut into rounded, oblong leaflets. These 18-in.-long leaves sprout from the top of a 6-in.-tall trunk, forming a somewhat rounded dome. Hardy in zones 10–11; marginal in zone 9b. ✦✦✦

Cyperus (SIGH-per-us)
Papyrus, Umbrella Plant, Paper Rush
Tropical and subtropical perennial bog plant, to 3 to 15 ft tall; can grow almost to its full height in a season. Hardy in zones 8/9–11.

These water-loving plants are tall, airy creatures that form beautiful, see-through clumps of grasslike stems topped with a starburst of brown or green flowers. All find a home in boggy soil along the edge of a natural pond or beneath several inches of standing water in a real or artificial pond. You can grow them in containers submerged in a garden pool or in a tub of water displayed on a deck or patio. Although they will be less lush, some adapt to moist soil in a garden border as long as they are never allowed to dry out. Combine papyrus with water lilies, water cannas, and lotus to create a romantic, tropical setting. The stems look quite exotic when cut and used in an arrangement.

Cultivation
Grow these plants in full sun in boggy or wet soil and do not let them dry out. To use in a water garden, plant papyrus in containers of rich soil and submerge them 1 to 2 in. beneath the water surface. Incorporate high-nitrogen fertilizer into the soil at planting time and add more once a month by feeding plants grown in tubs in a water garden with fertilizer tablets pushed into the soil. You can overwinter papyrus as houseplants or in a conservatory by placing their pots within a saucer or decorative container of standing water.

Species and Cultivars
C. alternifolius (**umbrella plant**): This easy-to-grow bog plant produces leafless stems that grow 4 ft tall or more and are topped with numerous, 6- to 10-in.-long, leaflike bracts that radiate outward like a starburst. Fertile stems produce a similar starburst decked out with tiny brown flowers. Umbrella plant grows well in moist soil in a garden or in a boggy site. This plant is fun to propagate: cut off the stem and stick it bract-end down into the soil about 1 in., so the bracts rest on very moist soil; within a few weeks, roots and new stems will form. 'Stricta' is more compact and has narrower leaves. The leaves of 'Var-iegata' are variegated with green and white. Hardy in zones 9–11.

C. haspan (**dwarf papyrus**): Use this 18-in.-tall species along a pond edge, where it will form a dense thicket of rounded, leafless, green stems topped with 2-in.-diameter puffs of feathery flowers. Hardy in zones 8–11.

C. papyrus (**Egyptian paper plant, papyrus**): Use this large plant to make a dramatic statement in a good-size pond or garden pool. Its narrow, green stems can reach 15 ft tall and are topped with large sprays of radiating, threadlike bracts that create an airy, 1- to 2-ft-wide ball. The ancient Egyptians pressed the pithy stems of this plant into paper, hence the common name "Egyptian paper plant." 'Nanus' (also sold as *C. prolifer*) grows 2 to 3 ft tall. Hardy in zones 9–11. ✦✦✦

Cyperus papyrus

Datura (da-TUR-uh)
Thorn Apple, Angel's Trumpet

Tropical or subtropical shrub, to 3 to 4 ft tall;
grows to its full height in a season.
Hardy in zones 9–11;
to zone 8 with winter protection.

These boldly beautiful tropicals bloom from early summer right up until frost, covering themselves with 6-in.-long, trumpet-shaped blossoms whose mouths flare into five lobes with curled-back, tail-like points. Rather than dangling in the manner of the bell-like blooms of *Brugmansia,* to which they are related, these flowers stand upright or at right angles to the stems. Seedpods follow the blossoms, forming attractive, prickly balls that resemble small, spine-covered apples and split open in fall to reveal brown seeds. Blooms open at twilight and close up by noon the next day, lasting for only one day, but are replaced by new ones on an almost daily basis. Most types emit a haunting, sweet perfume that carries well in the evening air. Hummingbirds visit the flowers during the morning hours. These tropicals grow quickly into sprawling mounds that look perfect planted in groups of three or more so they can weave into each other to form an appealing mass. Use them in garden beds at the feet of taller tropicals such as *Canna* and *Tibouchina* or in front of hardy grasses such as *Arundo donax* and bamboo. They perform poorly in containers unless the container is very large. Thorn apples often reseed from year to year but are not weedy. All plant parts of these species are extremely poisonous.

Cultivation

These plants need full sun. They bloom best in rich, moist soil but tolerate poor, dry soil. Improve the soil at planting time, and apply liquid fertilizer once or twice a month during the growing season. Allow the soil to dry somewhat between waterings. Don't bother trying to overwinter this plant—it grows quickly from seed sown in spring. You can collect seeds in fall from the pods when they split open, but they will need a cold stratification in your refrigerator before they will germinate. Sow stratified seeds in late winter and transplant to the garden after danger of frost has passed.

Species and Cultivars

D. inoxia (D. meteloides) **(thorn apple):** This bushy species grows 3 to 4 ft tall and 4 to 5 ft wide and is covered with 8-in.-long, dark green, oval leaves with scalloped edges. The fragrant flowers bloom continually during the growing season. 'Evening Fragrance' bears gorgeous, sweetly scented flowers that are glistening white with a lavender flush along the edges and have 8-in.-wide mouths. The leaves make an elegant contrast, since they are a muted gray-green.

D. metel **(downy thorn apple):** Similar to *D. inoxia,* this species reaches a height of 3 ft and can be distinguished by its eggplant-pur-

Datura meteloides

ple-colored stems. Flowers are white, purple, or yellow and are often double or triple, ruffled trumpets set within each other, hose-in-hose style. 'Purple Ruffles' ('Cornucopia', 'Hindu') is a sultry and fragrant cultivar whose double flowers have purple exteriors and white interiors. 'White Ruffles' offers exceptionally beautiful, double white blossoms that open from yellow buds. 'Yellow Ruffles' bears light yellow, upward-facing, triple blossoms that are highly ruffled along their mouths and make a stunning color combination with the purple stems.

◆ ◆ ◆

Duranta erecta (door-ANT-uh air-rect-uh)

(D. repens)

Skyflower, Pigeon Berry, Golden Dewdrop

Tropical shrub or small tree, to 3 ft tall or more;
grows almost to its full height in a season.
Hardy in zones 10–11; to zone 9 with winter protection.

Duranta erecta 'Pigeon Berry'

Dainty in leaf and flower, this graceful plant delivers the full measure of its beauty month after month, because it blooms throughout the year on new growth. Delicate-looking, 6-in.-long, arching sprays consisting of hundreds of tiny, five-petaled, slightly ruffled, pale blue or white flowers with yellowish green throats bloom at the tip of every stem, splashing the plant with color. The ¼-in. flowers turn into green berries that ripen into ½-in. golden globes. In fall these strands of gold glisten all over the plant, inspiring the common name "golden dewdrop." Skyflower grows quickly—a plant from a 4-in. pot will be 3 ft tall by the end of summer. And it blooms eagerly—flowers form even on small young plants in 4-in. pots. But the impact is most remarkable on large plants, which look stunning used as specimens in decorative containers or incorporated into a border to create a lacy veil in front of bolder plants. Skyflower grows in a spreading to upright mound as wide as it is tall. You can prune it to take the form you want or even train it to have a single trunk and grow as a small tree or standard with arching branches. Use untrained plants to billow over the edge of a large container or at the feet of the large, sweet-smelling ginger *Hedychium coronarium*. Standard forms work alone or as the tallest element in the center of a container with pastel shades of verbena at their bases.

Cultivation

Provide full sun and average to rich, well-drained soil. Enrich the soil at planting time with compost, and fertilize monthly to encourage new growth and thus flowers. Be cautious when pruning, because the branches may have small thorns. You can overwinter skyflower as a houseplant or in a conservatory, where it will keep on blooming if it has sufficient light. If you do not have room for it in the house, you can encourage a containerized plant to go dormant over winter by cutting it back to 6 in. tall and keeping it in a cool, dark place.

Cultivars

'**Cuban Gold**': This electrifying cultivar has bright chartreuse leaves and sky blue flowers. Try using it with *Canna* 'Pretoria' to pick up the gold variegations or with *Colocasia esculenta* 'Jet Black Wonder' for a color and size contrast.

'**Grandiflora Blue**': This improved cultivar features bright blue flowers with slightly lighter centers that bloom in very large sprays.

'**Grandiflora White**': Pure white flowers in large, lacy sprays characterize this selection. It looks elegant arranged with other plants with either pastel flowers or variegated leaves such as *Breynia* and *Plectranthus minima* 'Variegata'.

'**Variegata**': This beautiful variety has green leaves splashed with white and lilac-blue flowers. Arrange several plants at the base of a big plant with bold foliage and large flowers such as *Brugmansia*.

◆◆◆

Erythrina × bidwillii
(air-ee-THREE-nuh × bid-WILL-ee-eye)
Coral Tree

Tropical and subtropical shrub, to 3 to 10 ft tall or more;
grows 2 to 3 ft tall in a season.
Perennial that dies to the ground in zones 8–9 and possibly with winter
protection in zone 7; evergreen shrub or small tree in zones 10–11.

If you think a few hummingbirds zipping around your tropical-style garden will add to its exotic allure, plant a coral tree—these birds, which are drawn to tubular red flowers, find its flowers irresistible. In their native tropical habitats, several species of coral tree create a sensation in spring or summer when their large, vivid red or orange-red blossoms burst into bloom. In tropical-style gardens in northern climates, this hybrid coral tree, which is a cross between *E. crista-galli* and *E. herbacea*, makes a better choice than either of the species because it is smaller, blooms more, and has many fewer thorns. Hybrid coral tree blooms prolifically in six-week cycles from spring through fall, and it grows naturally into a bushy shrub—rather than a tree—that can be easily maintained with pruning. The velvety red, 2-in. flowers of this bean-family plant have several curled petals and a long, banner-shaped lip, and bloom in many-flowered, 18-in.-high spires at the tips of the branches. The waxy, green leaves grow about 1 ft long and consist of three large, pointed leaflets. These fan out from the arching branches, creating an entrancing texture even when the plant is out of bloom. Bean-pod-like fruits develop after the flowers. Use this red-flowered beauty to bring sensational color to a hot-colored garden. Grow it in a con-tainer and either plunge it into the border among cold-hardy shrubs such as oakleaf hydrangea (*Hydrangea quercifolia*), grape holly (*Mahonia* spp.), and smokebush (*Cotinus* spp.), or use it with other big tropicals such as *Canna* or *Senna*. Capitalize on the unusual red flowers by echoing their hue with a drapery of cypress vine (*Ipomoea quamoclit*), whose flowers make an exact color match.

Cultivation

Grow coral tree in full sun in rich, well-drained soil. Keep the soil evenly moist; water consistently during the summer to encourage blooming, which may cease if the plant dries out. Since flowers appear on new growth, keep the plant growing vigorously by applying liquid fertilizer weekly from spring into fall. Coral tree naturally goes dormant during winter, so you can easily store it over winter by cutting the stems of a potted plant back to a few inches above the soil and setting it in a cool, dark place. Repot in fresh soil and resume watering in spring. If you plant coral tree against a south-facing wall and mulch it heavily, the roots may survive the winter in zone 7.

Similar Species

E. variegata var. *picta:* Bright red flowers and green leaves with pronounced, golden yellow or creamy white veins make this coral tree a vivid specimen for a sizzling garden scene. Hardy in zones 10–11. ✦✦✦

Erythrina × bidwillii

Eucalyptus cinerea (you-kal-LIP-tus sin-air-EE-uh)
Silver-Dollar Plant, Gum Tree

Tropical tree, to 50 ft tall; can be maintained as a shrub;
grows 6 to 8 ft tall in a season.
Hardy in zones 8–10; possibly root-hardy into zone 7

Although it grows into a tower-ing tree in its natural habitat, you can enjoy this plant's silvery foliage and reddish brown bark in a cool-climate garden by keeping it pruned into a shrub, small tree, or standard with a stout trunk and a head of radiating branches. This tree form shows off the beautiful bark. The unusual leaves are sil-very blue and as round as coins. They grow opposite each other along long stems, creating an open arrangement that displays their

Eucalyptus cinerea

form and color to perfection. The leafy stems are so beautiful that florists sell them in bundles; you can harvest your own whenever you prune. An easy way to grow silver-dollar plant is to stool it—cut it to the ground at the beginning (or end) of the growing season to encourage it to send out long, fast-growing shoots. When they are grown like this in a container, you can plunge overwintered specimens into a border to make pleasing combinations with blue, purple, or red foliage and flowers. Use silver-dollar plant as the tallest element in the center of a large container with *Colocasia* 'Jet Black Wonder', *Breynia disticha* 'Roseapicta', and *Mandevilla*. In a garden bed or border, combine it with billowy blue *Hydrangea macrophylla* flowers and large spiky *Phormium* leaves.

Cultivation

Grow silver-dollar plant in full sun in well-drained, moist soil. Allow the plant to dry somewhat between waterings; it tolerates drought without ill effect but stops growing. Fertilize once a month to encourage new, attractive growth. This plant responds well to pruning, so prune it to maintain the

plant shape you desire. Growing rapidly from seed sown in spring, this eucalyptus turns into a small, 6- to 8-ft-tall tree by midsummer, so it need not be overwintered. But you can easily do so to get larger plants with especially nicely formed heads earlier in the season the next year. Overwinter stooled plants by cutting them to the ground and storing them in their containers in a cool, dark place. Cut branches of standards back to the top of their trunks and store them likewise, unless a conservatory is available. Prune standards back by two-thirds. Planted in a

sheltered spot and heavily mulched for the winter, silver-dollar plant may be root-hardy in zone 7.

Similar Species

E. neglecta (**Omeo round-leaved gum**): With silvery leaves similar to those of silver-dollar tree but more elliptical in shape, this cold-hardy eucalyptus creates a tropical effect without your having to worry about how to overwinter it. Its bark is silver-gray and green. Use it the same way you would *E. cinerea*. Hardy in zones 7–11; to zone 6 with winter protection.

◆◆◆

Eucharis × grandiflora
(you-KARE-us gran-dih-FLOOR-uh)
Amazon Lily, Eucharis Lily
Tropical bulbous perennial, to 2½ ft tall;
grows to its mature height in a season.
Hardy in zones 10–11.

Exotic yet elegant, Amazon lily creates an enchanting display when it blooms, which it does as many as four times a year. The flowers look somewhat like pure white daffodils, because they have a cup resting in the center of a petal-like corolla. However, unlike daffodils, these flowers bloom in a whorl of up to six, 4- to 5-in.-wide blossoms atop a 2½-ft-tall stem and nod gracefully downward. Scented with a light, lemony perfume, Amazon lilies last well in the garden or as cut flowers. The 1-ft-long leaves are glossy green and oval to elliptical, growing directly from the underground bulb and forming a large, attractive clump. Mature bulbs may produce as many as 20 flowering stems a year, in flushes every few months. Use

this easy-to-grow plant in containers on a porch grouped with other tropicals or plunged into the border with large-scale plants as a backdrop, where its lovely flowers can stand out without competition.

Cultivation

This jungle dweller needs light, dappled shade such as that under a

Eucharis × grandiflora

tree or on a porch. Provide rich, moist soil and fertilize monthly when it is growing actively. The trick to getting this bulb to bloom several times a year is to keep it moist before and during blooming but to allow the soil to dry out a bit after each flush of flowers. This induces a rest, and when after a month's rest the plant is watered again, flower buds form and it begins to bloom. Since the key to repeat blooming is to manipulate the soil moisture, you'll have the most success by growing this bulb in a container so that you can easily keep tabs on watering. Bring containers inside and grow your Amazon lilies as houseplants during the winter; allow the soil to dry out a bit in autumn, and then water more generously to induce a beautiful show of winter flowers. Otherwise, allow the bulbs to dry out and go dormant, then store them as you would dahlias until spring. Repot and divide bulbs every few years, planting them just a few inches below the soil surface.

◆◆◆

Eucomis bicolor (you-KOME-us BYE-kul-or)
Pineapple Lily

Subtropical bulbous perennial, to 2 ft tall;
grows to its mature height in one season.
Hardy in zones 7–10; to zone 6 with winter protection.

Surely one of the weirdest plants in the garden, pineapple lily looks like vegetation that might have invaded your garden from Mars or an alien galaxy. The bulb produces a tight whorl of pointed, hyacinth-like leaves from which a tall, leafless stalk of tightly packed, star-shaped, honey-scented flowers emerges.

Crowning the flowering stem is an odd-looking tuft of leaves. A purple band marks the edge of each pale green petal, setting off the flowers' purple anthers. Stems are mottled with purple, and the margins of the crown of leaves atop the flowering stem have a narrow purple edge, adding to the plant's eerie presence. Before the flowers open, their tightly closed buds and tuft of leaves on top resemble a pineapple fruit in miniature form, which explains the common name. This odd plant deserves to be displayed where you can see it—plant it in groups of three or more bulbs in the foreground of a border, where it can pop out of a low ground cover of

Eucomis bicolor

Tradescantia, Verbena, or *Wedelia trilobata.* You might also try planting three bulbs closely together in a low, 8- to 10-in. pan to display up close on the patio. Although in its native South African habitat it does not grow in a freezing climate, pineapple lily can endure cold winters and return to bloom again the following year as long as the soil is well drained.

Cultivation

Plant pineapple lily bulbs 6 to 8 in. deep in the garden once the psoil has warmed or in a container of well-drained potting medium. They perform well in full sun to part shade. Enrich the soil at planting time with compost and then fertilize once a month. Allow the soil to dry somewhat between waterings. You can leave the bulbs in the ground to overwinter in zones 7–8, provided you mulch them well, or dig them in fall after the tops have been killed by frost and store them until spring.

Cultivars and Similar Species

'Alba': This form has pale greenish white flowers, and its stems and leaves are green, lacking contrasting speckles. Use it for its unique appearance where a quieter color is needed in a pastel color scheme.

'Sparkling Burgundy' ('Sparkler') (purple pineapple lily): Deep burgundy stems, leaves, and flowers make this recently available form a fabulous choice for jazzing up a color scheme. For a harmonious effect, try it with *Coleus* 'Kiwi Fern'—it matches the purple in the ruffled leaves to perfection.

And for an eye-popping color scheme, plant it to grow through the golden leaves of golden creeping Jenny (*Lysimachia nummularia* 'Aurea').

E. comosa: This species looks similar to *E. bicolor,* and shares the same hardiness range, but its flowers are larger and taller and the undersides of the green leaves, as well as the stems, sport purple markings. The plant grows 2½ to 3 ft tall.

◆◆◆

E*uphorbia* (you-FOR-bee-uh)

Euphorbia, Red Spurge, Crown-of-Thorns, Pencil Cactus

Tropical shrub or perennial, to 3 ft tall or more; grows to about half its mature height the first growing season. Hardy in zones 9–11.

Euphorbia cotinifolia

Hailing from tropical Africa and South America, this vast genus includes some real curiosities for the tropical-looking garden, as well as old garden standbys for the perennial border. The best-known euphorbias are often mistaken for cacti because they have thorny, succulent stems. One way to tell the difference is that plants in this genus exude a milky sap from any injuries to their stems and leaves. Also, euphorbias tend to be leafier, often producing several sets of leaves a year when rainfall is plentiful and dropping them during periods of drought. Their inflorescences are made up of clusters of tiny flowers surrounded by colorful bracts, and they may be tiny and inconspicuous or large and showy, depending on the species. Other euphorbias are leafy throughout the growing season and usually thornless—these make excellent foliage plants. Whether grown for their novel architecture or for their enchanting leaves, euphorbias add wonderful contrast to mixed containers.

Cultivation

Full sun and well-drained soil are necessary ingredients for success with this genus. Succulent types tolerate drought and suffer if overwatered; leafy types are drought-tolerant but need more soil moisture and richer soil. Provide water accordingly. Fertilize lightly only once or twice during the growing season. Because they thrive in low-water situations and dry air, both succulent and leafy types make marvelous houseplants and if overwintered turn into wonderful specimens for the summer garden. Overwinter them in a cool, very sunny window and water sparingly. Euphorbias rarely need pruning, but if you do prune them, wear gloves and avoid contact with your eyes because the milky white sap may cause skin irritations and can cause blindness if it gets into the eyes.

Species and Cultivars

There are a vast number of species of *Euphorbia* to tempt gardeners in both temperate and tropical climates. Here are several favorite tropical species for tropical-style gardens, but if you fall in love with these plants, be sure to seek out other types for your collection.

Leafy Types

E. cotinifolia (**red spurge, tropical smoke tree, bronze euphorbia**): This elegant plant features a loose arrangement of rounded leaves on slender stems. The leaves, which are 2 in. across, are imbued with a glowing coppery red color, similar to that of the hardy smoke tree, *Cotinus coggygria.* Red spurge provides a gorgeous color contrast and a graceful texture throughout the growing season. Use this bushy plant, which can grow to 3 ft or more in a season, in beds or containers combined with *Oxalis* 'Copper Glow' or any of the fancy-leaved pelargoniums to create pleasing color echoes.

E. marginata (**snow-on-the-mountain**): Often grown as an annual, this is a charming, 3-ft-tall foliage plant from Grandmother's garden. The 3-in.-long, oval leaves are heavily marked with very wide, bright white bands along the edges. New leaves may be almost entirely white. Green-and-white flower clusters add another snowy cap to the stems in late summer, and the plant may reseed. The sap is extremely irritating, sometimes causing burns.

Succulent Types

E. ingens (**candelabra tree**): Use this upright grower for its vertical architectural effect in a combination planter or plant it in a xeriscape garden. It eventually reaches many feet tall but grows only a few inches per year. The thick, fleshy branches are angular in cross section, with a few sparse leaves at their corners. Terminal clusters of small greenish yellow flowers may appear in spring.

E. milii (**crown-of-thorns**): The stout gray stems of this bushy succulent are crowded with lethal thorns and usually studded with bright green, 1 1/2-in.-long, oval leaves. In spring and summer, clusters of small, but pretty, red flowers decorate the plant. Forms with yellow, white, orange, or salmon-pink flowers are available. Crown-of-thorns grows to 3 ft tall or more, adding a foot or so a year.

E. tirucallii (**pencil cactus**): Another shrubby, open-branched succulent that grows to several feet tall, pencil cactus features very narrow, bright green branches growing from its cylindrical main stems, which are also green. Grow this exotic as a specimen on a patio, or group it with *Agave parviflora, Echeveria, Aeonium,* or other succulents or cacti. ✦✦✦

Ferns, Tropical species

Tropical and subtropical perennials and treelike plants,
from 2 to 20 ft tall; growth rate varies, but tree-fern types
grow slowly, adding only a few inches every year once they mature.
Hardy in zones 8b–11.

About 10,000 species of ferns inhabit the earth, dwelling in all types of climates and growing conditions, and enduring both heat and cold, dampness and drought—some even grow as epiphytes attached to trees. Most ferns, however—especially the tropical types—grow in moist soil in shady, humid conditions. Summers in most temperate gardens afford the same growing conditions, so that a shady grove of trees in a northern garden can be transformed into a rain forest with a few large tropical ferns. No other plants evoke the forest primeval as much as do ferns. They are, after all, ancient plant forms. The sheer abundance of their greenery and their sometimes huge size make these leafy denizens of cool, moist forests the perfect choice for painting a jungly scene dripping with moisture and lush growth.

Platycerium bifurcatum

Fern leaves are fronds that unfurl gracefully from a central growing point. The leaf blade has a central midrib and is usually divided into leaflets, which in turn may be further divided one or more times, producing a very fine-textured effect. Some tropical ferns grow quite large and their fronds become huge, so they create the contradictory impression of being both bold- and fine-textured. The tree ferns look the most exotic of all, their enormous, feathery fronds growing very quickly to be as tall as or taller than a person. Growth slows once the tree fern reaches its mature spread. If you can overwinter a tree fern and place it in the garden during the summer, the impact will be instantly tropical. Otherwise, use any of these tropical ferns in groups in a shady bed, either planted directly in the ground or as containerized plunge plants. They also make marvelous specimens on a cool porch or patio, and they can be quite effective in hanging baskets, bringing their lushness to eye level. Ferns combine well with almost any other shade-loving plant, contributing muted color and texture.

Cultivation

Grow tropical ferns in humus-rich, moist soil in dappled shade. To prevent the leaves from browning or shedding, water plentifully, do not let the soil dry out, and protect the plants from drying winds. Feed monthly with a high-nitrogen liquid fertilizer such as fish emulsion. Tropical ferns are best overwintered in a greenhouse or conservatory. They can be grown as houseplants only if you can provide cool, humid conditions, away from heat sources. Tasmanian tree ferns will overwinter in Pacific Northwest gardens in zone 8b.

Species and Cultivars
Tree-fern Types

Blechnum brasiliense (**Brazilian tree fern**): This small tree fern from South America attains a height of only 3 to 4 ft and looks more like a sago palm than a fern because its leaves are bold and leathery dark green and have lighter undersides. They reach to 2 to 2½ ft long. 'Crispum' has slightly ruffled or wavy leaves that, if grown in a little morning sun, are light red as they unfold, adding an eye-catching note. This species needs moist conditions. Hardy in zones 9b–11.

Cyathea cooperi (**Australian tree fern**): The bright green fronds of this elegant tree fern are up to 6 to 10 ft long and are triple-cut, forming huge, lacy triangles. The stout trunk features round leaf scars, giving it an attractive texture. In the wild this fern might reach 40 ft in height, but in a container it grows so slowly that it will usually remain a manageable size. Use this exquisite species as a single specimen on a shady terrace or in a mixed border. It tolerates some sun as long as it has a moist, humid site. Hardy in zones 9b–11; to 9a in a protected location.

Dicksonia antarctica (**Tasmanian tree fern, Australian tree fern, New Zealand tree fern**): The 6- to 8-ft-long, oblong leaves of this tree fern are triple-cut into lacy segments and have hairy, reddish brown stems. Fibrous brown material covers the stout trunk, giving it a shaggy texture. This species grows slowly to 40 ft in the wild but typically only to 10 ft in cultivation. Use it as a container specimen on a cool, shady patio,

or plunge it into the shade garden with lower plants to add structure to a tropical-style setting. Be sure to keep the soil moist; humid air helps, too. This is the most cold-hardy of the tree ferns. It survives winters in zone 8b in the coastal Pacific Northwest, but it is very sensitive to heat and dry winds, so it is not suited to growing outdoors in hot, arid climates. Hardy in zones 8b–11 where the climate is humid and not too hot.

Other Types

Nephrolepis acutifolia (**Australian sword fern**): Sword fern resembles a Boston fern (see below) in leaf shape, but its fronds are more upright and grow taller: 2 to 3 ft in a container and 3 to 4 ft in the ground. It also tolerates full sun provided the soil remains evenly moist. Use this clump-forming fern alone or in groups in the ground or in containers to provide a vertical accent and a lush tropical feel to set off plants with big, exotic flowers such as *Hibiscus* or *Brugmansia*. Hardy in zones 10–11.

N. exaltata 'Bostoniensis' (**Boston fern**): Easy to grow and quite common, this fast-growing fern

Dicksonia antarctica

reaches a height of 2 ft in a single season. It features bright to dark green, feather-shaped fronds, which stand upright at first and then gracefully arch over with age, hanging downward 3 ft or more. Fancy-leaved cultivars may be curled and more finely cut. Use this dense grower as a pretty filler in beds and containers with other shade lovers such as *Abutilon, Fuchsia, Caladium,* and *Begonia*. It performs well in shade or morning sun. Boston fern will shed its leaves if it dries out. If this happens, cut it back to the ground and water it to force bright new growth. Hardy in zones 9b–11.

Platycerium bifurcatum (**common staghorn fern**): An oddball among ferns, staghorn fern is an epiphyte with large, flat, antler-shaped leaves covered with grayish white felt. When mounted on a bark slab or grown in a hanging moss basket, the plants form large rounded balls of angular, 3-ft-long leaves that grow from a central crown. Use these attention getters hanging from trees or mounted on a shady wall. Water with a hose every few days, making sure to soak the leaves and the growing medium. Bring the fern into the house in early fall and water by placing it in the shower. Hardy in zones 9–11.

Pteris cretica 'Albolineata' (**tabletop fern**): The fronds of this low, clump-forming fern are dissected into slender, 10-in.-long leaflets with a broad, silvery white stripe down their centers. Growing only 6 to 8 in. tall, this selection makes an excellent filler combined with *Begonia, Anthurium, Fuchsia,* and other ferns in a shady container. Hardy in zones 9–11.

◆◆◆

Ficus (FYE-kuss)
Fig, Ficus, Rubber Tree

Tropical and subtropical shrub, tree, or vine, some types to
180 ft tall in their natural habitat, lower in cultivation;
most grow a few feet taller each year.
Hardy in zones 8b/9–11.

This huge genus of primarily tropical plants includes some of our most popular houseplants: the rubber trees. Grown for their gorgeous, highly polished leaves, these are big, bold foliage plants extraordinaire. When plunged into a border with more colorful plants, a rubber tree adds a jungly note. Other species, however, have smaller leaves and make less of a statement but work well as pretty little fillers and weavers. Some *Ficus* have variegated leaves or reddish new growth for surprising dashes of color. None have showy or interesting flowers, so use them solely for the impact of their foliage. Those with large leaves make wonderful contrasts with fine-textured plants—try using a rubber tree as a focal point in a bed of *Pennisetum villosum,* where its glossy, bold foliage is accentuated by the white, fuzzy flowers and thin, grassy leaves.

Cultivation

These tropicals do well outdoors in part shade to full sun. Provide rich, moist but well-drained soil. Keep the soil evenly moist; they may drop leaves if the soil dries out. Apply a liquid fertilizer every two weeks during active growth. All types respond well to pruning, so cut them back as needed; they will readily regrow and become fuller. To keep tree-type species a manageable size for container culture, top- and root-prune them

yearly. Then every five years or so, air-layer them to start new, smaller plants. You can even stool a *Ficus* plant so it forms a dense, bushy shrub. These species make excellent houseplants and are easily overwintered in a well-lit room.

Species and Cultivars

There are about 800 species of *Ficus.* The few described here adapt well to being used outdoors in a tropical-style garden and to being overwintered as houseplants.

F. elastica (**rubber tree**): Very shiny and dark green, the beautiful leaves of the rubber tree grow into 1- to 1½-ft-long, oblong affairs with lighter undersides. Often the new growth is reddish. This fast grower can add 2 to 3 ft in height a year. It ultimately becomes tree size but can be pruned to keep it in scale with a tropical-style garden. 'Burgundy Knight' has dark burgundy leaves with scarlet midribs and light red undersides; it makes pleasing textual contrasts and color echoes with *Breynia disticha* 'Roseapicta' and red-flowered *Verbena.* 'Tricolor', the most colorful of the rubber tree cultivars, features green leaves splashed with white, cream, yellow, and pink that have prominent red midribs; it combines well with *Alternanthera dentata* 'Rubiginosa' and almost every other plant imaginable. 'Doescheri' is softly mottled with pale green, gray-green, and creamy white and has pink stems

and midribs. All *F. elastica* are hardy in zones 10–11 and root-hardy in zone 9.

F. lyrata (**fiddle-leaf fig**): The glossy, dark green leaves of this African plant are shaped rather like the outline of a fiddle and are puckered around their prominent veins. This very coarse plant looks good pruned as a small tree, which shows off its rough bark. It is fast growing, adding 2 to 3 ft in a season. Hardy in zones 10–11.

Ficus pumila 'Variegata'

F. pumila (**creeping fig**): You might never guess that this small, creeping ground cover or clinging vine is a fig, but it is. The 1-in. oval leaves are dark green and densely cover narrow brown stems. 'Variegata' has a bright white edge to the leaves and grows more slowly than the all-green form. Use creeping fig as a fast-growing annual ground cover in shade or part sun to weave among taller plants or to spill over the edge of a container. Hardy in zones 9–11; to zone 8b in a warm microclimate. ✦✦✦

F*uchsia* (FEW-shuh)
Fuchsia

Tender perennial or hardy shrub, from 1 to 4 ft tall;
grows 6 to 12 in. during a single season.
Tropicals are hardy in zones 9–11 and root-hardy in zone 8;
cold-hardy types survive to zone 6.

Blooming nonstop from spring until fall—and year-round if grown indoors in winter—a fuchsia's enchanting flowers masquerade as clusters of exotic ornaments suspended from the branches. The flowers of these highly hybridized plants are intricate affairs made up of brightly colored petals that overlap to form a cup from which protrudes a prominent set of anthers, and this is all deeply set into a long tube of colorful sepals that flares open and sweeps back into a curly saucer. Often the blossoms are bicolored, with the sepals and petals painted in brightly vying or pleasantly serene shades of red, pink, purple, or—what else—fuchsia! Some types have semidouble or double flowers that lend a fuller, frillier effect. The simplest forms are cultivars of *F. triphylla* and have long, slender tubes of sepals that almost engulf the petals, for a more subdued natural effect. Flower size varies from large, rather gaudy 2½-in. concoctions to simple ½-in. tubes. Foliage is deep green but of little interest when compared with the flowers, although you might find variegated forms with tricolored or bright golden yellow leaves. Whether grown in a hanging basket, trained as a small standard tree form, or allowed to grow into a bush, a blooming fuchsia cannot be ignored. Use it to add an exotic note to a tropical-style garden, combining it with such plants as

Fuchsia 'Mrs. J. D. Fredericks'

ferns, *Begonia*, *Phygelius*, *Osteospermum*, and *Abutilon*.

Cultivation

Fuchsias usually perform best in afternoon shade and morning sun, because for the most part they prefer cool temperatures. In hot, humid climates they bloom best in spring and fall when nights are cool and may go out of bloom in midsummer. The soil must be humus-rich and moist; keep it evenly moist and do not let it dry out or blooming suffers. Water frequently, especially fuchsias in hanging baskets. Incorporate fertilizer into the soil at planting time and then apply liquid fertilizer weekly when plants are actively growing. You may find it difficult to overwinter a fuchsia as a houseplant, because it languishes with-

out high light and high humidity. If you cannot provide ideal conditions, force the plant into dormancy by cutting it back to a few inches and keeping it in a cool, dark place until spring. Keep the soil fairly dry until you bring the plant out into the light. This is an especially valuable trick for carrying over expensive standards and large plants.

Species and Cultivars

There are thousands of cultivars and hybrids of fuchsia, so we list here only a few choice ones. You can choose from among those available at your local nurseries to match your garden's color scheme, or shop through specialty catalogs for the odd and exotic.

Upright Growers

'Hidcote Beauty': This bushy plant has graceful, single, 2- to 3-in.-long flowers that are bicolored coral and white. It performs well in hot, humid summers. Try it as a standard underplanted with white caladium or fancy-leaved geraniums.

'Mrs. J. D. Fredericks': The bright, pink-on-pink, 1-in.-long flowers of this cultivar are bell-shaped and single, blooming in sprays on arching branches that grow to 2 ft tall. The plant tolerates more sun than do most fuchsias.

'Schneckerl': This low-growing form, whose name is German for "snail," gets to be only 12 to16 in. tall but is bushy and well branched. The frilly flowers are 1½ in. long and display bright lilac corollas tucked inside pure white, curling sepals. A very sun-tolerant plant, it blooms all summer.

F. triphylla 'Gartenmeister Bonstedt': This upright, bushy plant produces incredible numbers of 2-in.-long, tubular, salmon-orange flowers. New foliage emerges reddish burgundy and matures to dark green with a burgundy flush, making for a hot-colored specimen. Combine it with *Alternanthera* 'Purple Select' or with the ducksfoot coleus 'Thumbelina' to pick up on the burgundy tones.

Weeping Types

There are hundreds of types of weeping fuchsia, but most grow and bloom well only in cool, sunny regions such as northern California. Where temperatures rise into the 80s, they usually stop blooming and succumb to fungal disease. The following types are exceptions to this rule, and some even have colorful leaves to carry through the flowerless periods.

'Curtain Call': This large-flowering hybrid stops the show with its huge, ruffled, light pink and deep lavender flowers. Although blooming may slow down during really hot weather, this cultivar stands up better to stressful growing conditions than do most large-flowered hybrids.

'Golden Marinka': This trailing fuchsia has an exceptional leaf color as well as brightly colored flowers. The 2-in. leaves are warm gold marked with bright red and cream variegation. The bell-shaped, red-on-red blossoms are 1½ in. long. Although blooming may cease with summer's worst heat, the colorful leaves keep the plant looking good.

'Island Sunset': This cascading fuchsia is a sparkling beauty with bright red, single, 1½-in. blossoms set off against silvery gray-green, white-edged leaves. It looks very nice tumbling over the edge of a container or draping from a hanging basket.

❖❖❖

*G*alphimia glauca (gal-FEE-me-uh GLOUW-kuh)
Mexican Gold Bush

Tropical shrub or tender perennial, to 10 ft tall;
grows 3 to 4 ft in a single season.
Hardy in zones 9–11.

The bright yellow, ¾-in. blossoms of Mexican gold bush have a pretty frill of red anthers, and the stems have reddish hairs, which gives them a hot aspect that goes well with other plants sporting red or orange flowers. Dense, upright clusters of these flowers smother the shrub from summer through fall, standing out against the waxy, blue-green, oval leaves. Use this compact shrub as a specimen in a container, or plant it directly in a sunny garden, where it will attract butterflies and hummingbirds. Its neat texture makes a great contrast with bigger, bolder tropicals such as *Canna, Ficus elastica, Musa, Sanchezia,* and *Codiaeum.* You might also try plugging it into a perennial or hardy-shrub border, where you can enjoy its months of flowers. It's delightful combined with *Buddleia* 'Black Knight' or 'Harlequin'.

Cultivation

Mexican gold bush blooms best in full sun but is satisfactory with only half a day of sun. Give it fertile, well-drained soil and allow the soil to dry a bit between waterings. Feed once a month with liquid fertilizer during the growing season. This shrub is naturally compact, but to prevent it from growing too large, prune it hard in fall after flowering stops. To keep it looking its best and to encourage continual flowering, remove spent flower clusters when they fade. Because mature specimens look so stunning,

Galphimia glauca

overwinter this plant in a sunny window or a conservatory so it can grow to a good size.

❖❖❖

Gardenia augusta (gar-DEAN-ee-uh awe-GUST-uh)

(*G. jasminoides*)

Gardenia, Cape Jasmine

Subtropical shrub, to 5 to 20 ft tall; grows 6 to 8 in. taller each year.
Hardy in zones 8b–11.

Gardenia jasminoides

A single gardenia flower in full bloom emits enough heady perfume to scent a room or intoxicate a garden party. These sophisticated-looking blossoms open from tightly wound buds to resemble full-blown, creamy white, 3-in. roses. Blooming occurs in flushes throughout the year but most heavily in spring and summer, with flowers opening several at a time for a month or so. The shrubs are evergreen, sporting very shiny and very dark green leaves. Gardenias can be plunged into the shrub border or garden bed or grown as container specimens on a terrace or deck. But wherever you choose to use this plant, there is only one rule to adhere to: Locate it where you will be sure to experience the exotic fragrance. A good place is near an outdoor sitting area or under a frequently opened window.

Cultivation

This species grows best in light or part shade but does well in full sun if temperatures aren't too hot. Provide humus-rich, moist but well-drained, acid soil. Keep the soil evenly moist; if the soil dries out or the plant is exposed to drafts, the leaves and flower buds may drop. Fertilize twice a month during the growing season with liquid fertilizer designed for acid-loving plants. Prune as needed in spring or summer to maintain the size of plant you desire. You can easily overwinter a gardenia in a conservatory or as a houseplant as long as it gets ample light and is kept cool, especially at night; given these conditions, it will continue to bloom. Plants do best indoors with high humidity.

Cultivars

'**Fortuniana**': This cultivar is the most floriferous, its heavily scented blossoms blooming freely throughout the year. The flowers open white and age to creamy yellow.

'**Radicans**': Use this low, mounding plant, which reaches only 2 ft tall, in a mixed planter. Although only 2 in. across, the flowers are intensely fragrant. 'Radicans Variegata' has gray-green leaves with creamy white edges.

◆◆◆

Gramineae (grah-MIN-ae-ee)

Grass Family, Tropical Grasses

Tropical and subtropical perennial and annual grasses, to 6 ft tall;
most grow to their mature height the first year.
Hardy in zones 8–11.

The vast grass family contains 400 genera and 4,500 species, some of which thrive in every climate and environment throughout the world. Grasses flourish in the tropics—their presence even defines some ecosystems. We experience them as towering stands of bamboo inhabiting the steaming jungles of Southeast Asia; the willowy reeds creating extensive marshlands that border the rivers and lagoons of South America; the golden, wheatlike fields forming the boundless savannas of Kenya; and the sugarcane fields in the neotropics. All grasses have linear leaves or blades whose bases wrap around a jointed, hollow stem that is called a culm. Their flowers are called florets and are borne in spikelets that can be quite showy in form, if not in color, especially when they ripen into feathery seed heads.

If you're attempting to create a tropical aura in your garden, the skillful use of ornamental grasses can set the mood. You can incorporate many large, cold-hardy grasses, such as *Miscanthus, Cortaderia,* and *Arundo donax,* and some of the cold-hardy clump-forming bamboos as a permanent structure; however, the beauty of certain tropical or annual grasses cannot be matched by their cold-hardy cousins. The tropicals and annuals grow faster and bloom longer, and some also offer unique textures and colors. Tall grasses work well for height in a container or in the garden, and they can be massed for a natural look. Use smaller types for their linear texture as effective foliage fillers.

Cultivation

Tropical grasses are easy to grow and undemanding. Most do best in full sun when grown in temperate climates. Provide well-drained, evenly moist soil. Fertilize monthly during the growing season. Most tropical grasses can be allowed to go dormant in fall and then be kept in their containers in a cool, dim place during winter. Some do well as conservatory plants. A few exotic grasses that are prolific seeders can become serious weeds that invade natural areas and out-compete native plants in the mild climates where they are hardy, so they should not be planted in those zones. Grow and enjoy them only as annuals in cold climates, where they cannot self-sow.

Species and Cultivars

Of the numerous ornamental tropical grasses available, the following prove to be easy to grow in northern gardens and can be used to great effect in tropical-looking designs.

Cymbopogon citratus (**lemon grass**): A clump-forming grass from India and Sri Lanka, lemon grass is beautiful as well as fragrant. All parts of this grass have a pungent lemon aroma, and the pith of the stems is used as an indispensable ingredient in Thai cooking. Plants grow to 5 ft tall and have 3- to 4-ft-long, gray-green, very narrow leaves. This is a very useful plant for adding height and texture to a mixed container; combine and contrast it with the foliage of *Solanum quitoense, Kalanchoe pumila,* and *Pelargonium* and the fine-textured flowers of *Lantana* and *Arctotis.* Overwinter in a cool, well-lit location. Hardy in zones 9–11.

Cyperus papyrus (**papyrus**): *See* Cyperus *entry.*

Muhlenbergia dumosa (**bamboo muhly grass**): Growing 4 to 5 ft tall and wide and forming arching clumps, this extremely fine-textured grass resembles a delicate bamboo. The stems are visibly jointed and are gracefully branched, sporting very narrow, light green, 3-in.-long leaves. The purplish flowers ripen into golden seed heads. The overall effect is very airy. This species prefers full sun and well-drained soil on the dry side. Use it in containers or massed in the garden for an exotic look. Overwinter on a cool sunporch, or cut it back and store it in the basement. Hardy in zones 8–10.

Pennisetum setaceum 'Rubrum' ('Atropurpureum') (**purple fountain grass**): The narrow, arching leaves of this deep burgundy, clump-forming grass form a beautiful fountain of color. Clumps can grow 3 to 4 ft tall and wide and are topped with pinkish purple, feathery plumes throughout the summer. These ripen to brownish pink seed heads in autumn. This is a wonderful grass to use as a color accent. For a harmonious color combination, pair it with silver-leaved plants, such as *Helichrysum petiolare,* or with plants with pink or lavender flowers, such as *Lantana, Pentas, Fuchsia,* or *Dahlia.* For an exciting, vivid color contrast, combine it with yellow-hued foliage and flowers, such as *Codiaeum, Allamanda,* or *Senna.* 'Burgundy Giant' is similar but grows to 6 ft tall and has wider leaf blades. Hardy in zones 8–11; treat as an annual elsewhere.

P. villosum (**feathertop, white-flowering fountain grass**): This 1½- to 2-ft-tall grass forms mounds of very thin, light green leaf blades that are topped from early summer until hard frost with

Setaria palmifolia

2-in.-long, feathery white plumes. An African native, it looks best planted in masses, creating a foamy sea that undulates in the breeze. Mass it in front of bolder plants so the different foliage and flower types can play off each other. This species does best in well-drained, rich, fertile soil. It is cold-hardy in zones 8–10, but it sows prolifically in those zones and can become a serious pest.

Rhynchelytrum repens (**ruby grass, natal grass**): Another creeping grass native to the savannas of Africa, ruby grass grows to about 2 ft tall, with the flowers rising up to a foot higher. It forms stands of very narrow, 4-in.-long, gray-green leaves at soft angles to the upright stems. Panicles of light reddish purple flowers tip the stems in early summer and ripen first to pink and then to silver seed heads, remaining showy until frost. This grass looks great mass-planted in the garden or used stuffed into a mixed planter, its stems creating a shower of fuzzy little flowers. Provide well-drained, moist soil.

Hardy in zones 9–11; to keep this grass from becoming a weed problem, grow only in colder climates, where it's an annual.

Setaria palmifolia (**palm grass**): Palm grass's leaf blades, which are crinkled into pleats, measure 2 to 3 in. wide and up to 1 ft long on stems reaching 2 to 3 ft in length and are arranged in such a way that they look very much like palm leaves. However, the stems are segmented like a bamboo. Throughout the summer, tall stalks tipped with fuzzy, green or tan foxtails add to the plant's bold good looks. Use palm grass as a single specimen in a container, where its unique foliage will really stand out, or plant it in the ground, where it will sprawl a bit. 'Rubra' has green leaves and purple midribs and stems; it looks wonderful underplanted with the waxy purple leaves of *Tradescantia* 'Purple Simitars'. 'Variegata' has white-edged leaves. Palm grass is hardy in zones 9–11 and in zone 8b with winter protection, but it seeds itself vigorously in zones 9–11 and can invade natural habitats. Use this grass only in cooler climates as an annual to prevent its spread into natural areas. It may be overwintered as a potted plant in a greenhouse. ✦✦✦

Caricature plant hails from the rain forests of Australia and the islands of the South Pacific and features glossy, oval leaves that are about 6 in. long, 2 to 3 in. wide, and tipped with a drip tip at their ends. New foliage emerges deep purplish brown accented with irregular, creamy white and pink splotches along the prominent red midveins. In midsummer short spikes of bright red, tubular flowers bloom at the tips of the stems, if they aren't removed by pinching. Use this fast-growing, shrubby tropical in a mixed container or in a border for height and structure. Its subdued variegations and metallic hue make it a versatile companion for plants with brighter purple leaves or flowers, such as *Tradescantia* 'Purple Heart' or heliotrope. Another great way to use caricature plant is to plant acidanthera (*Acidanthera bicolor* var. *murieliae*) beneath its boughs, so that the bulb's spiky foliage and

Graptophyllum pictum 'Tricolor'
(grap-toe-FYE-lum PIK-tum)
Caricature Plant

Tropical shrub, to 6 to 8 ft tall; grows 2 to 3 ft each year.
Evergreen in zones 10–11; root-hardy in zone 9.

purple-splotched white flowers poke up through the rounded leaves.

Cultivation

Caricature plant prefers part to full sun and rich, well-drained soil.

Graptophyllum pictum 'Tricolor'

Since the best foliage color occurs on new growth, your aim should be to keep the plant growing vigorously by watering, fertilizing, and pinching regularly. Apply liquid plant food once a month. Pinch the growing tips about once a month, or when needed, to promote colorful new growth and a bushy shape. Caricature plant makes a good houseplant and is easily overwintered in the house or in a conservatory or greenhouse. However, if you do not have room to keep a large plant over the winter, you can cut it back and store the resting plant in a cool, dim basement until spring.

✦✦✦

Gynura aurantiaca

(guy-NUR-uh are-an-ti-ACK-uh)

(*G. sarmentosa*)

Purple Velvet Plant, Velvet Plant, Purple Passion Vine

Sprawling or upright tropical perennial, to 2 to 3 ft tall; reaches mature height during the first growing season.
Hardy to zone 10.

Gynura sarmentosa

The leaves and stems of this pretty trailing plant are covered with soft hairs that give them a velvety finish so soft to the touch that you cannot resist reaching out and stroking them with a finger. Although the leaf surface is green, the long, dense hairs are a brilliant violet or reddish purple that shimmers in the sun and gives the plant an overall purple glow. The relatively fine-textured, oval leaves grow about 2 in. long and have toothed edges and a prominent network of purplish veins. Although purple velvet plant is grown for its luxurious foliage, it does bloom in winter, producing clusters of daisylike flowers in a happy contrasting golden hue. Use this sprawling plant in a hanging basket or to spill over the edge of a planter. It makes a good color echo with the fine-textured purplish leaves of *Leea amabilis* 'Splendens' and the bold-textured fronds of *Ensete* 'Maurellii'. You might also enjoy creating a jolting color combination with hot orange or gold flowers, such as those of *Lantana, Phygelius,* or *Cuphea.*

Cultivation

Purple velvet plant grows well in part to full sun, but the brightest purple color develops in full sun. It is not fussy about soil as long as it is well drained. The plant is best kept evenly moist when actively growing. Incorporate a timed-release fertilizer at planting time and add liquid fertilizer every two weeks. To keep the plants from getting leggy, pinch the growing tips every few weeks. This plant thrives as a houseplant in a sunny window, so it's easily overwintered indoors. It also roots readily from cuttings.

Similar Species

G. bicolor: This 2-ft-tall cousin to *G. aurantiaca,* which is also hardy to zone 10, has larger, coarser leaves that grow 6 to 8 in. long and are scalloped like an oak leaf. Although the leaves are as velvety to the touch, their color is not as intense: gray-green with purple blotches and margins. Plant this species in a combination planter or in the ground. ◆◆◆

Hamelia patens

(ha-MEAL-ee-uh PAY-tens)

Mexican Firecracker Plant

Tropical shrub, to 3 to 4 ft tall; grows about 1 to 2 ft each year.
Hardy in zones 9–10.

Ablaze with fiery flowers all summer and well into fall, this tropical shrub has a nice rounded shape that fits into most garden settings. The bright orange or scarlet, tubular blossoms are about 3/4 in. long and bloom in clusters at the tips of the stems, attracting a horde of hummingbirds and butterflies. Shiny black berries develop after the flowers fade. The rusty-colored stems and green leaves with a reddish flush add additional sizzle to the plant's effect. Individual leaves are ellipti-

Hamelia patens

cal and about 2 in. long. Mexican firecracker grows well as a specimen in a container or matched up in the border with bold-looking hardy or tropical plants that lend themselves to warm color schemes. Perennials that combine well with this tropical shrub include *Ligularia,* with its tall stalks of gold blossoms and rounded leaves, and *Kniphofia,* which offers spires of orange, yellow, or gold blossoms and spiky green leaves. Tropical choices include *Sanchezia,* for its vivid green-and-gold leaves, and *Heliconia,* with its tall flower spikes and glossy green leaves.

Cultivation

Although Mexican firecracker blooms well in part sun, the best leaf coloration and blooming occur in full-sun conditions, so try to give it as much sun as possible. Provide well-drained soil and allow it to dry out a bit between waterings. Fertilize once a month during the growing season. Overwinter this tropical in a greenhouse or conservatory, since it does not do well as a houseplant, or grow it as an annual. ✦✦✦

Heliconia (hell-eh-KONE-ee-uh)
Lobster Claw, Parrot Flower

Tropical perennial, to 2 to 20 ft tall;
some grow to mature height during the first year.
Hardy in zones 10b–11.

The many members of the genus *Heliconia* look like the offspring of a banana plant and a bird-of-paradise and bring a wild note to any setting. Their large, smooth, bright green, paddle-shaped leaves display prominent parallel veins like those of a banana or canna. The showy inflorescences bloom throughout the year but are especially numerous when the weather is the hottest. Flowering structures top the tall stems and consist of gaudily colored, large bracts that are shaped rather like boats or birds' beaks and may grow as stiffly upright staffs or bizarre pendulous concoctions. The bracts are often stacked into tiers and are arranged either in a spiral or in a single flat plane. Colors are usually a combination of flaming hues, such as orange, gold, and scarlet, and the bracts are often marked with yellow-green bands. The actual flowers are tiny, blue- or lavender-petaled affairs that peek from between the bracts and do not last long, but the

Heliconia stricta

showy bracts remain colorful a month or more.

Naturally inhabiting the sunny edges of the rain forest along a riverbank or lagoon, these very tender tropicals look right at home with other lush plants. To succeed with *Heliconia* in a temperate garden, grow them in containers and plunge the containers into the ground, surrounding them with other exotic-looking plants to create a natural appearance. Intersperse heliconias among cold-hardy, clumping bamboos such as *Fargesia* or ornamental grasses such as *Arundo donax* or *Miscanthus.* They also look good planted with daylilies (*Hemerocallis* spp.), whose brightly colored, trumpet-shaped flowers accentuate their bold foliage.

Cultivation

These plants thrive on heat and humidity. Provide full to part sun. The soil should be rich and moist but well drained. Water regularly so that the soil stays evenly moist and never dries out. Feed monthly during the growing season. Bring the containers indoors in fall before temperatures dip into the 40s. Because they need so much heat and humidity, these plants do not make good houseplants, although you might try overwintering them this way if you don't have a sunny, humid greenhouse in which to do so. Cut stalks that have flowered to the ground, as they will die anyway. Repot overwintered plants in fresh soil in spring; at this time you can also divide the rhizomes and pot them up as separate plants.

Species and Cultivars

H. indica 'Spectabilis': This heliconia from Papua New Guinea has understated inflorescences with green bracts but makes up for that with foliage that resembles wildly colored banana leaves. The 7-ft-long leaves are green and maroon with maroon undersides and white to rose stripes extending from their wine-colored midribs. This cultivar grows 4 to 5 ft tall in a season; it matures at 20 ft but is lower in a container.

H. psittacorum (**parrot flower, parrot's-beak heliconia**): The easiest of the heliconias to grow, parrot flower tolerates cooler temperatures and is easier to overwinter as a houseplant. Blooming constantly during warm, humid weather, the inflorescences look like elongated bird-of-paradise flowers held in a zigzagging arrangement. Leaves are narrower than those of other species and often have red stems. Many cultivars are available with flower colors ranging from orange to red to pink, including brightly bicolored versions. The bracts usually sport green, white, and black tips or bands. Dwarf types grow to 2 to 3 ft tall; regular forms, to 4 to 5 ft.

H. rostrata (**lobster claw**): The most dramatic-looking of the heliconias, this Amazonian species produces flamboyant inflorescences whose bracts are arranged in 3-ft-long, dangling clusters in a flat plane. The young bracts at the bottom of the cluster look just like a lobster's claw. The bracts are vivid orange-red, edged with bright yellow and green. Plants grow to 5 ft tall in a single season; mature plants may reach 20 ft in height, but plants grown in containers typically remain about 5 ft. Dwarf forms are available.

H. stricta (**dwarf lobster claw**): The inflorescence of this species resembles an upright version of *H. rostrata*. The bracts are at first tightly packed, overlapping each other to form a rigid, flattened, orange torch with yellow and green markings. The structure eventually grows and separates into individual lobster-claw shapes with green flowers poking from each bract. Several cultivars with color variations including pink, maroon, and apricot are available. The 2-ft-long leaves are dark green with red midribs and undersides. Maturing at 3 to 8 ft tall, this species adapts readily to container culture and performs well in half a day of shade.

◆◆◆

Hibiscus rosa-sinensis
(hi-BIS-kuss ROH-zuh-sign-EN-sis)
Tropical Hibiscus, Rose-of-China
Tropical shrub or tree, sometimes to 20 ft tall; grows 3 to 4 ft each year.
Hardy in zones 10–11;
dies to the ground but regrows from the roots in zone 9b.

Despite its Asian origin, hibiscus is the state flower of Hawaii, where it grows with abandon in gardens everywhere. This beautiful blossom is the flower that we visualize tucked behind a hula dancer's ear as an essential ornament. Readily available and easy to grow, hibiscus belongs in every tropical-style garden from Florida to Vermont, for no other flower symbolizes a tropical paradise more than this one. The blooms range in size from 5 to 12 in. across and come in every shade imaginable except blue. Five petals, crinkled like crepe paper, make up the open-faced blossoms. Showy red anthers with fluffy yellow stamens form a long column that decorates the flower's center. Sometimes the petals are flushed darker in the center or have a contrasting color that forms a ring in the blossom's center. Flowers may even be bicolored or double-petaled, resembling a fluffy rose. As long as the temperature is warm, hibiscus blooms constantly, each blossom lasting only one day

Hibiscus rosa-sinensis 'Charles Knobloca'

but being replaced by fresh ones. The satiny flowers are well set off against shiny green leaves with toothed margins. Hibiscus grows well as a single specimen in a container, which can be set on a patio or plunged into a border. You might try using a standard or tree form to frame a formal entryway, underplanting with lower plants such as *Ficus pumila, Ipomoea batatas,* and *Russelia equisetiformis* to spill over the edge of the pot. For a jungly look, combine hibiscus with palms and bananas.

Cultivation

Provide full sun for the best blooming. The soil should be rich, moist, and well drained. Water regularly to keep the soil evenly moist. Fertilize monthly while the plant is actively growing; a fertilizer that is high in potassium and trace elements promotes the lushest bloom. Prune hibiscus as needed to shape it and to control its size. Hibiscus makes a fine houseplant in a sunny location, but it can also be stored in its container over winter in a cool, dark basement and kept on the dry side.

Cultivars and Similar Species

Tropical hibiscus is so popular as a garden plant in the tropics and as a houseplant in cold climates that there are literally hundreds of cultivars and hybrids in an array of colors. Here are just a few of the most interesting to try. Be sure to include the related species, which share the same hardiness range, in your tropical-style garden.

'Charles Knobloca': The huge, frilly pink flowers of this cultivar are suffused with an iridescent orange sheen that looks wildly tropical.

'Cooperi' ('Checkerboard'): This plant features 5-in., rose-red flowers and green leaves with pink, red, and white variegations.

'Double Pink': Luscious rose-pink and fully double, the large blossoms of this cultivar echo the variegations of *Coleus* 'Shocking Pink'.

'Jason': Huge yellow flowers with red centers make this cultivar a hot number to combine with gold-variegated plants such as *Codiaeum* or *Sanchesia.*

'Nagao 20': With blood red flowers the size of dinner plates, this one says "exotic." Flower centers darken to almost black.

H. acetosella 'Red Shield': This useful plant finds a home in tropical-style and traditional gardens because its coppery maroon leaves make such wonderful combinations with other plants. The plant grows to 4 to 8 ft tall and features deeply lobed, 6-in. leaves. The flowers, which bloom in winter, are about 2 in. across and the same color as the leaves. Use this foliage plant in the back of a mixed border, where it makes pleasing echoes with *Pennisetum setaceum* 'Rubrum' or 'Burgundy Giant'. Combine with *Canna* 'Pretoria' and hot-colored flowers for flamboyant color effects.

H. schizopetalus (**Japanese lantern hibiscus, candelabra hibiscus**): This exotic looker is similar to *H. rosa-sinensis,* but the red or pink flowers hang downward on long, graceful stems and have petals that are cut into frills and swept back into curls to reveal an extra-long, showy column of anthers.

◆◆◆

Homalocladium platycladum

(home-al-oh-KLAY-dee-um plat-ee-KLAY-dum)
(*Muehlenbeckia platyclada*)

Centipede Plant, Tapeworm Plant, Ribbon Bush

Tropical shrub, to 8 to 12 ft tall, 2 to 3 ft in cultivation; grows to 2 to 3 ft the first season.
Hardy in zones 10–11.

This plant's weird looks make it an oddity in the plant kingdom, for it has the striking appearance of a seaweed that moved onto land and began growing as a shrub. Green all over, the stems are

Homalocladium platycladum

as flat and thin as ribbon and are jointed into segments about 4 in. long and 2 to 3 in. wide. The upright to arching stems form a tight clump that grows 2 to 3 ft in height in a season, ultimately reaching 8 to 12 ft tall and developing a small, woody trunk. The small, pointed leaves, which are the same color as the stems, are sparse and insignificant, rarely remaining on the plant for long. Tiny green flowers sometimes bloom in the leaf joints in summer and are followed by black berries. Centipede plant is native to the Solomon Islands in the South Pacific. It makes a great upright foliage filler in a container; combine it with the showy flowers of *Angelonia, Mandevilla, Lantana,* and *Pelargonium* and with the colorful foliage of *Coleus, Oxalis, Tradescantia,* and *Cissus discolor.*

Cultivation

This plant adapts to almost any light conditions; it grows most vigorously in full sun but performs well in shade. It needs humus-rich, well-drained soil. Allow the soil to dry a bit between waterings. Fertilize once every two months when the plant is actively growing. Centipede plant makes a good houseplant if it can be kept in a sunny window.

❖❖❖

I*pomoea* (ip-oh-MEE-uh)
Morning Glory, Moonflower, Cardinal Climber
Tropical and subtropical twining vine, to 20 ft or more; grows to full size during the first season. Hardy in zones 8–10.

The gorgeous flowers of all types of *Ipomoea* last less than twelve hours and are either day- or night-blooming. Fortunately, once the vines start blossoming in midsummer there seems to be an unending supply of buds waiting their turn to open. Morning glories and cardinal climbers exhibit the charming habit of unfurling their funnel-shaped blossoms at dawn. The flowers last until noon or later and may remain open all afternoon if the weather is cool and cloudy. Moonflowers bloom nocturnally, unfurling their luminous blossoms at twilight. These last all night and into the early hours of the morning. If the weather is cloudy, they may stay open much of the morning. All species climb by twining their stems around a narrow support—such as a lattice trellis or fence. They make fabulous additions to the tropical-style garden because they grow quickly and drape and drip downward to add to the jungly aura. You can also include them for height in a con-

Ipomoea tricolor 'Roman Candy'

tainer, positioning a bamboo tripod in the center of the pot so the vine can grow upward. It's great fun to grow common morning glory and moonflowers on the same trellis—that way, you'll have flowers both during the day and at night.

Cultivation

You can start most morning glories and moonflowers from seed sown outdoors in warm soil or, to get a head start, purchase young plants already growing on tripods. For best germination, nick the seeds with a file and then soak them overnight in warm water. Grow these plants in full sun and well-drained soil. Water after the soil dries somewhat. Fertilize sparingly or the plants will produce lots of foliage but few flowers. These vines need a support to climb on; start them climbing on a narrow bamboo stake and then direct them to latch onto a fence, post, trellis, or arbor; they'll even hoist themselves into a shrub or low-branched tree. The vines grow rapidly and without your realizing it may attach themselves where you don't want them. If this happens, carefully uncoil the stems and direct them where you want them to grow. Treat all these vines as annuals where they are not hardy.

Species and Cultivars

I. alba (**moonflower**): This night bloomer opens its enchanting flowers near dusk, unfurling them before your eyes. The pure white, funnel-shaped blossoms measure 6 to 8 in. across, emit a lovely sweet perfume, and stand out beautifully against the large, heart-shaped leaves. Moonflower needs heat to bloom well. Where the growing season is long, it grows vigorously to 20 ft and forms a thick covering of foliage and flowers. Hardy in zones 9b–10.

I. batatas: See separate entry.

I. × multifida (**cardinal climber**): This vigorous climber is a hybrid between *I. quamoclit* and *I. coccinea* and can grow 12 to 15 ft high. Its 1-in.-long, funnel-shaped, red flowers have pretty white throats. The blossoms unfurl in the morning and last most of the day. The dark green leaves are cut into sharp lobes but are not as fine-textured as those of *I. quamoclit*. Hardy in zones 9–10.

I. purpurea (common morning glory): Climbing to about 15 ft, this vine has 2¹⁄₂-in.-long, funnel-shaped flowers in an assortment of cool colors, including blue, pink, and rose-red, often boldly striped with white. The stems and leaves are usually somewhat hairy. Leaves are oval or three-lobed. Many cultivars are available. Favorites include 'Chiacki', which has pink-throated, light blue flowers, and 'Kniola's Black', which bears velvety blossoms that open almost black and turn deep purple. Hardy in zones 9–10; will reseed itself in zones 6–10.

I. quamoclit (cypress vine): The dark green, deeply cut leaves of this South American vine create a fabulous lacy pattern that makes it an excellent foliage plant. Highlighting the leaves are 1-in.-long, bright red, funnel-shaped flowers with star-shaped faces. This species grows to 15 ft high. Tender, perennial, hardy in zones 8–10.

I. tricolor (morning glory): Adorned with blue or purple, funnel-shaped flowers that have white throats flushed deep down with yellow, this species produces the largest blossoms—3 in. or more across—and grows to 20 to 30 ft. Leaves may be oval to heart-shaped and are smooth-surfaced and medium green. 'Crimson Rambler' bears vivid red flowers with white throats. The best-known cultivar, 'Heavenly Blue', greets the morning with quantities of 6-in., velvety, sky blue flowers with white throats. 'Roman Candy' has blossoms that are bright cerise-pink with white edges and leaves that are green with white variegations; the plant sprawls more than it climbs, so you might need to tie it to a support. This tender perennial species is hardy in zones 8–10, where it dies to the ground in winter.

Argyreia nervosa (**woolly morning glory**): This massive climber, an *Ipomoea* cousin, makes a very impressive sight when trained to cover an arbor or to grow up a pillar. Its sinuous, strong stems twine their way upward, showing off 10-in.-wide, stiff, woolly, heart-shaped leaves with a thick white down covering their undersides. Flowers come in the typical morning-glory shape and are lavender with a dense, woolly coat. This vine can reach 30 to 40 ft in areas with long, hot summers; in cooler areas it can grow to 15 to 20 ft. It needs a large, strong support; the massive weight of this plant can crush a fragile or unstable structure. Originating in India, woolly morning glory is hardy in zones 9–10 but has naturalized in most of the tropics.

◆◆◆

Ipomoea batatas (ip-oh-MEE-uh baa-TAH-tuss)
Sweet Potato Vine

Subtropical sprawling vine or ground cover, trailing to 2 to 5 ft; grows to full size during the first season.
Hardy in zones 10–11; dies to the ground but regrows from the roots in zones 8–9.

You can have your foliage and eat the tubers, too, when you grow the ornamental cultivars of sweet potato vine. The tubers of this vine are actually edible, orange-fleshed sweet potatoes, but you'd never recognize this plant as a vegetable from the colorful forms and attractive shapes of its leaves. The leaves are commonly about 6 in. long and heart-shaped, although in some cultivars they are cut into three to five sharp lobes like an oak leaf. This rapid grower sends out many sprawling stems, which can spread out quickly over the ground, drape down from a hanging basket, or, if helped, twine up a post or tree trunk. The ornamental-foliage types described below rarely produce the tiny morning-glory-like flowers of the species. Sweet potato vine lends itself to many uses in a tropical-style garden, where its bold leaf colors can hold their own. It can make a blanketing ground cover

Ipomoea batatas 'Blackie'

beneath taller plants or act as an accent plant to spill over the edge of a container.

Cultivation

For the brightest leaf colors, grow sweet potato vine in full sun, although it performs well with part or light shade. Rich, evenly moist soil is best. Fertilize twice a month to encourage lush growth. You may have to prune back vigorously growing plants to keep them in bounds; simply snip them back as needed and they will quickly rebound. Don't try to grow this one as a houseplant, but either treat it as an annual or dig up the tubers and store them as you would dahlia bulbs until planting time in early summer. Alternatively, you can take stem cuttings and root them.

Cultivars

'Blackie': As befits its name, this cultivar boasts very dark purple, almost black, leaves. New leaves are greenish black with dark veins and quickly deepen to velvety black. They are deeply cut into sharp lobes, giving the foliage both color and textural interest. You can use 'Blackie' with almost any other color, depending on the effect you're after. It looks stunning combined with hot red or yellow flowers or with cool blue and silvery lavender blossoms.

'Margarita': A brilliant chartreuse, the heart-shaped leaves of 'Margarita' are sure to bring sizzling color to any garden. This is one of the hottest plants around and works well with any other color. Combine it with scarlet, red, and orange to make flaming effects, or cool it down with blues and purples. Allow it to sprawl over the ground or to cascade from

a hanging basket. This very rapid grower may need to be pruned to be kept within bounds.

'Pinkie' ('Pink Frost', 'Tricolor'): Prettily decorated with bright lavender and white streaks, the leaves of this cultivar have a silvery background. They are only 2 in. long and are deeply lobed. This plant is excellent combined to echo lavender or pink flowers.

It's a slow grower that behaves itself without pruning.

'Vardaman': The new, heart-shaped leaves of this cultivar emerge deep plum and mature to medium green, creating a pleasant two-tone effect in a mass planting. 'Vardaman' makes a good foliage filler for subtler arrangements and is especially pleasing with purple and lavender flowers. ◆◆◆

*J*asminum (JAZZ-min-um)
Jasmine

Tropical and subtropical vine or shrub, sometimes growing to 25 ft high; grows to half the full size during the first year. Hardy in zones 8–10.

Jasminum polyanthum

*T*he essence of paradise, the sweet perfume of jasmine floating through the air is as intoxicating as any liqueur. Blooming year-round, all species feature clusters of funnel-shaped white, pink, or yellow flowers with star-shaped faces and small, glossy green leaves. These vining plants climb by twining around a support or simply leaning against it. Enjoy their fragrance by growing jasmine in tubs placed around a patio where their branches can climb up a nearby trellis or fence, or plunge them into a border near an appropriate support. You can also use small plants in a mixed container, window box, or hanging basket to spill over the edge of the container. Jasmines look great with other sun lovers such as *Felicia, Pelargonium,* and *Mandevilla* 'My Fair Lady' and with sword ferns (*Nephrolepis* spp.) around their feet.

Cultivation

Jasmines thrive in full sun and need humus-rich, moist soil. Keep the soil evenly moist; dry soil may cause the leaves to drop. To encourage new growth and more blossoms, fertilize weekly with a liquid fertilizer when plants are blooming. Jasmines can be overwintered as houseplants or in a conservatory. Prune back long vines as needed and overwinter them as houseplants in a sunny location. You can also wrap the vines onto a topiary form to create a compact plant that takes up less space.

Species and Cultivars

Unfortunately, no matter how beautiful their flowers appear, not all species of jasmine are fragrant. They lure you with their beauty, beckoning you to bury your nose in their flowers, but ultimately disappoint if it's only an aroma you're after. The species described below are all highly fragrant.

J. nitidum (**royal jasmine**): Rather than being star-shaped, these flowers are pinwheel-shaped, the petal tips curling back in a frilly manner. The very fragrant blossoms bloom in clusters of three from purple-tinged buds. This is a shrubby grower that needs to be tied in place to climb. Leaves are oval, to 2 in. long. Hardy in zones 8–10.

J. officinale (**common jasmine**): Probably the most fragrant of the bunch, common jasmine produces terminal clusters of white flowers set off against dark green leaves that are divided into five to nine, 2-in.-long, pointed leaflets. It twines vigorously to 25 ft. Hardy in zones 9–10.

J. polyanthum (**jasmine**): This very fragrant species climbs to 20 ft and produces dense clusters of flowers in the leaf axils. The blossoms have white petals with rose-colored undersides and open from rosy pink buds. The leaves are divided into five to seven, lance-shaped leaflets. Hardy in zones 8–10.

J. sambac (**Arabian jasmine, Arabian tea jasmine**): This is the jasmine used to scent tea in the Orient. Clusters of very fragrant, waxy-white flowers adorn this shrubby vine throughout the year but are most prolific in summer. The glossy green leaves are oval and about 3 in. long. Tie this species to a support to help it climb, or allow it to sprawl. 'Belle of India' has creamy yellow, citrus- and spice-scented flowers. 'Grand Duke of Tuscany' bears double white flowers. 'Maid of Orleans' has semidouble white flowers. Hardy in zones 9–10.

❖❖❖

Jatropha integerrima
(jah-TROH-fah in-teh-JEER-ih-mah)
Peregrina
Tropical shrub, to 10 to 12 ft tall; grows 3 to 4 ft the first year.
Hardy in zones 10–11;
dies to the ground but regrows from the roots in zone 9.

Jatropha integerrima

Lipstick red blossoms adorn peregrina throughout the summer, blooming most prolifically when the weather is the hottest. The 6-in.-wide clusters of five-petaled blossoms form pretty stars with a frill of yellow anthers in their centers. The flowers stand out beautifully against the dark green, leathery leaves, which are typically oval but are sometimes lobed. Native to the West Indies, peregrina grows naturally into a small, well-branched tree or large shrub, but it adapts readily to container culture and can easily be pruned into a small shrub. It looks great as a specimen container plant, located on a sunny patio, where it can bask in the heat and bloom its head off. Or you can plunge it into a dry, sunny border. Group this vibrant bloomer with heat-loving foliage plants, such as *Agave*, *Aloe*, or *Euphorbia*, to contrast its color and shape to best effect.

Cultivation

Peregrina flourishes in full sun in a hot location. Because it resents having its roots disturbed, grow it as a specimen in a container of well-drained soil. Allow the soil to dry somewhat between waterings; if the soil dries out too much, however, the plant may drop its leaves. Fertilize once a month during the growing season. Prune in spring to train it into a shrub form, but watch out for the sap, which can irritate the skin. Because it needs so much heat, peregrina does poorly, dropping a lot of leaves, when grown as a houseplant, but it can be overwintered in a warm greenhouse. Otherwise, encourage the plant to go dormant by moving it to a cool location and withholding water. Then store the containerized shrub in a cool, dark spot until spring, when you can resume watering it and return it to the garden. This species grows easily and rapidly from seed, attaining a height of 3 to 4 ft the first year, although it may not bloom until the second year.

Similar Species

J. multifida (**coral plant**): The blossoms of this species form very large clusters made up of long-stemmed, bright orange-red or deep coral-red flowers. These adorn the branch tips all summer long, standing out dramatically against the large leaves, which are 1 ft wide and divided into seven to eleven linear segments. The trunk forms a thickened base, giving the plant a somewhat bizarre character. Even when it's not in bloom, this is one extraordinary plant, because the leaves and trunk are so decorative. This species blooms the first year from seed. Hardy in zones 10–11. ✦✦✦

J*usticia* (jus-TISS-ee-uh)
Shrimp Plant

Subtropical and tropical shrub, to 8 ft tall; grows to 2 to 3 ft the first year.
Hardy in zones 9–11; sometimes dies to the ground but regrows from the roots in warm areas of zone 8.

Spires of showy inflorescences glow like candles at the branch tips of these shrubby plants, creating a flowering display as alluring and exotic as any gardener could dream of. In some species the spire consists of tightly packed, two-lipped, tubular flowers. In others colorful bracts create quite a spectacle, while the actual flowers appear, a few at a time, from in between the bracts. Depending on the species, the inflorescence may be shades of red, pink, rust, or yellow, and in types with showy bracts, the overall appearance is often bicolored. Leaves look rather ordinary, but since the plants bloom almost constantly, they perform their necessary role as a backdrop admirably. With pruning, shrimp plants form well-branched shrubs that make a startling impact when planted in a group of five or more in a tropical-style bed or border.

Cultivation

Shrimp plants flower best in full sun but perform acceptably in half sun. Provide humus-rich, moist soil. Keep the soil evenly moist. Enrich it with compost at planting time and fertilize monthly during the growing season. To keep the plants attractive-looking, cut off spent inflorescences and prune branches back by two-thirds, a few at a time, to encourage a denser branching pattern. Shrimp plants make excellent houseplants if they can be grown over winter in a sunny location. They can also be encouraged to go dormant if water is withheld and they are then stored in a cool, dark place for the winter.

Species and Cultivars

The genus *Justicia* recently became a taxonomist's playground; it now includes plants once classified in the genera *Beloperone* and *Jacobinia*. Similar-looking plants in the genus *Pachystachys,* which were once in the genus *Justicia,* are also described here.

J. brandegeana (**Beloperone guttata**) (**shrimp plant**): This sprawling shrub from Mexico produces gently arching inflorescences made up of showy, yellow-tipped,

Justicia carnea

muted cinnamon-pink bracts and purple-spotted white flowers. Use as a midrange plant in beds or containers, combined with *Hedychium, Brugmansia, Leonotis,* or *Ipomoea batatas* 'Margarita'. This species is a tender perennial, dying to the ground in winter but regrowing from the roots in zone 8.

J. carnea (Jacobinia carnea) **(pink shrimp plant, Brazilian plume)**: Pomponlike clusters of 6-in.-tall, brilliant clear pink flowers tip the branches of this exotic-looking shrimp plant. The dark green leaves may grow to 10 in. long. Use this compact shrub in combinations with *Fuchsia, Plectranthus argentatus,* or a pink-patterned *Coleus*. This species is hardy in zones 10–11; perennial in zone 9.

Pachystachys coccinea **(cardinal's guard)**: The bright scarlet, two-lipped flowers of this bold-colored shrimp plant are tightly packed into 6-in.-tall spikes. This shrub can grow to 6 ft tall but is best kept pruned to 3 to 4 ft tall. Play up its flaming colors with companion plants such as *Sanchezia* or *Coleus* 'The Line', 'Lime Frills', or 'Solar Sunshine', and contrast its shape with sword-shaped *Phormium* leaves. Grow in part sun. Hardy in zones 10–11.

P. lutea **(yellow shrimp plant, golden lollipops)**: The bright yellow inflorescences of this Peruvian shrub make it an attention getter in the garden. The 6-in.-tall spikes consist of showy yellow bracts from which peek tubular white flowers. Blooming continuously, this compact shrimp plant grows best in part to full shade, where it combines effectively with the yellow-striped leaves of variegated shell ginger (*Alpinia zerumbet* 'Variegata') and with bright green ferns and hostas. Hardy in zones 10–11. ◆◆◆

Kalanchoe (KAL-an-choe-ee)
Kalanchoe

Tropical succulent perennial or subshrub, to 1 to 12 ft tall, depending on the species; grows 6 to 12 in. a year. Hardy in zones 10–11.

Kalanchoe pumila

Although some are appreciated for their flowers, most *Kalanchoe* species draw admiring glances for their unusual leaves, whose beauty derives from a practical source—a water-conserving strategy. These succulents from the arid regions of Madagascar and Africa store water in their stems and leaves. The leaves may be thick and fleshy with a smooth, waxy coating or covered with a downy fur that helps keep them cool and slows water loss. Use these drought-tolerant plants in decorative containers on a sunny terrace or in the hot, dry part of your garden to evoke the mood of a desert island. Their spare beauty combines well with plants that require similar conditions, such as *Agave, Aloe, Euphorbia,* and *Rhipsalis*.

Cultivation

Grow these plants in full sun in a warm part of the garden. Because they are sensitive to overwatering, it is best to grow kalanchoes in containers so you have more control over moisture conditions. The soil must be well drained and on the sandy side. Water only after the soil dries out. Feed monthly during spring and summer. Kalanchoe can be overwintered as a houseplant in a south-facing window.

Species

There are hundreds of species of *Kalanchoe*. The following three make excellent additions to an arid, tropical-style garden.

K. beharensis **(felt bush)**: Triangular in shape with scalloped margins, the thick leaves of this weird-looking species measure 12 to 14 in. long and are covered with felty hairs. The leaves have a two-tone effect, since the hairs are rusty cinnamon on the top surface and silvery white on the lower. The plants can grow to 12 ft tall but are easily and best pruned to a manageable 3 to 4 ft tall. If the plant gets too tall, take cuttings from the top and root them to create a replacement plant.

K. daigremontiana **(maternity plant, devil's backbone)**: This is another odd-looking plant. Its lance-shaped, 10-in.-long, fleshy leaves are brownish green on top and have purplish splotches on the undersides. The leaves grow only a few at a time at the tips of 3-ft-tall stems. Even more bizarre, tiny perfectly formed plantlets grow all along the leaf margins, giving the leaves a frilly effect. You can propagate these plantlets by removing them from the leaf edge and growing them in small pots or flats of moist soil—they will root and grow into new plants.

K. pumila: Silvery powder blue, the leaves of this succulent species make an elegant color statement. It is a small species, growing only to 1 ft tall, and has 1-in.-long leaves with scalloped edges. When overwintered as a houseplant, it bears lovely clusters of light pink flowers. ✦✦✦

Lantana camara (lan-TAN-uh kam-AIR-uh)
Lantana

Tropical and subtropical upright or sprawling shrub,
3 to 6 ft tall; grows 3 ft during the first year.
Hardy in zones 10–11;
dies to the ground but regrows from the roots in zone 9.

A popular flowering annual in gardens everywhere, lantana is actually a tropical South American shrub that has long found a home in North American gardens. Blooming from early summer right up until frost, this floriferous plant makes a vibrant statement in the garden. Tiny, five-lobed flowers with long tubes arrange themselves into tight domes measuring about 1 to 1 1/2 in. across. The species produces multicolored flower heads containing yellow, pink, orange, and red flowers in bands circling through the dome. How-ever, the many cultivars exhibit blossoms in almost any color imaginable, in heads of a single color or multiple ones. The hairy, scalloped leaves are small and exude a citrus scent when crushed. Although the shrub is blanketed with flowers, the overall effect is fine-textured, making this a plant for all occasions. Yellow- and orange-flowered types are especially welcome additions to tropical-style gardens with hot color schemes. Upright forms of lantana make low, bushy plants that can be massed to produce a sea of color. They are also easy to train as a tree form (standard) with a woody trunk and a full, rounded head of vibrant blossoms to create an elegant container plant. Use weeping types to drape from a window box or hanging basket or to form a ground cover beneath taller tropicals.

Cultivation
Lantana thrives on heat and full sun. Any well-drained soil is fine. Best growth occurs in evenly moist soil, but if the soil dries somewhat between waterings no harm is done. Fertilize weekly during the growing season. Deadhead faded flower clusters and pinch back leggy growth to keep the plant blooming and good-looking. Lantana performs poorly as a houseplant because it is highly susceptible to whiteflies, but mature standards are worth keeping year to year. You can overwinter a standard as a dor-mant container plant in a cool, dark location and treat smaller plants as annuals.

Cultivars and Similar Species
Easily 30 to 40 cultivars of this popular plant are available. Some types, however, go by several names, even though the plants are identi-

Lantana camara 'Greg Grant'

cal. Here are some of the most useful and colorful ones for tropical-style gardens.

Upright Types, to About 18 to 24 In. Tall in a Season

'Confetti': This cultivar makes an eye-catching sight, offering multicolored flower heads that are painted deep red, pink, and wine.

'Greg Grant': Beautifully subtle, this form has light pink flowers that fade to soft yellow, and dark green leaves with yellow and cream mottling.

'Honey Love': Bicolored with golden honey and peach flowers, this lantana is quite bright but never gaudy.

'Irene': Multicolored in red, yellow, and fuchsia, this tempts you to call it gaudy, but combine it with a brightly colored croton and the effect is brilliant.

'Patriot's Rainbow': With this name one would expect a combination of red, white, and blue, but instead this cultivar blooms in a riveting blend of yellow-orange and magenta.

'Pink Caprice': Light pink and pale yellow, this lantana is easy to pair with other plants.

'Radiation': Orange-red flowers make this one a sizzler for a hot color scheme. It really turns up the heat when combined with yellow flowers or variegated leaves.

L. trifolia: The flowers of this species grow in 2-in.-tall cones rather than domes and are light purple. Lavender berries follow the flowers. The plant grows fast, reaching 3 ft tall by the end of the season.

Dwarf Types, to 1 Ft Tall

'Dennholm Pink': Light pastel pink flowers on compact, upright plants make this one an excellent subject for stuffing into a mixed container on a patio.

'Dennholm White': This is a pretty white version of 'Dennholm Pink'.

Weeping and Mounding Types

'New Gold': Golden yellow blossoms bloom on a mounded plant with small leaves.

'Samantha': Bright creamy yellow flowers set off against green leaves with subtle creamy white variegations make this a beautiful plant for combining with white flowers or plants with broad, dark green leaves.

L. montevidensis 'Lavender Cascade': Blanketed with light lavender flowers on trailing stems, this is a cool-colored beauty that easily heats up when commingled with plants with orange and yellow blossoms .

L. m. 'White Cascade': Snowy mounds of pure white flowers characterize this plant, which is an elegant partner to silvery-leaved plants.

◆ ◆ ◆

*L*eea amabilis 'Splendens'
(LEE-uh ah-MAH-bill-us SPLEN-denz)
Leea
Tropical shrub, to 6 to 8 ft tall; grows 2 to 3 ft each year.
Hardy in zones 10–11.

Although the species is a nice plant with glossy green leaves, the cultivar 'Splendens' is more desirable because of its rich coloring. With dark burgundy bark and gorgeous leaves, it performs its part as a good-looking exotic foliage plant. The leaves grow up to 2 ft long and wide but are cut and then recut into pointy segments about 2 in. long, creating a lacy pattern that the shrub's open branching

Leea amabilis 'Splendens'

pattern accentuates. New leaves gleam a lustrous burgundy-red and mature to bronze with purplish undersides and dark purple petioles and stems, bringing rich color along with an elegant texture to the garden. The plant's blossoms, although hardly a necessary embellishment to the beauty of this shrub, add to the effect. The 6-in.-wide, lacy, flat-topped flower heads are made up of tiny, pinkish red flowers that create a veil over the tops of the plants. Leea makes a graceful specimen in a container and can also be planted in a bed or border. Use it to pick up the wonderful deep red variegations of *Breynia disticha* 'Roseapicta' or other showy foliage plants such as *Acalypha* or *Coleus*. It also works well with the vivid flowers of *Dahlia, Lantana,* and *Cuphea.* Large overwintered plants can be plunged into the border to great effect—they play well with hardy, bold-textured plants such as *Hydrangea* and *Viburnum.*

Cultivation

Leea grows well in full sun to part shade. Provide humus-rich, well-drained soil. Water regularly so the soil remains evenly moist, and fertilize monthly during the growing season. To encourage colorful new growth and to prevent legginess, prune leea back by two-thirds to create a lower well-branched shrub; let it grow tall and thin for an airier look. Container-grown plants can be overwintered in a bright window or a greenhouse.

❖❖❖

Leonotis leonurus (lee-oh-NO-tuss lee-oh-NUR-us)
Lion's Ear

Tropical shrub or tender perennial, to 6 to 8 ft tall;
grows to mature height in a single season.
Hardy in zones 8–11.

Leonotis leonurus 'Lion's Ear'

A bizarre-looking plant from South Africa, lion's ear gets its common name from the fuzzy orange flowers that, if you use your imagination, might resemble the ears of a large cat. The flowers bloom from midsummer into fall, growing in knobby whorls that encircle the 6-ft-long stems. The whorls form tiers separated by several inches of lanky, leafless stem, giving the whole structure a strong architectural presence. Lion's ear is in the mint family and therefore features square-sided stems and oval to lance-shaped, aromatic, gray-green leaves. Because these plants are so tall and spare, plant lion's ear in groups in front of more substantial plants, such as *Datura* 'Double Yellow' or *Alpina zerumbet* 'Variegata', the variegated shell ginger. Lion's ear combines wonderfully with ornamental grasses, emphasizing the tall grassy lines while adding flower color to their graceful texture. 'Dwarf' is a 2-ft-tall selection that has a well-branched, bushy habit; dense spires of flowers, rather than stretched-out ones; and smaller leaves, creating a more solid look lower down. Use it in the front of a bed or border.

Cultivation

Grow lion's ear in full sun in average to sandy, well-drained soil. Evenly moist soil produces the best growth, but if the soil dries between waterings no harm will be done. Fertilize once or twice during the growing season. This plant is best treated as an annual, which grows rapidly from seed started in late spring.

❖❖❖

Lotus (LOW-tuss)
Parrot's Beak, Lotus Vine, Gold Flash

Subtropical trailing subshrub, to 8 in. tall and several feet long.
Hardy in zones 9–10.

These fine-textured beauties make extraordinary fillers, for they send their delicate stems and dense feathery foliage out in all directions to create waves of gray-green or silvery, needlelike leaves. The sickle-shaped blossoms are 1 to 1 1/2 in. long and may be bright red, scarlet, or gold, all with black centers. They have been variously described as resembling a parrot's beak or a lobster's claw and adorn

Lotus berthelotii

the trailing stems when growing conditions are right. The short days and cool night temperatures (into the 40s) of late spring promote bud set, which results in summer flowers as long as nights cool off. This trailing plant rarely blooms during summer's worst heat, however, so you need not concern yourself about matching its flowers to a color scheme. It makes a fine foliage plant when contrasted with the prolific soft pink flowers of *Lantana* 'Pink Caprice' or sun-loving cultivars of *Fuchsia* and *Orthosiphon,* or hope for blossoms and use it with hot-colored *Hibiscus* and *Jatropha.* It works as a ground cover in a bed or border or as a cascading plant in a window box, hanging basket, or other decorative container. Lotus vine hails from the Canary Islands, off the coast of Africa, and is a member of the vast pea family, which contains many tropicals.

Cultivation

Parrot's beak grows vigorously in full to part sun. Provide well-drained, evenly moist soil. Fertilize every two weeks when the plant is actively growing. Pinch back the stems every few weeks if they grow too long. Lotus vine can be over-wintered in a cool greenhouse or porch where it receives bright light and 40°F temperatures. When given these conditions, it will start blooming in spring.

Species and Cultivars

L. berthelotii (parrot's beak): Fine-textured, silvery leaves and red or scarlet flowers decorate this dainty plant.

L. maculatus (gold flash): The leaves of this species are a bit thicker and more gray-green than silver when compared with *L. berthelotii* and the flowers are yellow with red or orange tips. ◆◆◆

numerous trailing stems, which can spread out to form a low mound 2 ft across. Sunset plant looks great planted in the ground where it can weave around the bases of taller, bolder plants such as palms or *Ficus.* To create an especially hot combination, mass sunset plants under *Phormium* 'Yellow Wave' to emphasize its yellow-striped leaves, and add groups of *Pelargonium* 'Vancouver Centennial' to pick up the red in the flowers with its brick-colored leaf variegations.

Cultivation

Sunset plant grows and blooms well in full sun to light shade. The soil should be humus-rich, moist, and well drained. Water regularly so the soil remains evenly moist, especially in sunny conditions. Fertilize monthly with liquid fertilizer. You can easily overwinter sunset plant as a houseplant in a sunny window.

Cultivars

'Aurea': The new growth on this trailer emerges soft peach and matures to bright golden yellow. It bears golden flowers, of course.

'Golden Globes': This green-leaved form blooms all summer, producing a wonderful display of golden blossoms that stand out like pretty little globes against the dull green leaves.

'Outback Sunset': Truly spectacular, the lime green leaves of this cultivar are splashed with peach and golden yellow variegations. Red-throated yellow flowers complement the color scheme throughout summer, but they are hardly needed to make a color impact, given the razzle-dazzle of the foliage.

◆◆◆

Lysimachia congestiflora
(lie-sih-MAH-key-uh con-jes-tih-FLOOR-uh)
(*L. procumbens*)
Sunset Plant

Trailing subtropical or tender perennial, to 3 in. high and 2 ft wide.
Hardy perennial in zones 8–9; to zone 7 with winter protection.

This fast-growing plant, which blooms throughout spring and summer, makes a superb ground cover or a trailer for the edge of a pot or a hanging basket, brightening lightly shaded spots with its sunny flowers. Several of its cultivars offer exciting foliage color in addition to the flowers, for a riveting effect. The cup-shaped, five-petaled, golden yellow blossoms sometimes have red throats, and they measure about ¾ in. across. They bloom in clusters at the tips of the stems. Pointed oval leaves, about 2 in. long, densely cloak the

Lysimachia congestiflora 'Outback Sunset'

Mandevilla × amoena 'Alice du Pont'

Mandevilla (man-duh-VILL-uh)
(*Dipladenia*)
Mandevilla Vine, Dipladenia Vine
Tropical vine or sprawling shrub, to 3 to 20 ft high;
grows to 2 to 6 ft during the first year.
Hardy in zones 10–11;
dies to the ground but regrows from the roots in zone 9.

If it's a spectacle of flowers you're after, mandevilla vine is the answer. Freely borne and grand in scale and color, the big trumpet-shaped flowers bloom almost non-stop from late spring into fall. The short tube of each blossom flares out into five points that overlap a bit to form a spiraling twist. Shocking pink is the color of the day, although some species and cultivars come in red, pale pink, or white. The vining types grow aggressively, so if you train one to an arbor, to cascade from a stake, or to hoist itself into a tree, you can revel in the lush junglelike effect of flower-filled branches dripping down from overhead. The more sprawling forms make excellent fillers and cascaders in beds and containers.

Cultivation
Best growth and blooming occurs in full sun. Provide humus-rich, moist soil and enrich it at planting time with lots of aged compost or manure. Water regularly to keep the soil evenly moist, and fertilize twice a month during active growth to keep these vines growing vigorously. Provide a sturdy support for vining types to grow up and tie them in place to get them started. The low sprawling forms (originally in the genus *Dipladenia*) make great houseplants that will bloom all winter. The vining types grow too large to be overwintered but can be stored as dormant plants. Leave them outside until frost kills the top; then cut the plant back and store the tuberous root system in a container of soil in a dark place at about 35° to 40°F over winter. The soil should not completely dry out.

Species and Cultivars
M. × amabilis (Dipladenia × amabilis): This bold-flowered hybrid boasts rose-pink flowers with rounded lobes, red centers, and yellow throats. It can climb to 12 ft.

M. × amoena 'Alice du Pont': This free-flowering beauty has deep pink, funnel-shaped blossoms that flare to 4 in. wide and form in clusters of up to 12 blossoms. The leaves are rough-textured and leathery, to 8 in. long, and have a prominent network of veins. This vigorous grower can twine to 15 ft high.

M. boliviensis (Dipladenia boliviensis) (**white dipladenia**): Slenderer and more graceful than the other climbing types, this white-flowered beauty from Bolivia and Ecuador features 2-in. blooms with canary yellow throats. The leaves shine with a dark green gloss and grow to about 4 in. long. It climbs to 12 ft, but you can prune for a bushy shrub form.

M. sanderi (Dipladenia sanderi): The species has small, rose-pink flowers and can climb to several feet high, but its cultivars have large flowers and the plants tend to sprawl more than climb. They are easily pruned into a bushy form. 'My Fair Lady' bears pale porcelain pink flowers that glow almost white and are complemented by a gentle yellow throat. 'Red Riding Hood' has large, deep rose-pink flowers with bright yellow throats that stand out against the glossy green, 2-in.-long leaves. 'Scarlet Pimpernel' sears the eyes with its large, bright scarlet flowers.

◆◆◆

Melianthus major (mee-lee-AN-thus MAY-jur)
Honey Flower, Honey Bush

Subtropical shrub, to 4 to 5 ft tall; grows 2 to 3 ft each year.
Hardy in zones 9–10; dies to the ground
but regrows from the roots in zones 7–8.

This handsome plant with commanding foliage hails from the grasslands of southern Africa, where it tolerates somewhat arid conditions. Steely blue-gray and up to 1 ft long, the leaves divide into 9 to 11 segments that are folded down their centers to create a V-shaped trough. The toothed leaf margins add further to the foliage's jagged appearance. These big leaves radiate like branches from short stems, giving the plant an open, palmlike shape with a striking silhouette and texture. Mature bushes bloom in spring, producing nectar-laden, brownish red blossoms in 2-ft-tall spikes that attract droves of hummingbirds. The leaf color is so beautiful that it agrees with almost any other hue you might pair it with. Honey flower needs space to show off its architectural beauty; you can train it to a palm-tree-like form by staking several stems to the straight and narrow, or allow it to sprawl a bit and grow more shrublike. Combine it with a sea of *Pennisetum villosum* to re-create an African savanna effect, or put it together with flowers such as *Mandevilla* or *Hibiscus* for a lusher scene. It also looks great as a single specimen in a decorative container or plunged into a perennial border.

Melianthus major

Cultivation

Honey flower grows well in full sun to part shade. The soil should be well drained and sandy but kept moist. Water regularly. Fertilize once a month during the growing season. If the plant becomes leggy, you can cut it back severely, to just a few inches above soil level. It will resprout readily. Container-grown plants can be overwintered in a cool greenhouse. Alternatively, let a hard frost knock back the tops and then store the dormant plants in a cool, dark cellar until spring.

Similar Species

M. minor: This is a small version of honey flower with downy, 8- to 10-in.-long, gray-green leaves and brick red flowers. Plants grow about 3 ft tall.

◆◆◆

Musa (MOO-suh)
Banana, Plantain

Tropical and subtropical perennials, from 2 to 25 ft tall;
grows to about half its mature height in one season. Most types
hardy in zones 9–11; a few to zone 5 or 6 with winter protection.

Banana trees and palm trees go hand in hand, for no other plants can cast a tropical spell the way these do. And it is entirely possible to grow bananas outdoors in almost any climate to create that tropical feel right in your own backyard. They are fast-growing and easy to overwinter, and even offer many interesting leaf colors beyond basic green. Big, bold, and majestic, a paddle-shaped banana leaf can grow as long as 20 ft. It is slick-surfaced and polished to a high sheen and exhibits a beautiful pattern of veins angling out from a prominent central midrib, adding texture to the gloss. The leaves radiate into an umbrella-like form that arches upward and outward to great architectural effect. They have very long bases, or sheaths, that wrap around each other to produce a stout, fleshy structure that looks like a short trunk but is actually no such thing: this pseudostem is neither woody nor permanent. It sprouts from a spreading root system that sends up new suckers that form clumps of more pseudostems. Each stem produces half a dozen leaves and eventually a flowering structure and edible or inedible bananas, and then dies. It is, however, replaced by more suckers. The flowers appear quite bold and dramatic, often made up of colorful, boatlike bracts. You can easily grow a banana right in the ground or in a tub, which you can plunge into a border or arrange in groups on a terrace or patio. Line a path that winds through the garden with banana trees rising up all around and you'll surely create a magical tropical experience with hardly any effort at all.

Cultivation

Bananas thrive in full sun to part shade. Their fast growth demands moist but well-drained, humus-rich, fertile soil. Provide plenty of water, never allowing the soil to dry out. Enrich the soil at planting time with rotted manure or compost. Incorporate fertilizer at planting time and thereafter apply plant food every week. Use a thick, organic mulch to conserve soil moisture. Banana leaves are easily tattered by the wind, so locate banana plants in a protected site to preserve their appearance. Cut off unsightly leaves at the base, if needed. Where it is not hardy, you can move a banana indoors (if there's room) to overwinter as a houseplant, or dig up the fleshy root system and store it like a canna. Or for a container-grown plant, simply cut the top back to a

few inches above ground level and store the container in a cool, dark place until spring. (See the sidebar "Banana Wars" on page 96 for more on strategies for overwintering these plants.)

Species and Cultivars

These readily available, true bananas will grow rapidly in a summer garden in almost any climate. Most will not survive a frost, but a few are surprisingly cold-hardy.

M. acuminata (**Cavendish banana**): This big banana grows to 20 ft tall and has 10-ft-long, narrow green leaves that sometimes have reddish undersides. The fruits are edible and commercially valuable. 'Dwarf Cavendish', a very popular clone, grows to 4 to 6 ft tall and its small yellow bananas can be easily handpicked. It looks great in a tub and is small enough for houseplant culture. 'Super Dwarf Cavendish' gets to be only 2 to 4 ft tall, but its leaves are lush and gorgeous, making an exotic low planting, and it even fruits. Hardy in zones 10–11.

M. a. **var.** *sumatrana (M. zebrina)* (**bloodleaf banana**): This

banana is a standout among the banana family for its colorful foliage. The top surfaces of the leaves are bright lime green with dark burgundy patches. The undersides are burgundy all over. It does not flower or fruit. Hardy in zones 10–11.

M. basjoo (**Japanese fiber banana**): This beautiful banana's claim to fame is its cold hardiness. It's root-hardy to −10°F, surviving the coldest temperatures of any banana, and therefore adaptable to year-round culture pretty far north. The 4- to 6-ft-long leaves are bright green and quite slender, forming a distinctive, upright, umbrella-like arrangement that can reach 6 to 14 ft tall. The yellow flowers are perhaps the most beautiful of all the bananas and are followed by small, green, unpalatable fruits. 'Variegata' has white-striped leaves. Japanese fiber banana is evergreen and hardy in zones 9–10; in zones 5–8, it dies to the ground in winter but regrows. In these zones you can also wrap the stems with straw, black plastic, and burlap and mulch the roots heavily so that the stems survive

Musa velutina

the winter, resulting in larger plants.

M. ornata (**flowering banana**): Grow this small species in a container to show off its luscious growth and gorgeous flowers. Blossoms, which form in upright clusters and are followed by small, ornamental, inedible fruits, may be pink, orange, yellow, or lavender in many named cultivars. Leaves are dark olive green. This species grows 5 to 12 ft tall. Hardy in zones 10–11.

M. × paradisiaca (**edible banana**): This fast-growing banana can get to be at least 10 to 12 ft tall, and perhaps even 25 ft, in a single season. You can easily plant a row of these bananas for a tropical-looking screen. Don't expect this species to bloom or to form fruit if you grow it in the North, however. Stems need to grow for 8 to 24 months before blooming. 'Ae Ae' is a bright and eye-catching cultivar whose leaves display an irregular pattern of broad, white stripes and narrow, dark and light green stripes angling away from the midrib.

M. velutina: The 3-ft-long, dark green leaves of this attractive banana have dark red midribs on their undersides and grow on 5- to 7-ft-tall "trunks." Pretty, lavender-pink flowers bloom every year and are followed by curious, fuzzy pink, inedible bananas. Most banana fruits do not contain seeds; those of this species do, and they germinate easily, so you can save them and grow more plants. Hardy in zones 8b–11; to zone 8a with winter protection.

The following relatives of Musa *closely resemble true banana plants.*

Ensete ventricosum: This banana look-alike has great garden appeal. The leaves grow up to 10 to 15 ft long and 3 ft wide. Plants can reach 20 ft in height and do not sucker or form clumps. The broad green leaves of 'Maurelii' (red Abyssinian banana) are flushed partly or all over with deep reddish burgundy and have deep red "trunks" for a dramatic look. The bright green leaves of 'Red Stripe' feature a beautiful, deep burgundy-red midrib that's visible on the undersides. Evergreen and hardy in zones 9–11; root-hardy with winter protection in zone 8.

Musella lasiocarpa (**Chinese yellow banana**): This rare banana relative from China grows 4 to 5 ft tall and has narrow, dusky green leaves. A spike of golden starburst-like flowers that resemble artichokes decorates the plant for months. Hardy in zones 8b–11; in zones 7–8a with protection. ✦✦✦

N*epenthes mirabilis* (neh-PEN-theez mi-RAB-ill-iss)
Pitcher Plant, Monkey Cup

Tropical scrambling or shrubby vine, to 1 ft long and 2 to 3 ft wide; grows to about half its mature size the first year.
Hardy in zones 10–11.

Nepenthes mirabilis

*D*enizens of tropical rain forests, these insectivorous plants cling to tree branches or clamber over nearby shrubs, forming a clump of weird, 2-ft-long leaves that drape downward to display water-filled, bug-catching cups at the tips of long, straplike tendrils.

The "pitchers" are actually swollen areas at the leaf tips that have transformed themselves into inflated cylinders that can catch a small amount of rainwater. These pale green pitchers are freckled with red spots and have a red lip, and they grow to be 6 to 8 in. long and 2 to 3 in. wide. The lip of this bizarre structure contains nectar glands that attract insects, luring them to the water-filled pitcher, where they fall in and drown. Projecting from the leaf is a "lid" that stands open above the pitcher and acts as a roof to prevent too much rain from filling the pitcher below. By digesting the insects in the pitcher, the plant supplements its spare nutrition. Arching sprays of pale yellow or white flowers may be 1½ to 2 ft long and bloom sporadically throughout the year. Use this plant oddity to create a jungly feel in your garden by growing it in hanging baskets secured in the crotches of trees or suspended in groups from an arbor. Add epiphytes such as orchids, anthuriums, or ferns for an even lusher effect.

Cultivation

Grow this exotic in full to light shade or part sun. The potting mixture must be fast-draining but humus-rich. Water regularly so that it never dries out. Pitcher plant thrives in hot, humid conditions. You can overwinter it in a greenhouse or as a houseplant in a bright window, but since it needs a lot of humidity, a bathroom or kitchen is probably best.

Similar Species

N. rajah: This species from Borneo is a climber that sends out 1-ft-long, green pitchers with red or purplish red mottling that dangle from the leaf tips. The interiors of these squat, cup-shaped pitchers are almost black, creating a most interesting effect. Hardy in zones 10–11. ✦✦✦

Nerium oleander (NEAR-ee-um OH-lee-an-der)
Oleander, Rosebay

Tropical and subtropical shrub, from 4 to 20 ft tall;
grows to 3 to 5 ft during the first year.
Hardy in zones 9–11; dies to the ground
but regrows from the roots in zone 8.

*U*biquitous shrub in tropical gardens around the world, this species actually originated in the Mediterranean region, which explains why it can tolerate dry conditions once it is established. Blooming in big clusters, the beautiful 1- to 3-in.-wide flowers are short funnels that flare open to a five-lobed face with a jaunty twist to the petals. The hundreds of cultivars come in an array of floral hues, including red, pink, salmon, white, and yellow, and may be single or double, but they are always decorated in the center with a yellow throat with a pretty fringe. The blossoms appear prolifically in spring and summer and have a pleasant, though slight, fragrance. Leathery, dark green, and oblong to 4 to 8 in. in length, the glossy leaves have a pretty light green stripe marking their midribs. In northern gardens, oleander flourishes in a container, and it can be plunged into a border or grown on a patio. Since it thrives on heat, it makes a great heat-proof plant for a stone terrace or patio. Pair it up with other heat lovers such as *Lantana, Cuphea, Arctotis,* and *Pelargonium.*

Cultivation

Oleander needs full sun and heat to bloom. Provide average to sandy, well-drained soil. It's best to allow the soil to dry somewhat between waterings. Established plants can tolerate drought. Fertilize lightly only once or twice during the summer. Oleander blooms on new growth, so to encourage new growth and more flowers, you should remove spent blossoms before they turn into seedpods. Prune the plant as needed to keep it at the shape and size you desire. All parts of this plant are poisonous if eaten, and even the smoke of burned plants is highly toxic. Wear gloves when pruning to avoid getting the sap on your hands—it may cause a rash. Overwinter oleander as a houseplant or in a greenhouse, or force it to go dormant by placing the container in a cold (35°F), dark garage or shed. The tall forms are the most cold-hardy and if sited well and wrapped in winter will survive outdoors in zone 7b.

Cultivars

There are hundreds of cultivars of this popular tropical. Here are some of the best and most readily available to gardeners outside of the tropics.

Dwarf Types That Grow About 4 Ft Tall; Excellent in Containers or in a Garden Bed

'Peach Blossom': Double-flowered, soft pink, frilly flowers make this small plant a stunner that combines well with purples and cool reds. In addition to their beauty the blossoms possess a very sweet, intense scent.

'Petite Pink': This low, bushy plant with very bright pink flowers is perfect for a container. Combine it with the silver foliage of *Heli-*

Nerium oleander

chrysum petiolare or *Plectranthus argentatus.*

'Petite Salmon': The beautiful, pale salmon-pink flowers of this floriferous cultivar are easy to pair with yellow or orange blossoms for a sizzling effect.

Midsize Cultivars, to 6 to 8 Ft Tall; Good for Containers

'Casablanca': The flowers of this pretty plant are pure, glistening white.

'Ruby Lace': Big bundles of light red blossoms decorate this oleander, which really sizzles when combined with other brightly colored flowers or leaves.

Tall Cultivars, to 10 to 20 Ft Tall; Great as Plunge Plants in a Perennial or Shrub Border

'Cherryripe': The bright cherry red flowers are borne on 12-ft plants.

'Hardy Pink': This selection grows to 12 ft tall and has deep pink blossoms.

'Sister Agnes': This is a big one; it grows to 20 ft tall and covers itself with pure white flowers.

◆ ◆ ◆

Orthosiphon stamenius
(or-thoh-SIGH-fon stah-MIN-ee-us)
Cat Whiskers
Tropical subshrub, to 3 to 4 ft tall; reaches mature height the first year.
Hardy in zones 10–11.

This exotic member of the mint family hails from the South Pacific. Individual flowers are two-lipped tubes colored white or lavender that are adorned with very long, curving stamens that extend an inch or two beyond the blossoms, the same way a cat's whiskers extend from its face. The flowers group themselves into short spikes at the tops of the stems, giving the plant a very lacy, airy appearance. The lance-shaped leaves are very dark green and lustrous, measure about 2 to 3 in. long, and densely cloak the stems beneath the flowers. Cat whiskers works very well massed to create a veil through which to see other bolder plants, especially those that grow tall and tend to lose their lower leaves. The dense lower part of the plant effectively hides the bare knees of *Brugmansia* and *Tibouchina,* which tend to become leggy, while the flowering tops create a scrim that softens without hiding.

Cultivation

Cat whiskers blooms well in part to full sun. Provide rich, fertile, evenly moist soil and enrich it at planting time with rotted compost or manure. Water regularly and fertilize every two weeks with liquid plant food. Deadhead spent flowers and prune branches back to keep the plant in shape, if needed. Although it continues growing and blooming as a houseplant, you can store *Orthosiphon* as a dormant plant in the basement. Allow frost to kill the tops and then move the containerized plant into a cool (40° to 45°F), dark location until spring.

Cultivars

'Lavender': This form's beautiful lavender-blue flowers look cool and elegant. It combines well with purple-foliage plants such as *Coleus* or *Strobilanthes.*

'White': Snowy white with yellow stamens, this fluffy plant softens any planting with neutral color and airy flowers. ◆ ◆ ◆

Orthosiphon stamenius

Osteospermum × hybrida

(os-tee-oh-SPERM-um × hi-BRIH-duh)

African Daisy

Subtropical shrub or tender perennial, from 12 to 30 in. tall.
Hardy in zones 8–10.

Blanketing itself with many-petaled, daisy-shaped flowers during cool weather, this popular plant makes a great season extender in a tropical-style border. Because it needs cool night temperatures (as cold as 30° to 40°F) to set flower buds, African daisy blooms most heavily in spring and early summer and again in fall, with sporadic blossoms in summer. The day-blooming flowers usually grow singly on long, leafless stems and vary from 2 to 4 in. across, with ray petals painted in shades of pink, yellow, lavender, purple, or white, often with a contrasting darker central disk. A metallic sheen coats the flowers, and the undersides of the petals are frequently bronze, which looks quite obvious—and gorgeous—when the blossoms fold up at night. African daisy grows as a small leafy shrub with oval, smooth- or jagged-edged, green or silvery leaves. Incorporate masses of it beneath other plants that do well in hot, dry conditions, such as *Phormium, Aloe,* and *Agave,* so that its pretty flowers can skip around the more architectural plant. It also does well in containers, contrasting its daisy shapes with the flowers of *Pelargonium, Salvia,* and *Phygelius.*

Cultivation

African daisy is a sun lover, so grow it only in full sun. It needs well-drained, average to sandy soil. Water when the soil begins to dry.

Once established it tolerates dry conditions. Fertilize only sparingly, because the lush growth that results from too much fertilizer occurs at the expense of flowers. This plant is best treated as an annual; it can be kept as a houseplant in a sunny, cool window, although it may become buggy. It is easily grown from cuttings taken almost any time of year, and some cultivars grow well from seed. If planted in well-drained soil, African daisy may survive outdoors in a mild winter in zone 7.

Cultivars

This popular plant is a complex hybrid of several species that are native to southern Africa and the Arabian Peninsula.

Compact, Upright Plants, to 2 ½ Ft Tall

'Nairobi': These brilliant white flowers have blue centers, creating an unexpected color scheme.

'Silver Sparkler': The glistening white blossoms feature steely silver-blue centers and the same color is echoed on the undersides of the petals. To make the effect even more dramatic, the green leaves have creamy variegations.

'Sparkler': This one's flowers grow quite large and are light lavender-purple.

'Sunny Girl': Pinkish lavender ray petals surround blue disks for a very feminine color scheme.

'Sunny Ingrid': Intense, deep violet-purple blossoms with black eyes give this selection a smoky look.

'Tetra' ('Pole', 'Star'): This pretty blue-and-white flower features white ray petals with a blue ring at their bases that encircles the blue disk.

'Zulu': This upright grower has rich yellow petals with golden disks. It combines beautifully with oranges and reds.

Sprawling or Trailing Types, to 1 to 2 Ft High

'Gweek Variegated': This cultivar's silver-and-green-variegated leaves create a pretty background for its shell pink flowers. The petals are coppery bronze on their reverse side, making for a beautiful color scheme.

'Pink Whirls': This pink-petaled version of 'Whirligig' is useful for combining with other pink or white flowers.

'Whirligig': Silvery white, spoon-shaped petals surrounding blue disks give this form an unusual pinwheel shape that is sure to attract attention. It grows to 2 ft. ✦✦

Osteospermum ecklonis

Oxalis vulcanicola 'Copper Glow'

(auck-SAL-us vul-kan-ih-KOLE-uh)

Sorrel, Shamrock

Tropical perennial, to 6 in. tall.
Hardy in zones 9–11.

Oxalis vulcanicola 'Copper Glow'

This small plant from Central America carries a big wallop in the garden because its brilliantly colored leaves shimmer like hot metal. The leaves, while shaped like a clover or shamrock with three distinct rounded lobes, are yellow flushed with a coppery glow and marked with an outstanding network of copper-colored veins. Small, five-petaled, funnel-shaped yellow flowers exhibiting a silky sheen bloom all summer on slender stems that hold them just above the leaves. The plant forms a compact mound that works wonders massed like a ground cover under taller plants or used at the edge of a container, where it will dribble over the edge. The coppery color creates a sunset when combined with purple-foliage plants such as *Strobilanthes* and *Leea* or with lavender or pink flowers of *Angelonia* and *Lantana* 'Pink Caprice'.

Cultivation

Sorrel grows best in full sun but will tolerate light shade. Provide very well drained soil and allow it to dry slightly between waterings. Fertilize monthly when the plant is actively growing. You can overwinter this and the other species as a houseplant in a sunny window

Cultivars and Similar Species

'Red Velvet': Similar to 'Copper Glow', this cultivar features green leaves with a decidedly burgundy flush and deep burgundy stems. The yellow flowers also grow on burgundy stems.

O. hedysaroides 'Rubra' (fire fern): This outstanding cultivar is called fire fern for good reason: the 1-in.-wide, clover-shaped leaves are scarlet and grow on a many-branched, bushy plant that eventually reaches 3 ft tall. Bright yellow, 1/2-in. flowers add to the fire. This selection needs full sun and warmth to perform well.

O. regnellii: This 10-in.-high, mounding plant from South America features shamrock-shaped leaves with purple markings and deep purple undersides, and the leaves fold up at night. The white, funnel-shaped flowers are about 1 in. across. Withhold water and allow the plant to go dormant, then dig up and store the rhizomes in a cool, dark place until spring. The cultivar 'Pink Princess' is an unsurpassable foliage plant, boasting leaves that are deep purple all over with light purple markings and lavender-pink flowers with darker veins. ◆◆◆

Palmae (PAUM-ee)

Palm Family, Palm Trees

Tropical and subtropical trees and shrubs, from 1 to 50 ft tall;
most stay much smaller when grown in containers.
Most types hardy in zones 9–11;
see page 207 for hardy palms.

Of all the members of this vast family, the coconut palm epitomizes the tropics like no other plant. Its graceful, tall, curvaceous trunks, tufted on top with an arching spray of feather-cut fronds, decorate the shores of the tropics the world over. Other palm species lodge themselves in teeming jungles or desert oases. Most have sturdy trunks that may be short or tall, with large, usually deeply cut leaves that arrange themselves in whorls at the tops of the trunks. The sprays of flowers shoot out from the leaf clusters and are sometimes quite colorful and may ripen into edible or beautiful fruits. While not all palms—there are over 4,000 species in 200 genera—work well in a tropical-style garden, many do. Even if they ultimately grow into towering giants in their native habitat, don't be afraid to start off with a few small ones. You can enjoy them for many years as 4- to 10-ft-tall specimens. Most palms look exotic and wonderful at any stage of their lives when used in a garden setting. Small, young palms grow slowly enough that when planted in a container and summered outdoors in a northern climate they perform their job of creating an exotic setting for many years. You can use a single container-grown palm as a specimen to create a vertical accent on a terrace or patio, or plunge it into the garden. A highly effective approach is to group several palms of different heights together to give a really lush feeling. And, of course, if you combine their deeply cut fronds with the huge, bold leaves of a few banana plants, your garden will surely resemble the stuff of a Rudyard Kipling tale.

Cultivation

Depending on the species, palms grow in full sun to dense shade. Young palms almost always need some shade, so you probably cannot go wrong by growing any palm in light to half shade. Most do well in well-drained soil that is enriched with humus. Keep the soil evenly moist but never wet. Some mature species can be grown on the dry side with no ill effects. Most palms have a compact, fibrous root system that adapts well to growing in a container. Because its top can act like a sail in the wind, locate a containerized palm in a protected site and weight the container to make the plant less top-heavy.

Although the vast majority of palm species are tropical and can-not survive freezing temperatures, a few can withstand light frost, and even fewer are cold-hardy into zone 6. In cool climates, you can grow the hardy types right in the ground; beyond their hardiness limit, try wrapping them during winter to keep them from freezing. Overwinter pot-grown tropical palms as houseplants or in a greenhouse or conservatory; most can be left out well into fall and brought inside just before frost is expected.

Species and Cultivars

Large Palms That Mature at 25 Ft or Larger in the Tropics

Archontophoenix cunninghamiana (**king palm**): With a very straight, gray trunk and a crown of 6- to 8-ft-long, bright green fronds, this is a stately species to use for an architectural statement. It matures at 50 to 60 ft. Grow it in full sun. Hardy in zones 10–11.

Cocos nucifera (**coconut palm**): This beautiful palm features large fronds up to 20 ft long that are cut into feathery leaflets and may be bright green to yellow-green with bright yellow bases. The golden yellow flowering sprays ripen into edible coconuts. In container culture, these trees are quite beautiful even when young. You can sprout them from coconuts placed in shallow container of soil. This species matures at 70 to 100 ft. Grow it in full sun. Hardy in zones 10–11.

Howea forsteriana (**kentia palm**): This species' dark green fronds are 4 to 12 ft long and are cut into many narrow segments that droop downward for a graceful effect. It is best in shade, especially when young, and makes an excellent houseplant. Kentia palm grows slowly to 40 to 50 ft. Hardy in zones 10–11.

Phoenix dactylifera (**date palm**): Native to the Middle East and northern Africa, this edible-fruited palm produces very stiff, upright, dark green leaves on top of a rough trunk. Use it for a bold, textural contrast. It matures at 60 ft. Grow it in full sun. Hardy in zones 9–11; sometimes to zone 8b.

Syagrus romanzoffianum (Cocos plumosa) (**queen palm**): Native to South America, this species has very delicate-looking, arching, 20-ft-long fronds cut into narrow, 3-ft-long leaflets. The smooth gray trunk is decorated with dark gray leaf-scar rings and has a bulging base. The white flowers ripen into small, showy orange fruits. Queen palm matures at 30 to 60 ft. Grow it in light to half shade. Hardy in zones 9–11. ✦✦✦

Phoenix roebelenii

Medium to Small Palms That Mature at About 4 to 20 Ft in the Tropics

Chamaedorea elegans (**parlor palm**): This native of Central America grows slowly to 4 to 5 ft tall. The leaves are only 1 to 2 ft long and are divided into numerous 2- to 6-in.-long leaflets. The trunks are green with green leaf scars and it produces sprays of yellow flowers that ripen to black fruits. It grows in full shade and so is the most commonly grown houseplant palm. Hardy in zones 10–11.

Neodypsis decaryi (**triangle palm**): This dramatic palm has only three ranks of fronds, making it triangular in cross section. The fronds, which are colored blue-gray to gray-green and have a crop of long threads hanging from them, are very stiff, 6 to 8 ft long, and arranged to form a dramatic triangle at the top of the trunk. The tree looks wonderful up close, where you can appreciate its dark brown trunk ringed with light gray. It grows in full sun to part shade and matures at 20 to 25 ft. Hardy in zones 10–11; perhaps to zone 9b.

Phoenix roebelenii (**dwarf date palm**): This lovely single-trunked palm from Southeast Asia has ferny, 3- to 4-ft-long, dark green leaves with spiny stems that form a soft, rounded head. New leaves emerge gray-green. This species matures at 8 to 10 ft and makes a good houseplant. Give it full sun to part shade and ample water. Hardy in zones 10–11.

Rhapsis excelsa (**lady palm**): The round, deep green fronds measure about 8 to 12 in. across and are cut into many fingerlike leaflets. These fronds grow up and down the entire length of the trunk, and the plant forms multiple trunks that grow into dense clumps. The bark is rough-textured with brown fibers. Lady palm matures at 10 ft. Grow it in shade to part sun. Hardy in zones 9b–11; marginal in zone 9a. ◆◆◆

Passiflora (pass-ih-FLOR-uh)
Passionflower

Tropical and subtropical vines, to 12 to 20 ft or more.
Hardy in zones 9–11; some types to zone 7 with winter protection.

Passiflora incarnata × 'Incense'

The exquisite flowers of the passionflower vines conjure up images of a heavenly garden, for they are surely the most beautifully unusual flowers produced by any tropical vine. The blossoms, which can measure 5 in. across, are complex arrangements of ten showy petals and sepals that form a ring around an inner ring of narrow, needlelike filaments, which sometimes twist themselves into frilly curls. Showy stigmas and anthers grow in the center and curve downward in a bizarre structure that forms the flower's centerpiece. Most passionflower blossoms come in shades of purple, lavender, and blue—a few rebellious species are scarlet—and all attract butterflies. Some species produce juicy, edible berries. The leaves are typically three-lobed and a nice green. Passionflowers normally bloom from spring well into fall, producing only a few flowers at a time. Although the plants are never blanketed by flowers, the individual blossoms are so attractive that one or two are enough to attract attention. These are vigorous vines that climb with abandon, coiling their sturdy tendrils around anything they can grasp. You can use these fast growers to twine into shrubs and trees to lend a lush, exotic look, or train them to climb up a trellis, fence, or arbor. In a container, plant them at the base of a stake or tepee to create a vertical element, or plunge the container next to a suitable fence or tree and let the vine climb.

Cultivation

These vines bloom best with full sun, although they grow well in part shade. They thrive on heat, so locate them in a warm microclimate for best performance. Provide moist, well-drained soil and let it dry somewhat between waterings. Fertilize at planting time and every two weeks thereafter during the growing season. Do not overfertilize, however, since too much nitrogen results in foliage at the expense of flowers. You can overwinter a passionflower in a greenhouse or as a houseplant. Or if you haven't room for it, allow the plant to be touched by frost, cut back the tops, and overwinter it in a container in a cool (35° to 40°F), dark place until spring. Passionflowers are easily propagated from stem cuttings.

Species and Cultivars

P. alata: The fragrant flowers of this species are probably the most spectacular of the lot, for they have deep purplish red petals with white undersides and very long, pink filaments that are banded with white, red, and purple. The green leaves are 6 in. long and unlobed. Hardy in zones 10–11; dies to the ground but regrows from the roots in zone 9.

P. caerulea (**common passionflower, blue passionflower**): This species probably blooms the most heavily of the lot, producing crops of 4-in.-wide, fragrant flowers with greenish white petals and filaments variously banded with purplish black, pink, and lavender. The handsome leaves are glossy and lobed. Given enough heat it can grow to 30 ft in a single season. Hardy in zones 9–11; and often root-hardy in zones 8 and 7 if well sited and heavily mulched in winter.

P. coccinea (**red passionflower**): Not as intricately formed as the blossoms of the blue-flowered species, but nevertheless quite stunning, the 4-in.-wide, scarlet flowers of this vine feature a ring of downswept, scarlet petals encircling rings of showy, short, purplish red, white-tipped filaments. The blossoms appear from spring through fall and stand out against the oblong leaves. Hardy in zones 9–11.

P. incarnata (**maypop**): The 3-in. flowers of this native vine feature pale lavender to greenish white petals surrounding very long, twisted filaments that are prettily banded with white, pink, and purple. This deciduous vine has lobed leaves and is native to the southeastern states, where it naturally dies to the ground each winter. Hardy in zones 7–11; to zone 6 with good siting and winter mulch.

P. × '**Incense**': A hybrid of the maypop, this vine has large, showier flowers but is not as cold-hardy. The deep lavender, 5-in.-wide blossoms have frilly violet-and-white filaments in the center and give off a heady, incense-like scent. Hardy in zones 8b–11.

P. × '**Jeanette**': The corolla of this hybrid is made up of alternating light lavender and dark purple petals and sepals surrounding dark purplish black filaments. The dark green leaves have three or five lobes. Hardy in zones 9–11.

P. trifasciata: Grown more for its foliage than its flowers, this vigorous vine will create a 12- to 15-ft-tall curtain of deeply lobed, green leaves that are dramatically marked with metallic lavender veins. New growth, stems, and tendrils are tinted maroon. The 1-in.-wide, fragrant blossoms are creamy green and styled in the typical passionflower construction. Hardy in zones 9–11. ✦✦✦

Pavonia × gledhillii
(puh-VOH-knee-uh × gled-HILL-ee-eye)
(*P. intermedia*)
Pavonia
Tropical and subtropical shrub, to 6 to 10 ft tall.
Hardy in zones 10–11.

Pavonia × gledhillii

Pavonia's flowers possess a powerful red-and-blue color scheme. Fuzzy, bright red, strap-shaped bracts gather tightly around a funnel of purple petals, creating a vase from which the vivid blue anthers explode like fireworks. Although the 1¾-in.-long blossoms grow between the leaves up and down the branch tips, they are not obscured and give this sparsely branched shrub a colorful presence throughout summer. Glossy, light green, and 6 to 8 in.

long, the elliptical leaves end in a point. This fast grower can add 2 to 3 ft of height each growing season until it matures at about 6 to 10 ft tall. Use this tropical as the tallest element of a mixed container, combining it with the purple flowers of *Angelonia* 'Hilo Princess' and with the bright red blossoms of *Pentas* 'Red Egyptian Star'. Or plant it right in a tropical-style shrub border with *Strobilanthes* or *Tradescantia* 'Purple Heart' to create a rather unconventional purple glow. 'Kermesina' is a sought-after dwarf form of pavonia that is more compact, growing to only 3 to 4 ft tall, but with equally vivid flowers.

Cultivation

Grow pavonia in full sun to part shade. Average well-drained soil that is kept evenly moist is best. Water regularly. Fertilize every other week during active growth. Prune if necessary to keep the plant lower and bushier. You can overwinter a container-grown pavonia as a houseplant in a sunny window, where it will continue to bloom.

✦✦✦

*P**elargonium** (pell-are-GO-knee-um)
Scented Geranium

Tropical shrub or tender perennial, to 1 to 3 ft tall.
Hardy in zones 9–11.

When their leaves heat up in the sun or are brushed up against, scented geraniums release aromas that mimic many familiar smells such as citrus, rose, lavender, apple, nutmeg, and peppermint. Depending on the species, the leaves may be small or large, lobed like a maple leaf, deeply cut like a fern, or crinkled up with sawtooth edges, and they are sometimes nicely marked with variegated patterns. A velvety texture finishes the leaf surface of most types, and oil-filled scent glands stud the leaves and stems. These species produce small, five-petaled pink, white, or magenta flowers borne in clusters on stems that rise above the leaves. Native to the rocky cliffs and dry veldts of South Africa, these aromatic plants endure hot days and cool nights without complaint. You can create a smorgasbord of scents with these wonderful plants by grouping them in containers. But they also perform perfectly in mixed groupings, where their leaf colors bring excellent neutralizing effects and a bouquet of aromas. Locate them along a walk or patio where they can drape into the pathway and release their aromas for the enjoyment of all who pass by. The scented geraniums are often trained into standards that make excellent formal accents in a container.

Cultivation

Grow scented geraniums in a full-sun location. The soil should be average and very well drained; allow it to dry between waterings. Fertilize once or twice during the growing season. The scented geraniums make good houseplants in a cool, sunny window. They can also be encouraged to go dormant if water and light are withheld; keep them in a cool, dark garage until spring. Standards do not overwinter well as dormant plants because they tend to send up new growth from the base rather than fill in the head.

Species and Cultivars

The Following Species Are Highly Scented Plants with Amazing Aromas

P. crispum (**lemon-scented geranium**): This is a very stiff, upright plant with a dense covering of tiny, dark green leaves that

Pelargonium 'Fair Ellen'

are crinkled up like a wad of paper and that emit a powerful lemon scent. 'French Lace' ('Variegatum') features a thin white edge outlining the leaves.

P. graveolens (**rose-scented geranium**): This upright grower has many 3- to 4-in.-long, velvety-textured, gray-green, somewhat triangular, rose-scented leaves. There are numerous cultivars with various leaf shapes and scents. Pale pink, purple-veined flowers add a pretty accent throughout the summer. 'Lady Plymouth' has beautiful cream-margined leaves with a lemony fragrance.

P. quercifolium (**oak-leaved geranium**): This plant usually grows as wide as it does tall and has balsam-scented, 3- to 4-in.-wide leaves that are deeply lobed and toothed. Purplish pink flowers bloom in summer. 'Fair Ellen' is a low-growing form with smaller, more rounded leaves that have nice dark markings along the veins.

These Species Have Musky-scented Leaves But Are Perhaps More Beautiful than Those with the Best Fragrances

P. cordifolium: This shrubby geranium has green, lobed, 2½-in.-wide leaves with toothed edges that resemble grape leaves with cinnamon brown stems. Light pink flowers with purple veins top the plants in summer.

P. echinatum (**cactus geranium**): A pretty little geranium, this species features gray-green, shallow-lobed leaves about 2½ in. across that create a neat form that shows off the tall stalks of bright magenta flowers, which are freckled with deep burgundy spots.

P. reniforme: This lovely small, compact species has velvety green, ½-in.-wide, rounded leaves above which rise clouds of dainty lavender flowers throughout the summer. It makes an excellent specimen when planted in a small container.

◆◆◆

Pelargonium × zonale
(pell-are-GO-knee-um × zone-AL-ee)
Fancy-leaved Zonal Geranium
Tropical shrub or tender perennial, to 1 to 3 ft tall.
Hardy in zones 9–11.

These cousins of the ever-popular bedding or zonal geranium (*Pelargonium × hortorum*), whose sturdy red, pink, or white flowers are ubiquitous in gardens and parks the world over, bring rave reviews for their colorful foliage as well as for their flowers. Both bedding and fancy-leaved geraniums are hybrids with *P. zonale* in their lineage, explaining the horseshoe-shaped band, or zone, that usually appears in the centers of their round, scalloped-edged, fuzzy-surfaced leaves. However, the fancy-leaved forms go all out when it comes to leaf color, and their flowers are quite showy as well. The background leaf color varies from a predictable green to some surprising colors, marked with a contrasting yellow, gold, orange, or pink band. More than one colorful zone may decorate the leaves. The leaf colors are so electric that the rounded clusters of flowers, which have orange, red, or pink, broad or strap-shaped petals, aren't really needed—but they develop anyway, adding additional icing to the cake. With their origins in South Africa, these colorful plants tolerate heat and make excellent choices for containers on a sun-drenched patio, but they can also be massed in a bed or border around the feet of taller plants. As with *Coleus,* choose their compan-

Pelargonium 'Vancouver Centennial'

ions carefully or the effect may be way too vivid.

Cultivation
Grow these plants in full sun in fast-draining, average soil. Allow the soil to dry somewhat between waterings, as wet soil may cause rotting. Fertilize weekly during the

growing season. Fancy-leaved zonal geraniums may be successfully overwintered as houseplants in a cool, sunny window. Or you can force them to go dormant by letting them dry completely in their pots and keeping the pots in a cool (45° to 50°F), dark location until spring. These geraniums are easily propagated from cuttings.

Cultivars

'Crystal Palace Gem': The dazzling yellow-green leaves of this cultivar feature irregular green zones, lending a two-tone effect. Coral flowers add to the unconventional color scheme. The cultivar got its name from the famous glass structure that housed the 1857 plant exhibition in England, when many new geraniums were introduced.

'Persian Queen': This large-leaved showstopper has unzoned chartreuse leaves topped with an abundant supply of magenta flowers.

'Skies of Italy': The tricolored, rounded leaves of this plant are banded with bronze, brick red, and creamy yellow, and the flowers are showy and scarlet. Maybe this is what a sunset looks like in Italy.

'Vancouver Centennial': Densely cloaked with colorful, 2-in.-wide, maple-leaf-shaped leaves, this cultivar is a real stunner for bedding or a container. The leaves are brick red near their bases and banded to the edge with bright yellow margins. Salmon-orange blossoms top off the foliage.

❖❖❖

Pentas lanceolata (PEN-tass lan-sea-oh-LAH-tah)
Star-cluster, Egyptian Starflower
Tropical subshrub, to 3 to 5 ft tall.
Hardy in zones 9–11.

These flowering beauties from the Arabian Peninsula reward gardeners in temperate areas with alluring flowers from spring right up until a hard frost. The 3- to 5-in.-wide clusters of five-petaled, star-shaped flowers bloom at the stem tips in shades of pink, red, lilac, lavender, or white and attract scores of butterflies. Upright and bushy or wide-spreading, these tropical subshrubs display dark green, lance-shaped leaves. Pair up those with red- or hot-colored flowers with equally vivid *Coleus, Wedelia,* or *Phormium* if you want an energetic color scheme. Pastel shades combine better with *Plumbago, Strobilanthes, Melianthus,* or *Datura* for calmer effects.

Cultivation

Flowers form abundantly in full sun, less so in part sun. Provide

Pentas lanceolata 'Ruby Glow'

average, well-drained soil and allow it to dry somewhat between waterings. Fertilize every other week during the growing season. Prune back leggy plants to encourage bushiness and more abundant flowers. Star-cluster does not fare well as a houseplant, as it attracts lots of whiteflies. It's best to treat it as an annual, although it is easily propagated from cuttings.

Cultivars

'California Lavender': Large heads of pastel lavender flowers smother this dwarf form, which grows to 8 to 12 in. tall.

'Kermesina': This selection's vivid magenta-pink flowers with red throats work wonders in sizzling color schemes. It grows to 5 ft in height.

'New Look Pink': Clear, bright pink blossoms are borne on an upright plant that reaches 2 to 2½ ft tall.

'Ruby Glow': Bright, clear red flowers adorn this bushy form, which grows to 2 to 3 ft tall.

'Tu-tone': The pretty pink flowers of this dwarf, 1- to 1½-ft-tall cultivar have red centers, making effective color echoes in combination with red-flowered plants.

❖❖❖

*P*hormium (FORE-me-um)
New Zealand Flax, Flax Lily

Subtropical perennial or subshrub, from 1 to 10 ft tall; grows from 1 to 4 ft during the first growing season. Hardy in zones 9–10; dies to the ground but regrows from the roots in zones 7–8 if given winter protection.

All it takes is one of these big, dramatic plants to create an exciting focal point in a tropical-looking bed or border. The focus is on foliage—its form and color. The leathery, sword-shaped leaves are folded down the middle at their bases, forming a sharp V shape, and they radiate upward and outward, creating a bold, stemless clump. The effect can be rather like that of a large *Agave,* to which this genus is related. Depending on the species, the leaves may be 1 to 10 ft long and 2 to 10 in. wide and vary from stiffly upright to somewhat broad and arching. The forms with colored or striped leaves are magnificent plants, since they bring color as well as structure to the garden picture. Leaf colors include green, blue-green, and bronze-purple, and there are many variegated forms with gold, pink, red, and cream stripes. Flowers rarely appear on plants grown in captivity, but in the plants' native New Zealand coastal habitat, panicles of tubular, yellow-green or reddish flowers bloom on 3- to 12-ft-tall stalks. Use New Zealand flax as a specimen container plant on a patio, or plunge it into a border among tropical or hardy ground-covering plants. These big plants take cool temperatures in stride, so they make great season extenders. They'll look attractive well into autumn until temperatures fall to the low 30s, when it's time to get them inside.

Cultivation

New Zealand flax adapts well to light conditions varying from full sun to mostly shade. These very tolerant plants grow in most soil types, from sandy to rich and from well to poorly drained. Fertilize once or twice during the growing season. New Zealand flax does best in cool, dry climates and suffers during extended periods of heat and humidity. Plants may be overwintered as houseplants in a cool, sunny setting or kept dry and cool in a low-light setting. If the soil is well drained and the site is protected from harsh weather, a *Phormium* planted in the ground may survive as far north as zone 7.

Cultivars

Two species—*P. tenax* and *P. cookianum* (*P. colensoi*)—are widely grown and have been hybridized to create the following outstanding cultivars.

'Atropurpureum': A rich purplish red, the narrow leaves of this useful cultivar are 3 to 5 ft long and grow stiffly upright when young, eventually arching downward.

'Bronze Baby': This small, compact form is an eye-catching plant with thin, curved, bronze leaves. It grows to only 1 to 1½ ft tall.

'Pink Stripe': This bushy plant gets to be 3 ft high and features bronze-green leaves beautifully marked with pink edges.

'Sundowner': Growing in an upright clump, this cultivar's broad, 3- to 5-ft-long leaves are pale bronze-green with pink stripes along the margins.

'Yellow Wave': This dramatic plant features broad, arching green leaves with a wide yellow stripe down their centers. It grows 3 to 4 ft tall. ✦✦✦

Phormium tenax 'Sundowner'

Phygelius × rectus (fye-GIL-ee-us × WRECK-tuss)
Cape Fuchsia, Cape Figwort

Subtropical perennial or subshrub or tender perennial, to 3 to 5 ft tall.
Hardy in zones 8–10;
to zone 7 with good siting and winter protection.

The pendulous trumpets of Cape fuchsia resemble small (2½-in.-long) foxglove or snapdragon flowers; they form tall, one-sided clusters that stand above the bushy plants. Flower colors range from creamy white to brilliant red, yellow, and salmon-pink. Blooming nonstop from early summer right through several light frosts, this attractive plant extends the garden's show through fall and sometimes into early winter. Dark green, lance-shaped leaves cloak the woody stems. Use this beautiful bloomer where its one-sided, floppy nature looks best—dripping over the edge of a container or low wall. Good companion plants include *Plectranthus argentatus, Ipomoea batatas,* and *Stipa tenuissima.*

Cultivation

Grow Cape fuchsia in full sun in rich, moist soil. Although even moisture is best, the plant can tolerate a bit of drying between waterings. Fertilize weekly if it's growing in a container, less often if it's growing in the ground. *Phygelius* can be grown as a blooming houseplant in a sunny window. Or allow the tops to be cut down by frost and then overwinter it as a dormant plant in a cool, dark place.

Cultivars

The following cultivars are hybrids between two South African species, *P. aequalis* and *P. capensis.*

'**African Queen**': This selection's pale red flowers with reddish orange lobes and yellow throats keep blooming for months.

'**Moonraker**': Pale yellow with deeper yellow lobes, the blossoms of this cultivar look good with any color scheme.

'**Pink Elf**': A compact, dwarf plant, only 12 to 18 in. in height, 'Pink Elf' produces prolific pink flowers with crimson lobes.

'**Trewidden Pink**': This lovely cultivar has light pink, 2-in.-long trumpets with contrasting dark pinkish red throats. ✦✦✦

Phygelius 'Trewidden Pink'

Plectranthus 'Green and Gold'

Plectranthus (pleck-TRAN-thus)
Spanish Thyme, Mexican Mint, Spanish Oregano

Tropical and subtropical subshrub or ground cover.
Hardy in zones 10–11;
dies to the ground but regrows from the roots in zone 9.

Members of the mint family, these pretty foliage plants add invaluable form and color—and sometimes aroma—to garden beds and containers. Depending on the species, leaves vary from perfectly round to oval, and most have a lovely scalloped edge that adds a highly decorative note. Smooth and glossy or soft and felty to the touch, the leaf surface may also be plain green, silver, or beautifully variegated. The flowers are small and two-lipped, blooming in short spikes in summer. These shrubby to trailing plants make excellent fillers that blend well with flowers and foliage of almost any color.

Cultivation

Grow these plants in full sun to part shade in any well-drained soil. Allow the soil to dry somewhat between waterings. Apply liquid fertilizer every two weeks during the growing season. *Plectranthus* performs well as a houseplant in a sunny setting. Tip cuttings root easily.

Species and Cultivars

P. amboinicus: The felt-covered, round leaves of this sprawling subshrub have delicate scalloped edges and give off an enticing herbal aroma when crushed. The leaves of 'Goldheart' are marked with gold in their centers. 'Green Gold' is a beautiful plant with a light green edge encircling the green leaves. 'Spanish Thyme' shows off with green leaves marked with gray-and-white splashes.

P. argentatus: Covered with a dense silvery coat, the oval leaves of this species make a stellar addition to an arid-looking garden. Plants are well branched, grow to 3 ft tall, and bear showy spikes of blue flowers.

P. forsteri (P. coleoides) 'Marginatus': This is one of the most beautiful forms of *Plectranthus*. Plants are upright and spreading and have hairy, light green, 2- to 4-in.-long leaves stunningly marked with a wide, creamy white, heavily scalloped edge. When crushed the leaves release a mild citrus scent.

P. madagascariensis 'Minimus Variegatus': Use this pretty trailer in a hanging basket or window box to show off its dainty, crinkled, green-and-white-variegated leaves. Crushed leaves give off a citrusy aroma. ✦✦✦

Plumbago auriculata
(plum-BAY-goe are-ick-you-LAH-tah)
Plumbago, Cape Leadwort

Tropical and subtropical sprawling or climbing shrub, to 3 to 6 ft tall; grows about 1 to 2 ft the first growing season.
Hardy in zones 9–11; to zone 8 with winter protection.

This gorgeous, fast-growing tropical shrub blooms nonstop, covering its long, arching branches with 6-in.-wide clusters of five-petaled, sky blue or white flowers that look like garden phlox. Leaves are matte green and oblong, about 3 in. in length. A versatile plant, plumbago is easily pruned to make a beautiful, bushy specimen in a decorative container or trained as a vine if tied to a support. Young plants tend to sprawl, while older plants can become quite woody at their bases. The flowers' delicate blue color combines with every color under the sun—use it to sweeten hot colors or to enhance cool silvery hues. An exciting combination of tropicals might team *Plumbago* with *Nerium oleander,* *Tibouchina, Hibiscus, Cestrum,* and *Breynia.*

Cultivation

Plumbago blooms well in full to part sun. Provide rich, well-drained soil. Keep the soil evenly moist for best performance. Plants that are overwintered as houseplants can be pruned almost to soil level in late winter to encourage a flush of new growth. Fertilize once in spring, in summer, and in fall, but not in winter. This tropical makes an excellent blooming houseplant in winter, but you can also force it into dormancy by letting frost take its top growth, then cutting it back and storing it in a cool, dark place until spring.

Cultivars

'Alba': This form's elegant, pure white flowers look like a snowfall in summer.

'Royal Cape': The light blue flowers of this cultivar feature a pretty dark blue star in the center, creating a more intensely blue experience. ✦✦✦

Plumbago auriculata

P*lumeria* (plue-MARE-ee-uh)
Frangipani, Plumeria

Tropical tree or shrub, to 10 to 25 ft tall.
Hardy in zones 10b–11; marginal in zone 10a.

Plumeria rubra

Gorgeous flowers that emit a wondrous fragrance characterize the exotic frangipani, a plant that hails from coastal areas of the neotropics but grows in tropical gardens the world over. The leaves are dark green and very glossy, grow to 1 ft long or more, and cluster around the stem tips, giving the plant a lean look that shows off the branching structure's great architectural beauty. Native to areas with a decided dry and wet season, these shrubs or small trees adapt themselves by losing their leaves during periods of drought and by storing water in their stout, gray-barked trunks and limbs. With the resumption of the rainy season, frangipani bursts into bloom even before the new leaves form. Blooming continues in waves of color and perfume until the dry season arrives, which triggers a rest period. The stunning blossoms are made up of waxy, five-lobed flowers with long tubes that grow in clusters a foot or more across. Individual flowers are 2 to 4 in. across and exhibit an enchanting pinwheel twist to the petals. Colors come from the rainbow, often with several hues blending into each other along the petal edges and a yellow flush seeping down the throat. Depending on the cultivar, the floral fragrance may be heady and sweet, fruity, jasmine-like, or a complex mixture of indescribable aromas. The fragrance is heaviest during the morning or late afternoon and early evening. Hawaiian leis are made from frangipani blossoms. Frangipani looks best when grown as a specimen in a container or used as a plunge plant with low plants around its feet so its candelabrum-like shape can be admired.

Cultivation

Grow these plants in full sun. The soil must be well drained, otherwise any type from sandy to humus-rich will do. Allow the soil to dry somewhat between waterings, although mature specimens tolerate drought. Prune as needed to keep the plants from getting leggy. Most frangipani plants go naturally dormant and drop their leaves during the winter months. You can overwinter a containerized plant in either a bright or dark location at temperatures between 40° and 70°F as long as you withhold water and allow the soil to completely dry out. When you resume watering in spring the plant will leaf out and bloom. If plants get too big, you can easily propagate smaller versions from cuttings. Simply cut off a nonflowering stem tip about 1 ft long and allow the cut end to dry and callus for a day or two, then stick it in damp sand—it will root readily.

Species and Cultivars

Most frangipanis offered in the nursery trade are hybrids of *P. rubra,* a shrubby species with rose-pink, red, or yellow flowers, and *P. alba,* a large West Indian species that grows to 25 ft and has yellow-centered white flowers. There are dozens of cultivars and hybrids available and some are quite expensive. The following are a few favorites.

'Hausten White': These white blossoms feature a yellow flush in the center, beautifully setting off the very wide petals. The fragrance is sweet and enchanting.

'Miami Rose': The flowers of this selection are smaller than most—only 2½ in. wide—but are flamboyantly colored rose-pink with light pink bands and yellow throats. Their exotic scent is a very strong coconut aroma.

'Puu Kahea': Individual flowers are 4½ in. wide and have long, nar- row, bright yellow petals marked with red bands. The blossoms give off a nice mild lemony scent.

'Yellow Jack': Very sweetly fragrant, this prolific bloomer exhibits clusters of 3½-in., yellow flowers with creamy white edges.

✦✦✦

Pseuderanthemum atropurpureum

(sue-de-RANTH-eh-mum at-troh-poor-POOR-ee-um)

Pseuderanthemum, Wax Acanthus, Chocolate Plant

Tropical shrub or tender perennial, to 3 to 4 ft tall.
Hardy in zones 10–11;
dies to the ground
but regrows from the roots in zone 9b.

Pseuderanthemum reticulatum

This Polynesian beauty adorns gardens throughout the tropics and adapts well to summer gardens in colder climates, where it offers its unusual leaves as a source of extraordinary foliage color. The waxy-coated, leathery leaves shape themselves into 6-in.-long ovals with a prominent network of veins and sometimes have a beautiful metallic sheen. New leaves often emerge bright red but quickly change to an irregular patchwork of burgundy, rose-red, pink, yellow, lime green, and chocolate brown, depending on the cultivar. Dense, 6-in.-tall spikes of tubular, 1-in.-long, white flowers with purple spots bloom in summer at the tips of every stem, adding a froth of contrasting color to the darker foliage. In the tropics, pseuderanthemum is often grown as a brightly colored hedge; you can mass plants the same way for a great effect, or use one for height in a mixed container.

Cultivation

Grow pseuderanthemum in part shade to preserve the leaf colors. Provide humus-rich, moist soil. Water regularly, never letting the soil dry out. Fertilize once a month during the growing season. Plants tend to get leggy and develop bare bases. To prevent this, pinch back plants when young to encourage a bushy shape, and prune them back hard, if needed, to overcome any legginess that does develop. Pseuderanthemum makes an excellent easy-to-grow houseplant during the winter months. It is also easily propagated from cuttings.

Cultivars and Similar Species

'Albo-marginatum': The long leaves of this hybrid are marbled green and gray and have a wide white border.

'Rubrum': This richly colored plant features wide, maroon-colored leaves with a polished-lacquer surface. It grows 3 to 4 ft tall.

'Variegatum' ('Tricolor'): The extra-long, pale pink leaves streaked with green and cream create a surprising color effect that combines effectively with deeper-colored foliage.

P. alatum (chocolate plant): This low-growing species reaches only 6 to 8 in. in height and spreads out like a ground cover. Its oval leaves are milk-chocolate colored with silvery markings along the midribs. It grows well in full shade to full sun. Hardy in zones 10–11.

P. reticulatum (golden-vein shrub): Brilliantly colored, the lance-shaped leaves of this species are rich yellow-green with bright golden veins and midribs. The plants grow to 3 ft tall. Hardy in zones 10–11. ✦✦✦

Ricinus communis (RIS-ih-nuss com-YOU-niss)
Castor Bean, Castor Oil Plant

Tropical shrub or tree, to 40 ft tall; 12 ft in cultivation.
Hardy in zones 10–11;
dies to the ground but regrows from the roots in zones 8b–9.

Growing from seed or young plants to as much as 12 feet tall in a single season, this huge tropical can turn your backyard into a jungle almost overnight. The huge, glossy leaves, which are 2 to 3 ft across, are long-stemmed structures that are cut into 5 to 12 pointed lobes like the fingers on a hand, and they stand out from the stout, trunklike stems like parasols. Although the species is green, several handsome cultivars offer maroon leaf coloration. Clusters of greenish yellow and red, cup-shaped flowers bloom in summer at the leaf bases and are followed by heavy stems of bright red, burr-like seedpods. All parts of this plant are poisonous if eaten, especially the seeds, which may drop from the pods. This mammoth grower works wonders when you plant it in groups as a fast-growing, tropical-looking screen. Combine it with hardy grasses such as

Ricinus 'Carmencita'

Miscanthus, Arundo donax, or *Cortaderia* to play up and emphasize the boldness of castor bean's leaves, or combine it with other big tropicals such as palms, bananas, and cannas for a jungly effect.

Cultivation

Castor bean needs full sun to perform well. Grow it in well-drained soil and enrich the soil with compost at planting time. It's best given plentiful water to spur its rapid growth, but it will not suffer too much if the soil dries a little between waterings. Keep the plants well mulched, and fertilize once a month during the growing season. Stake plants growing in windy areas. Treat this plant as an annual; it grows easily and rapidly from seed.

Cultivars

'Carmencita': This is a favorite cultivar with burgundy-red to brownish red leaves and stems. The flowering stems and seedpods are brilliant red. It grows 5 to 6 ft tall.

'Impala': The new leaves of this selection are especially big and bold, growing to 2 ft across, and emerge maroon but mature to dark green. The plants grow 6 to 10 ft tall.

'Zanzibarensis': This form's green, 3-ft leaves with white veins grow on towering stems that reach 8 to 12 ft tall. ✦✦✦

Russelia equisetiformis

Russelia equisetiformis
(russ-EEL-ee-uh eh-kwih-seat-ih-FOR-miss)
Coral Fountain, Fountain Plant, Firecracker Plant

Tropical trailing shrub, to 4 ft long;
grows 2 to 3 ft during the first growing season.

Resembling an asparagus fern decorated all over with exquisite, tubular, scarlet flowers, coral fountain puts on its show from late spring well into fall. Hummingbirds dart around the plant, seeking out the blossoms, which are 1 to 1½ in. long and bloom up and down the stems. The long, thin, arching, grass green stems are jointed and branched, rather like horsetails, creating a billowing, fine-textured mass that cascades like the spray of a fountain over the edge of a hanging basket, drapes over a wall, or flows down a slope. Inconspicuous needlelike leaves appear during the growing season. Coral fountain looks wonderful as a single specimen in a large hanging basket, which you might suspend by a window to enjoy the visiting hummingbirds. Or combine it with *Cuphea* 'David Verity' to echo the flower color and shape or with fancy-leaved geraniums to complement the floral hues with variegated foliage.

Cultivation

Grow coral fountain in full sun in well-drained, evenly moist to dry soil. Fertilize once a month during the growing season. It makes a good houseplant during the winter. You can also overwinter it by cutting it back to soil level and storing the container in a cool (40° to 50°F), dark place until spring. Rejuvenate plants by cutting them back to soil level, or by removing the oldest stems, every spring. ✦✦

Saccharum officinarum
(SACK-are-um oh-fish-in-AIR-um)
Sugarcane
Tropical grass, to 15 to 18 ft tall;
grows 4 to 6 ft during the first growing season.
Hardy in zones 9–11.

Although it's a commercial crop in the tropics, where it's grown for sugar and rum production, sugarcane makes an exotic-looking landscape plant when massed in tropical-style gardens. The colored-leaf forms are especially ornamental. Jointed rather like a bamboo, and with 2- to 6-ft-long, narrow leaf blades arching out from their joints, the stems, or canes, grow to 4 to 6 ft tall in a single season in a northern garden. Tall plants tend to lose their lower leaves, which shows off the stems to great effect. The flowers are tall, fluffy white plumes, but they rarely form in areas outside of the tropics. Group five or more plants together in a border to form a bamboo-like clump. Bold-leaved plants such as *Alocasia esculenta, Canna, Ficus lyrica,* and *Musa* make magnificent tropical-looking contrasts. Make up for sugarcane's lack of flowers and create a layered look by allowing lightweight vines such as *Ipomoea quamoclit, Solanum jasminoides,* or *Thunbergia* to wrap around their stems and climb toward the sky to show off their lovely blossoms.

Cultivation

Sugarcane thrives on heat and humidity. Grow it in full sun in rich, moist, well-drained soil. Enrich the soil with compost or manure before planting. Although it grows best with plentiful water, this species can tolerate periods of dryness. Fertilize every other week throughout the growing season. Overwinter sugarcane in a greenhouse or conservatory if there is no room in the house. Or force it to go dormant by cutting it back to 2 ft tall and keeping it in a dark, cool place during winter; it will resprout in spring.

Cultivars

'California Stripe': Creating a fresh green-and-white effect, the long leaves of this cultivar feature a bright white stripe running the lengths of their midribs, with thinner white stripes coursing through the blades. It grows from 10 to 16 ft tall.

'Violaceum' (purple-leaved sugarcane): The canes of this cultivar are a dusky purple, rather like the color of wine grapes, and are adorned with 2-ft-long, reddish purple leaves. This is a wonderful plant for creating color accents in mixed containers. It grows 10 to 16 ft tall.

✦✦✦

Saccharum officinarum 'Violaceum'

Sanchezia speciosa

(san-CHEEZ-ee-ah spee-see-OH-sah)

Sanchezia

Tropical shrub, to 6 to 8 ft tall;
grows 3 to 4 ft during the first growing season.
Hardy in zones 10–11; marginal in zone 9.

Sanchezia speciosa

Bright white or yellow veins stand out against a dark green or yellow-flushed background to create striking patterns on sanchezia's leaves. The new growth has the most colorful markings; older leaves may turn completely green or have only a white midrib. The glossy leaves are elliptical and grow to 10 to 12 in. long. Tall spires of 2-in. bright yellow flowers resting in red bracts bloom at the stem tips during summer, adding interest, but the plant is best known for its handsome leaves. Unpruned shrubs can reach 6 to 8 ft tall if overwintered. *S. s.* ssp. *nana* (dwarf sanchezia) is a compact shrub that is a miniature version of the species, reaching only 3 to 4 ft

tall. Use sanchezia in containers or garden beds, where its bold-textured foliage will look great combined with grasses and other fine-textured plants. Its gleaming yellow coloring adds sparks to hot color schemes when combined with the red and orange flowers of *Heliconia, Hibiscus,* or *Jatropha.*

Cultivation

Sanchezia grows well in full sun to part shade and tolerates most soil types but does best if kept evenly moist. Feed every two weeks during active growth. Prune or pinch back plants to encourage colorful new growth. They will withstand cool nights but not a hard frost. Although sanchezia can be overwintered as a houseplant, it needs fairly high humidity and thus does better in a greenhouse. Store containerized plants in a dark basement and cut back dead growth in spring to rejuvenate them; or cut them back before overwintering.

❖❖❖

Senecio confusus (sin-EE-see-oh kahn-FEW-sus)

(*Pseudogynoxys chenopodioides*)

Orangeglow Vine, Mexican Flame Vine

Tropical vine, to 15 to 18 ft;
grows 6 to 10 ft during the first growing season.
Hardy in zones 10–11.

Large clusters of 2-in.-wide, bright orange, daisy-shaped flowers with yellow centers decorate this vine from spring through fall, creating an electrifying sight. Leaves are 3 in. long, lance-shaped, and glossy medium green and have toothed margins. Native to Central America, orangeglow

vine grows rapidly and can get to be 6 to 10 ft high in a single season. Use it to spill out of a hanging basket, or plant it at the base of a trellis, bamboo tepee, tree, or shrub so it can weave its way upward to display its dazzling flowers at eye level and above. Both the flower color and shape

Senecio confusus

are unusual for a vine, so capitalize on this eccentricity by showing off the vine in combination with other hot-colored tropicals such as fancy-leaved geraniums, *Cuphea* 'Variegata', *Lysimachia* 'Outback Sunset', and *Canna* 'Pretoria'.

Cultivation

Orangeglow vine needs full sun for the best blooming and requires well-drained, average soil. Keep the soil evenly moist, or allow it to dry somewhat between waterings;

the plant is not too particular. Fertilize monthly during the growing season. This species can be overwintered as a houseplant in a sunny window. It is easily propagated from tip cuttings.

❖ ❖ ❖

*S*enna (SEN-uh)
(*Cassia*)
Candle Bush, Popcorn Bush, Shower Tree
Tropical and subtropical tree or shrub, to 10 to 30 ft tall; grows 4 to 8 ft during the first growing season. Hardy in zones 8b–10.

With big, bold leaves and tall spikes of flowers that are as golden as sunshine, these bushy, pea-family members bring excitement and a tropical aura to any garden. The leaves, although coarse-textured, divide themselves into rounded, fernlike lobes, which gives them a textural, frond-like appearance. Leaf color varies from bright green to gray-green, depending on the species. The plants grow very fast, thriving on heat, and, depending on the species, produce their upright spires of hooded, golden yellow blossoms in spring or mid- or late summer into fall. Flower stalks can be as much as 2 ft in height and are held upright—like candles—at the tips of the stems. The ripened seedpods resemble furry beans and add an intriguing texture to the landscape. Give these architectural plants plenty of growing space, but plant them in groups for the most dramatic effect.

Cultivation

Grow these plants in full sun in any well-drained soil. Average watering is fine, although once

established the plants tolerate drought. Fertilize once a month. Because they grow so fast from seed, you might not wish to bother overwintering them in a conservatory or greenhouse. In autumn, you can save the seed of species that bloom early and are able to set seed and sow it indoors from February to April. Plant outside once frost danger has passed. Space plants of large-growing species 2 to 3 ft apart in groups of five or more plants. Pinching or pruning these plants delays flowering and results in weak, bushy growth, rather than the desirable vertical effect.

Species

S. alata (**candle bush**): Easily grown from seed, by season's end candle bush will be 6 to 12 ft tall. In the tropics, it matures at about 30 ft tall, but you won't have to worry about its ultimate size if you treat it as an annual. If you overwinter containerized plants, prune and pinch the stems as desired in spring to encourage branching and to keep them compact. The gray-green leaves grow to 3 ft long but

Senna didymobotrya

are divided into rounded leaflets, giving them the appearance of branches on a small tree. If you start plants from seed indoors in February, bright yellow flowers will bloom on 2-ft-tall spikes in late September or October, unless frost stops the plants earlier. Even if your growing season isn't long enough to allow candle bush to bloom, grow it anyway for its wonderful bold leaf textures and architectural presence.

S. didymobotrya (**popcorn bush**): Growing from seed to its full height of 4 to 6 ft in a single season, this fast grower is an upright, bushy shrub with a bold look. Leaves are gray-green, about 1 1/2 ft in length, and divided into rounded leaflets. The golden blossoms unfold from shiny, brownish black buds on 1-ft-tall spires and bloom throughout summer. A whiff of the blossoms may evoke the smell of freshly popped popcorn, hence the common name. The buds even resemble unpopped kernels. ✦✦✦

*S*olanum (so-LAY-num)
Nightshade, Potato Tree, Potato Vine

Tropical and subtropical shrub or vine, from 2 to 20 ft tall. Most types are hardy in zones 10–11 and die to the ground but regrow from the roots in zones 8–9.

Solanum pyracanthum

This huge genus of South American plants contains both valuable commercial crops, such as eggplant and potato, and some desirable ornamentals. As a group the members are united by their similar flowers, which are five-lobed, bell- or trumpet-shaped affairs with a column of fused yellow-tipped anthers and pistils in their centers, and by their fruits, which are colorful seed-filled berries. The ornamental species bring a beautiful show of flowers, berries, or leaves to a tropical-style garden. Some species arm their stems and even their leaves with colorful thorns, which gives them a weird but lovable aspect. Grow these plants as single specimens in a container or combined with compatible plants in beds and borders. The plants shrug off a light frost and remain decorative well into fall; even after a hard freeze, their beautiful fruits cling to the dried stems, providing winter interest well past Valentine's Day. Most members of the genus *Solanum,* the nightshade genus, are poisonous if eaten and are best not grown in gardens visited by young children who might be tempted to taste their fruits.

Cultivation

Grow these plants in full sun to part shade. Any well-drained soil will do, but enriching the soil at planting time with compost gives them a boost. They tolerate a range of soil moisture, from evenly moist to dry. Fertilize every two weeks. Overwinter them as houseplants, or let a light frost toughen them, then cut back the tops to about 1 ft high and store the plants in a cool (35° to 40°F), dark place until spring.

Species and Cultivars

S. atropurpureum: This Brazilian shrub, best treated as an annual, is a colorful plant grown for its foliage, flowers, and fruits. Dark purple, 1-in.-long thorns cover both the stems and the lobed leaves and are so close together that they resemble a bristly fur. Don't pet this plant, however—it will bite. Plants are tall and slender, maturing at about 4 ft in one season. The 1-in.-wide, light purple flowers bloom in summer and are followed by bunches of bright yellow berries. The berries remain showy on dried plants most of the winter. Hardy in zones 10–11.

S. jasminoides (potato vine): This is one of the few vining species in the genus *Solanum.* It's a vigorous twiner than can grow to 6 to 10 ft long in a single season. The vine produces clusters of starry white, fragrant flowers all summer. Leaves are lance-shaped or lobed and have winged leaflets at their bases. The highly ornamental 'Variegata' has green-and-gold-variegated foliage. Use these vines to cover a trellis or to scramble into a tree or shrub. Hardy in zones 10–11.

S. pyracanthum: Another thorny species, this remarkable-looking plant is a well-branched shrub that reaches about 2 to 3 ft tall and is cloaked with narrow, 6- to 8-in.-long, deeply lobed, gray-green leaves. A line of bright coppery orange, 1-in.-tall thorns marches down the leaves' midribs, adding a stunning ornament. Pale lavender flowers in heavy clusters enhance the plant's color scheme.

This shrub combines well with purples and blues or with yellows and oranges, whatever your fancy. Hardy in zones 10–11.

S. quitoense (**naranjilla**): The ornamental leaves of this species are rounded in outline, have scalloped edges, and get to be 1 to 2 ft wide. Best of all, a coating of velvety, deep purple hairs covers the leaf surface. As an added bonus, small white flowers followed by yellow-and-red berries decorate the plants. Naranjilla grows to 4 ft tall the first season. Combine it with *Tibouchina, Strobilanthes,* and ornamental grasses for beautiful color and textural contrasts. Hardy in zones 10–11.

S. rantonnetii (Lycianthes rantonnetii) (**blue potato bush**): Blooming year-round if brought indoors, blue potato bush produces gorgeous, deep royal blue, yellow-centered, 1½-in.-wide blossoms in copious quantities. Red berries follow the flowers. Leaves are glossy dark green and lance-shaped, to 4 in. long. Ultimately reaching 6 ft in height, this small, floppy shrub grows 2 to 3 ft in a season and looks best tied to a support like a vine or staked and trained into a tree form, or standard. Hardy in zones 10–11.

❖❖❖

*S*tigmaphyllon ciliatum
(stig-mah-FIE-lon sill-ee-ATE-tum)
Brazilian Gold Vine
Tropical vine, to 20 ft; grows 4 to 6 ft in a single season.
Hardy in zones 10–11.

A delicate-looking, twining vine with threadlike stems and showy flowers and foliage, this fast grower resembles an *Oncidium* orchid transformed into a vine. The blossoms look every bit as intriguing as orchid blossoms and have the same golden yellow color as an *Oncidium*. Each long-stalked flower is 1½ in. wide and made up of five fluted petals with fringed edges. These bloom in 5-in.-wide clusters between the leaves. Emerging rusty red, the heart-shaped leaves mature to deep green with rust-colored hairs decorating their edges. This vine blooms from spring through fall but most heavily in summer. Enjoy its intricate texture and form by growing it on a trellis, wire obelisk, or tripod in a border or mixed planter near a sitting area so you can view it up close. Brazilian gold vine is lightweight enough to allow it to twine into trees and shrubs to display its beauty in a naturalistic way. The glowing yellow hue with hints of rust enhances any hot-colored combination, and the flowers' exotic look increases the appeal of other tropicals such as bromeliads and gingers.

Cultivation
This easy-to-grow vine performs well in full sun to part shade. Provide rich, well-drained soil kept evenly moist. Fertilize monthly during the growing season. This twiner does best if given a narrow support to grow on, such as a trellis or slender poles. Overwinter it

Stigmaphyllon ciliatum

as a houseplant in a sunny window; it will continue to bloom if it is warm enough. Prune it back to the desired height at the end of winter. ❖❖❖

*S*trelitzia reginae (stree-LITZ-ee-uh REH-gin-ee)
Bird-of-Paradise
Tropical perennial, to 5 ft tall; grows to 5 ft in one season.
Hardy in zones 10–11.

N aturally growing in big clumps along the rivers and streambanks of South Africa, bird-of-paradise can bring a tropical look to any setting and is grown in tropical gardens throughout the world. Its bizarre-looking flowers resemble the beaked face of a big

Strelitzia reginae

'Humilis' (dwarf bird-of-paradise): This compact grower reaches 1½ ft tall but has full-size flowers, making it perfect for creating a tropical effect where space is limited. The small plant also has the decided advantage of being easily moved from indoors to out.

S. nicolai (white bird-of-paradise): Similar in shape to the flowers of *S. reginae*, the flowers of this species have brownish red stalks and bracts with white-and-blue petals, but the plants must reach a large size before they bloom and rarely bloom in northern climates. Instead, the plant is appreciated for its huge, banana-like leaves and immense size. It can reach 20 ft in height, forming a trunklike pseudostem like a banana. Overwinter it as a houseplant or in a greenhouse. It is hardy in zones 10–11, marginal in zone 9b.

❖❖❖

colorful bird and stand on long, leafless stalks above the foliage. The "flowers" actually consist of a leathery green, beak-shaped bract from which grow orange-and-blue petals and sepals that look like a crown of feathers. These long-lasting blossoms appear most heavily in spring, fall, and winter and sporadically in summer, although you can trick bird-of-paradise into heavier bloom in summer. They make excellent cut flowers. The leathery leaves are paddle-shaped, have a waxy blue coating, and grow in attractive dense clumps. Because *Strelitzia* blooms best if potbound, use it as a container plant on a patio, or plunge it into the border, grouped with other tropicals.

Cultivation

Grow bird-of-paradise in full sun. It needs humus-rich, moist soil, although it can stand a bit of drying between waterings. Fertilize monthly in spring, summer, and fall. Plants may not bloom until they are five years old and bloom best if potbound. They must be overwintered and carried from

year to year to get to flowering size; they make excellent houseplants and are also quite happy in a sunporch or in a conservatory. To encourage heavy summer blooming, reduce watering in winter so that the soil dries out but does not shrink away from the sides of the container, and stop fertilizing. Resume watering and fertilizing in spring.

Strobilanthes dyeranus
(stroe-bih-LANTH-eez die-ur-AN-us)
Persian Shield
Tropical shrub, to 3 to 4 ft tall; grows 3 ft in one season.
Hardy in zones 10–11.

With a beautiful metallic silver gleam to the leaves, this exquisite foliage plant makes a colorful impact without being at all gaudy. The oval leaves grow to 8 in. long and have pointed tips. Their vein pattern and leaf margins are stamped out in dark green and stand out boldly against the shiny silver coating, which is suffused with a pink-and-purple iri-

Strobilanthes dyeranus

descence. The leaf undersides are deep purple. Small, funnel-shaped, light purple flowers bloom along the stems in winter but are insignificant compared with the foliage impact. Plant Persian shield in groups of three or more with a dark green background to really show off the leaves' metallic sheen. Contrast their shape and color with the sword-shaped leaves of *Acidanthera, Strelitzia,* or *Iris* or with ornamental grasses. The purple and silver hues intensify when combined with the purple flowers of *Tibouchina* and *Verbena* or with the silvery leaves of *Helichrysum* and *Lotus* weaving around this shrub's feet. For a riveting color scheme, try using Persian shield with chartreuse foliage, such as *Ipomoea* 'Margarita', *Lysimachia nummularia* 'Aurea', or *Xanthosoma* 'Chartreuse Giant'.

Cultivation

Persian shield grows best and has the best leaf colors in part sun. In northern areas it can tolerate full sun. Provide humus-rich, well-drained, moist soil. Water regularly so the soil remains evenly moist. Fertilize every two weeks when the plants are in active growth. To keep Persian shield full and bushy and to promote colorful new growth, pinch back the stems whenever the plant becomes leggy. You can overwinter *Strobilanthes* as a houseplant, but the leaves may lose their luster; take cuttings in spring. ✦✦✦

Thunbergia (thun-BURR-gee-uh)
Black-eyed Susan Vine, Blue Glory, Blue Trumpet Vine, King's Glory

Tropical vine, to 6 to 20 ft; grows 2 to 8 ft in a single season.
Hardy in zones 10–11;
dies to the ground but regrows from the roots in zone 9.

These tropical vines form curtains of flowers, adding layers of color and foliage to a garden and creating that essential lush, overgrown look that is so essential to a tropical aura. The different species vary in flower color, including blue, purple, orange, gold, and

Thunbergia battiscombei

creamy white blossoms, but all the flowers are variations of a trumpet shape with five flaring lobes and yellow throats. Leaves are usually large and glossy dark green. The vines climb by twining and do not have tendrils. These species will twist their way into a shrub or tree, climb an arbor or trellis, and even descend from a large hanging basket to display their glorious blossoms throughout summer and fall.

Cultivation

Grow these vines in full sun. The soil can be average to humus-rich but must be well drained. Enrich the soil at planting time and then fertilize every two weeks with liquid plant food. These plants grow rapidly from seeds or small plants and are best treated as annuals and not overwintered.

Species and Cultivars

T. alata (black-eyed Susan vine): This vigorous but delicate climber from Africa is not a newcomer to northern gardens; it's been a popular annual for years. The 2- to 3-in.-wide, funnel-shaped flowers have a five-lobed face with a dark, purple-black eye and throat, accounting for the common name. The blossoms are typically golden orange or bright yellow, but creamy white forms are also available. Because of the dark center, the flowers are magnificent with purple foliage plants such as *Pennisetum* 'Burgundy Giant'. Or combine them with *Duranta* 'Cuban Gold', *Lysimachia* 'Outback Sunset', or *Lantana* to continue the orange-and-yellow flames. This species grows up to 8 ft in a single season.

T. battiscombei (blue glory): This cascading shrub is suitable for a hanging basket or can be tied to a trellis so that it will grow upward and then drape downward. The 3-in.-long, trumpet-shaped flowers are an incredible deep royal blue with bright golden yellow throats. The plants bloom most heavily in summer and fall, more lightly in spring and winter. A well-grown plant in full bloom is an incredible sight. Blue glory grows up to 2 to 3 ft in a single season.

T. grandiflora (**blue trumpet vine, skyflower**): Growing up to 6 to 8 ft in a single season, this massive vine from India reaches 50 ft in its native habitat. The pale lavender-blue flowers have pale yellow or white throats and are shaped like a trumpet that flares open to five frilly, sweptback lobes. Chainlike clusters of three to ten flowers open during several flushes in summer and fall. The 8-in.-long leaves are lustrous green, are oval to lance-shaped with a long point, and create a beautiful sight even when the plant is not in bloom. 'Alba' is an elegant form with pure white flowers. Skyflower needs full sun. It combines well with almost any other tropical, echoing either its blue or yellow hues.

❖❖❖

Tibouchina (tih-boo-CHEE-nuh)
Princess Flower, Glory Bush

Tropical and subtropical shrub or subshrub, to 12 to 15 ft tall;
grows 3 to 8 ft in a single season.
Hardy in zones 10–11;
dies to the ground but regrows from the roots in zones 8–9.

Tibouchina grandifolia

Glorious in both flower and foliage, these Brazilian plants draw attention wherever they grow and prove to be indispensable to any tropical-style garden. In northern climates they grow rapidly into tall, open-branched shrubs with magnificent velvety leaves and stems. From early summer into fall, clusters of royal purple to violet or pink, saucer-shaped flowers with a silky texture adorn the plants. Princess flowers keep on blooming through light frost, and cold temperatures turn the foliage pumpkin-colored. These sizable plants find a home in the back of a tropical border or as the tallest element in a big planter. They look especially good combined with burgundy-hued foliage plants such as *Coleus, Strobilanthes,* and *Pennisetum setaceum* 'Rubrum' and large-flowered plants such as *Dahlia* and *Mandevilla*.

Cultivation

Grow *Tibouchina* in full to part sun and fertile, humus-rich, well-drained, moist soil. Water regularly. Fertilize every few weeks during the growing season. These plants are rather large to be overwintered as houseplants, but they are easily pruned and so can be cut back and then grown indoors. Or overwinter them by allowing frost to wither the top growth, then cut back the stems to 6 in. and store the root ball in a container of soil in a cool, dark place until spring.

Species and Cultivars

T. grandifolia (**large-leaved princess flower**): Magnificent in both foliage and flower, this commanding plant would be desirable even if it didn't bloom. The 10-in.-long, oval green leaves seem to be quilted out of velvet, because they are covered with silver hairs and have prominent veins that give them a puckered look. The violet-purple, red-centered, 1½-in.-wide blossoms grow in 18-in.-tall panicles at the ends of the branches. Each panicle can have up to 30 flowers. Blooming begins in midsummer and keeps on until frost. Plants grow to 6 to 8 ft tall and wide in a single season. Overwinter this plant and use it as plunge plant to enjoy its mature beauty.

T. nandina (**pink princess tree**): This lovely, slender, bushy species produces copious clusters of light pink, ½-in. flowers throughout the year. The silvery green, velvet-coated leaves are 2 in. long, creating a delicate appearance. If overwintered as a houseplant, prune it back hard in spring; it will grow to 3 to 4 ft tall during the growing season.

T. urvilleana (T. grandiflora, T. semidecandra) (**princess flower, glory bush**): Deep satiny purple, 4-in.-wide blossoms with pinkish purple anthers bloom in clusters all over this tall plant during summer and fall. The oval leaves are a gorgeous velvety green with prominent veins and a halo of red hairs along their edges, and they turn brilliant orange in fall. Reddish hairs also cover the dark green new growth, changing to cinnamon brown on the older branches. The species grows 4 to 5 ft tall in a single season. It can get a bit leggy, but 'Edwardsii' is an improved free-flowering cultivar with larger flowers that is more compact and bushier and makes a great standard or tree form. ✦✦✦

Tradescantia (trah-dess-KAN-tee-uh)
Inch Plant, Wandering Jew, Moses-in-a-Boat

Tropical ground cover, trailing to 3 to 4 ft;
grows 3 to 4 ft wide in a single season.
Hardy in zones 9–11;
dies to the ground
but regrows from the roots in zone 8.

Tradescantia pallida 'Purple Heart'

These delicate-looking foliage plants are probably the easiest and fastest-growing ground covers you can use in a tropical-style garden. They send out their jointed stems, densely cloaked with colorful leaves, in all directions, which root as they go to form a 6-in.-tall mat. The leaves are oval to lance-shaped and 1/2 to 3 or 4 in. long, depending on the species. These choice garden subjects feature brightly colored or variegated leaves. The flowers are small pink or lavender blossoms that tuck up against the stems cradling at the leaf base, which explains one common name for this genus, Moses-in-a-boat. Although the flowers are not important, they add a nice touch. Because inch plants tolerate damp soil, you can use them along a pond edge, or simply allow them to weave around the bases of bushy plants or between the stones in a steppingstone path. When the plants are grown in a hanging basket or container, their stems drape gracefully downward.

Cultivation

These adaptable plants grow in almost any conditions from full shade to full sun. Provide moist but well-drained soil; it should be evenly moist to damp. Fertilize every few weeks during the growing season. Prune back as needed. All species make excellent houseplants and are easily overwintered or started from cuttings.

Species and Cultivars

T. fluminensis (**wandering Jew**): The species has pointed, light green leaves up to 4 in. long, but the cultivars are showier and more commonly grown. The leaves of 'Albovittata' are irregularly striped with bright white on top and have purple undersides. Green and yellow stripes decorate the leaves of 'Aurea'. 'Orchid Frost' ('Variegata') features leaves striped with white, purple, pink, and green. Combine wandering Jew with *Fuchsia* and *Begonia* in a lightly shaded garden.

T. pallida (Setcreasea pur-purea) 'Purple Heart' (purple heart vine): The smooth leaves of this luscious ground cover are an unbelievable deep purple color. They grow in dense tufts around the succulent stems, forming a wonderful grapey mass. Tiny pink flowers bloom all summer at the leaf bases. Use 'Purple Heart' to weave around *Coleus* or *Strobilan-* *thes* to pick up on those plants' purple and violet hues.

T. sillamontana (white velvet): Silvery white hairs cover the 1-in.-long leaves and trailing stems of this compact inch plant, giving it the feel of velvet. Bright pink flowers appear in summer at the stem tips. It grows more slowly than the other species and needs full sun to keep it glistening. ✦✦✦

Tradescantia sillamontana

Vigna caracalla (VIG-nuh kare-uh-KALL-uh)
Snail Flower, Corkscrew Flower
Tropical and subtropical vine, to 18 ft;
grows 6 to 10 ft in a single season.
Hardy in zones 9–11.

The fascinating flowers of this twining vine from South America are made up of colorful petals that are coiled corkscrew-fashion into the shape of a snail's shell, explaining the plant's common names. The 2-in.-long flowers bloom in 12-in.-long clusters and may be light lavender-pink, white, or creamy yellow. This vine thrives in hot weather and blooms most heavily in summer. A member of the bean family, snail flower produces small green pods and has the three-parted leaves typical of its clan. Use this lightweight vine to decorate a trellis or to twine into a shrub or tree. It can grow up a tripod in a border or large planter. It's best planted near a path or patio where you can see the unusual flowers up close.

Cultivation
Grow snail flower in full sun in average, well-drained soil; allow the soil to dry between waterings. Fertilize once a month from spring through fall. Prune back the vines as needed if they get too long. Although it can be grown over winter as a houseplant, snail flower may become infested with spider mites. Cut the plant to the ground and store in a cool, dark basement until spring. ✦✦✦

Vigna caracalla

Wedelia trilobata

(weh-DEAL-ee-uh try-low-BAH-tah)

Golden Creeping Daisy

Tropical ground cover, spreading to 3 to 4 ft and growing 4 in. tall;
spreads 3 to 4 ft in a single season.
Hardy in zones 10–11;
dies to the ground but regrows from the roots in zone 9.

Wedelia trilobata

The charming, yellow, daisylike flowers of this ground cover are about 2 in. across and stand above the mat of bright green foliage on 4-in.-high stems. Native to Florida, the West Indies, and Central and South America, this dense plant spreads rapidly in gardens to provide a glorious green-and-yellow carpet. Blooming starts in spring and keeps on until frost. Golden creeping daisy works perfectly planted so it can weave around the stones in a stepping-stone path or under the stalks of taller tropicals. Use it to emphasize the yellow variegations in the leaves of *Coleus, Sanchezia, Canna,* and *Erythrina* or to paint a pretty picture with the large flowers of *Hibiscus* and *Brugmansia.* It also performs delightfully in hanging baskets and planters, where it will spill over the edge in a softening wave of color. 'Outenreath Gold' offers the same charming yellow daisies, but in addition its green leaves are splashed with gold flecks for a very pretty effect.

Cultivation

Grow this creeper in full to part sun. It is very adaptable as to soil type, even tolerating the dry shade under trees. For best growth, allow the soil to dry a bit between waterings. Fertilize every two weeks during the growing season. You can overwinter golden creeping daisy as a houseplant in a sunny window and take cuttings in the spring or fall to increase its numbers.

❖❖❖

Xanthosoma (zan-tho-SO-muh)

Elephant's Ear, Taro

Tuberous perennial, to 2 to 3 ft tall;
grows 2 to 3 ft in a single season.
Hardy in zones 9–11; to zone 8b with winter protection.

Xanthosoma sagittifolium

This luxurious foliage plant grows big enough to hide a small child behind its leaves and is essential to giving a jungly look to a tropical-style garden in a northern climate. Its huge, shield-shaped leaves grow on long stalks directly from the ground and create a lush, bold look. The flowers are composed of a spathe and spadix—a colorful cup-shaped bract (spathe) that shields the tall, cigar-shaped spike of tiny flowers (spadix)—and appear at the bases of the leaves on and off during the summer. This genus of elephant's ears is related to *Colocasia* and *Alocasia,* which also go by the common names of elephant's ear and taro. All have edible tubers, which need to be cooked before they are eaten. Plants in the three genera look very similar and it takes a botanist to tell them apart.

An effective way to use *Xanthosoma* is to combine it with ferns and grasses to showcase its dramatic presence. It can also be massed with elephant's ears from the other genera to create a happy alliance of varying colors and heights in similar, sumptuous forms.

Cultivation

Grow elephant's ear in full to part sun and humus-rich, moist soil. Enrich the soil with compost before planting. Keep the soil very moist, as these plants are fast growers and need a lot of water. Fertilize every other week for the lushest growth. Containerized plants can be overwintered in a cool, dark place after frost has cut down their leaves; keep the soil dry until spring. Or dig and store the tubers of plants growing in the ground as you would a canna.

Species and Cultivars

X. lindenii (Caladium lindenii) '**Magnificum**': The leaves of this small elephant's ear are strongly arrow-shaped and grow 8 to 12 in. long. A beautiful pattern of silvery white veins is stamped out on the olive green surface, making this a highly desirable specimen.

X. sagittifolium '**Chartreuse Giant**': The heart-shaped leaves of this rare cultivar grow about 2 ft long on 1- to 2-ft-long stalks, but the best part is their fabulous color—vibrant, golden yellow-green. The foliage literally glows in the garden, especially when combined with grass green or purplish red foliage. When the plants are grown in part shade, the colors are richer and the leaf blades can get to be 3 ft long. This selection makes a scintillating combination with *Colocasia* 'Jet Black Wonder'.

X. violaceum (**blue taro**): The 2-ft-long, triangular leaf blades of this species grow on 2- to 3-ft-long, dark purple stalks. Dark reddish purple margins and veins stand out against the dark green background, creating a powerfully attractive pattern. ✦✦✦

For additional elephant's ears, see Alocasia *and* Colocasia *entries.*

Zingiberaceae (zin-ji-bah-RAY-see-aye)
Ginger Family
Subtropical and tropical perennials, from 1 to 8 ft tall;
grow to mature height in a single season.
Hardy in zones 8–10; some to zone 7.

Hailing mostly from the rain forests of Indonesia, Malaysia, and South and Central America, the ginger family represents a diverse group of plants that are grown for their wonderfully lush, often brightly variegated leaves and captivating flowers. Planted in a large clump, any of the ornamental gingers casts a tropical spell over a garden. An enchanting fragrance makes *Hedychium,* the butterfly gingers, especially desirable for a tropical-style garden, because their sweet perfume adds one more dimension to its allure. Although their origin is tropical, many gingers are surprisingly cold-hardy, overwintering in zone 7b and flourishing all year in gardens in the Deep South. Tropical gingers—those that are hardy only in zones 9–10—are usually evergreen and make good houseplants in winter. Subtropical ones—those hardy into zone 7—can go dormant in winter and should be overwintered as you would a canna; if space allows, they can also be grown as houseplants. Both types, however, adapt well to summer gardens in almost any climate. Use them in the ground or in containers.

Cultivation

Some gingers need more sun than do others. Those with thin, straplike leaves do best in part to full sun. Gingers with wide, flat leaves prefer part shade to all-day, light dappled shade. All need moist, rich, acid soil. Water freely, never letting the soil dry out, especially in the sunnier locations. These plants feed heavily, so incorporate a timed-release fertilizer when planting and fertilize them with a well-balanced liquid fertilizer every two weeks. Overwinter evergreen gingers as houseplants or in a conservatory in a sunny, warm, humid location to keep them in constant bloom. The more cold-hardy types go dormant when hit by a frost. Dig them up and divide the rhizomes, which will normally separate readily, and store them in a cool, dry place until planting time in spring. Plant the rhizomes 2 in. below the soil surface. Where gingers are winter-hardy, leave them in the ground and be sure they are well mulched for the winter, especially near their hardiness limit.

Species and Cultivars

Some 45 genera of gingers abound in the tropics, but gardeners in temperate climates have the best luck with the following types in summer gardens. Once you've succeeded with these, you can seek out rarer types.

Globba winitii

Tall Types

Alpinia zerumbet (**shell ginger, cone ginger**): This ginger's 2-ft-long, glossy green, oblong leaves grow on reedlike stems that can reach 6 to 7 ft tall. Fragrant flowers bloom in 1-ft-long, arching clusters, their porcelain white flower buds looking like a string of shells. These open into pink-and-white, 3-in. blossoms with red-and-yellow mottled throats. 'Variegata' is a choice plant whose green leaves are shot through with clusters of narrow, creamy yellow stripes that form angles to the midrib, creating an exciting pattern and an eye-catching color scheme. The variegated form makes a hot combination in a container with *Ipomoea* 'Blackie' draping over the pot's edge or used with flowers such as *Lantana* or *Pentas*. Grow shell ginger in the ground as a specimen in a mixed border. The roots are hardy to zone 7 with winter protection and good siting.

Costus amazonica '**Variegata**' (**variegated spiral ginger**): The showiest of the numerous types of *Costus,* this plant features lance-shaped leaves with numerous bold, pure white stripes radiating from the leaf bases. The plant's stems are twisted into spirals, which gives the foliage an attractive whorled appearance. Frilly white flowers bloom, several at a time, from green conelike structures at the stem tips. Use this beautiful plant in a container or in the ground, perhaps planting *Ficus pumila* 'Variegata' at its feet. It grows to 8 ft in the ground and to 3 to 5 ft tall in a container. Hardy in zones 9–11.

Hedychium coccineum (**orange bottlebrush ginger**): Only faintly fragrant, the spidery flowers of this 6-ft-tall species compose themselves into 10- to 12-in.-tall bottlebrush-shaped spikes at the tips of the stems. Colors include scarlet, orange, and gold. The narrow leaves are blue-green and quite attractive in their own right, but paired with the sumptuous flowers they create a lush tropical aura. Use bottlebrush ginger in beds or large containers. This showy ginger is native to India and Myanmar (Burma) and is hardy in zones 8–10.

H. coronarium (**white butterfly ginger**): Gorgeous orchidlike white flowers with an entrancing, far-reaching fragrance adorn this popular ginger in late summer and fall, blooming until night temperatures drop into the low 30s. The foliage is bold and dark green and grows 4 to 5 ft tall. Plant this ginger in clumps in the garden for the outstanding leaves and season-extending blossoms. Good combinations include hardy plants with rounded leaves such as *Hosta* and *Ligularia* and tropicals such as *Sanchezia, Melianthus,* and *Ricinus.* Many species or hybrids of *Hedychium* with orange, yellow, or pink flowers are available from specialty growers, although not all are as cold-hardy as this one. Hardy in zones 7–10.

Zingiber zerumbet (**shampoo ginger, pinecone ginger, beehive ginger**): This green, leafy ginger grows to 6 to 8 ft tall and its oblong leaves form two ranks on either side of the reedlike stems, giving it a strong architectural quality. Small yellow flowers bloom from midsummer on, forming in between the bracts of showy, green, pinecone-like structures. Once blooming has finished, the cone turns bright red. When squeezed the cone releases a thick sap that is used in the tropics as a shampoo, hence the common name "shampoo ginger." Use this tall ginger as a vertical accent in a container or border in part to full sun. 'Darceyi' has white-edged leaves. Hardy in zones 8–10.

Low Types

Curcuma alismatifolia (**Siam tulip, summer tulip**): Grown for its prolific flowers, this charming ginger creates a clump of lance-shaped, green leaves from which sprout stems of pink flowers. The whole arrangement seems reminiscent of a tulip but looks much more exotic. The flowering stalk is actually topped with whorls of showy, bright pink bracts stacked together to resemble a 3-in.-tall flower. The true flowers are tiny lavender-and-white blossoms that peek, a few at a time, from between the bracts. Borne on a 2-ft-tall, straight stem, the inflorescence lasts a month and is supplanted by more blossoms all summer and fall. Unlike most other gingers, this one does best in part to full sun in rich, well-drained soil. White, pink, and rose forms are available. Hardy in zones 8–10. *C. gracillima* 'Chocolate Zebra' is similar, with maroon-and-green striped inflorescences. Plant these gingers in the ground or in containers so that several plants grow out of a low ground cover such as *Ficus pumila* 'Variegata', *Tradescantia*, or *Alternanthera*. Hardy in zones 9–10.

Globba winitii (**dancing ladies**): The lush, green leaves of this 2-ft-tall ginger have a pretty shape—long lances with heart-shaped bases. These curve over gracefully, and from where they clasp the stems grows an arching spray of unusually beautiful flowers. The individual flowers are made up of bright pink, mauve, or purple bracts, from which extend long stems with yellow petals and curling yellow stamens. This ginger does best in light shade and is an excellent plant for softening the front of a container. It blooms from midsummer until frost and the sprays make lovely cut flowers. 'Mauve Dancing Ladies' has mauve-purple bracts. 'Red Leaf' is similar, but its leaf undersides are painted maroon. 'White Dragon' has yellow petals growing from pure white bracts. *G. schomburgkii (G. marantina)* 'Yellow Dancing Girl' has yellow bracts and petals, creating a golden look, and is hardy in zones 7b–10. *G. winitii* is hardy in zones 9–10.

Kaempferia pulchra (**peacock ginger**): This showy, low foliage plant forms 6- to 8-in.-high, dense clumps of rounded, green leaves that are painted and spotted in lovely subtle patterns. Tiny white or lavender flowers peek from between the leaves, adding a dash of color, but these pretty little things pale when compared with the lovely foliage. One of the intriguing things about peacock ginger is the way the leaves unfurl. New leaves constantly form all summer and as they emerge are rolled up into cylinders. As they slowly unfold, they lie flat to reveal their expanse of color. The shapes and patterns of the juxtaposed young and old leaves make for an intriguing texture. This shade lover flourishes in moist soil in dappled shade with ferns and begonias. Use it massed as a ground cover, or grow it in a container on a porch or patio. 'Bronze Peacock' has heavily textured leaves with bronze backs. 'Mansonii' is green with ridged leaves. 'Silver Spot' has blue-green leaves with soft silvery splotches. *K. gilbertii* '3-D' features leaves variegated green, pale green, and creamy white like a hosta. All are hardy in zones 8–10. ◆◆◆

Kaempferia pulchra

Appendix **O**ne

Plant **L**ists

TENDER PLANTS THAT EXTEND THE FALL SEASON

These tropical, subtropical, and tender plants grow vigorously all summer and keep performing beautifully throughout the fall months. Leave these outside until frost so your garden will be as glorious in autumn as it is in summer.

Abutilon spp.
Agapanthus spp.
Agave spp.
Alpinia zerumbet
Anisodontea × *hypomandarum*
Arctotis hybrida
Aristolochia spp.
Colocasia esculenta
Cordyline spp.
Crinum spp.
Cuphea ignea
Curcuma alismatifolia
Curcuma gracillima 'Chocolate Zebra'
Cyathea cooperi
Cycas spp.
Cymbopogon citratus
Dicksonia antarctica
Eucalyptus cinerea
Eucomis bicolor
Euphorbia spp.
Fuchsia spp.
Galphimia glauca
Gardenia augusta (G. jasminoides)
Globba winitii
Hamelia patens
Hedychium coccineum
Hedychium coronarium
Kalanchoe spp.
Leonotis leonurus
Lotus spp.

Melianthus major
Muhlenbergia dumosa
Musa spp.
Nerium oleander
Nephrolepis acutifolia
Osteospermum × *hybrida*
Passiflora spp.
Pelargonium zonale
Pennisetum setaceum 'Rubrum'
Pennisetum villosum
Phoenix dactylifera
Phoenix roebelinii
Phormium spp.
Phygelius rectus
Plumbago auriculata
Rhapidophyllum hystrix
Rhynchelytrum repens
Sabal minor
Saccharum officinarum
Serenoa repens
Setaria palmifolia
Solanum spp.
Tibouchina spp.
Trachycarpus fortunei
Tradescantia pallida 'Purple Heart'
Wedelia trilobata

TROPICAL PLANTS WITH BIG LEAVES

Whether they feature clear, simple outlines or are cut into feathery segments, the gigantic leaves offered by these plants give a garden an indisputably tropical air.

Acalypha wilkesiana
Alocasia spp.
Alpinia zerumbet
Anthurium spp.
Argyreia nervosa
Begonia × *rex*
Blechnum brasiliense
Caladium bicolor (C. × *hortulanum)*
Canna × *generalis*
Colocasia esculenta
Costus amazonica
Cyathea cooperi
Dicksonia antarctica
Ensete ventricosum
Eucharis × *grandiflora*
Ficus elastica

Ficus lyrata
Graptophyllum pictum
Hedychium spp.
Heliconia spp.
Musa spp.
Musella lasiocarpa
Palmae
Ricinus communis
Sanchezia speciosa
Senna (Cassia) spp.
Solanum quitoense
Strelitzia reginae
Strobilanthes dyeranus
Tibouchina grandifolia
Xanthosoma spp.
Zingiber zerumbet

TROPICAL PLANTS WITH COLORFUL LEAVES

Use these foliage plants as your basic plant palette to paint your garden with vivacious colors.

Leaves silvery or blue-gray all over

Aechmea fasciata
Agave americana 'Glauca'
Agave macroacantha
Agave parryi
Agave stricta
Argyreia nervosa
Eucalyptus cinerea
Eucalyptus neglecta

Kalanchoe pumila
Lotus berthelotii
Lotus maculatus
Melianthus spp.
Plectranthus argentatus
Solanum pyracanthum
Tillandsia spp.
Tradescantia sillamontana

Leaves solid-colored golden yellow, yellow, or chartreuse

Acalypha wilkesiana 'Ceylon'
Alternanthera ficoidea var. *amoena* 'Yellow Fine Leaf'
Alternanthera ficoidea var. *amoena* 'Yellow Wide'
Duranta erecta (D. repens) 'Cuban Gold'
Ipomoea batatas 'Margarita'

Lysimachia congestiflora 'Aurea'
Oxalis vulcanicola 'Copper Glow'
Pelargonium × *zonale* 'Crystal Palace Gem'
Pelargonium × *zonale* 'Persian Queen'
Xanthosoma sagittifolium 'Chartreuse Giant'

Leaves variegated with green and gold or yellow

Abutilon megapotamicum 'Variegata'
Abutilon pictum 'Thompsonii'
Alocasia 'Hilo Beauty'
Alpinia zerumbet 'Variegata'
Breynia disticha 'Thimma'
Canna × generalis 'Pretoria' ('Striata', 'Bengal Tiger')
Coleus blumei (Solenostemon scutellarioides)
Cuphea ignea 'Variegata'

Erythrina variegata var. picta
Fuchsia 'Golden Marinka'
Lantana camara 'Greg Grant'
Lantana camara 'Samantha'
Phormium 'Yellow Wave'
Sanchezia speciosa
Solanum jasminoides
Tradescantia fluminensis 'Aurea'
Wedelia trilobata 'Outenreath Gold'

Leaves variegated with green and white

Abutilon × 'Souvenir de Bonn'
Acanthus montanus 'Frielings's Sensation'
Agave americana 'Marginata'
Agave americana 'Mediopicta'
Agave parviflora
Alocasia macrorrhizia 'Variegata'
Ananas bracteatus 'Albomarginata'
Ananas bracteatus 'Striatus'
Anthurium crystallinum
Bougainvillea 'Raspberry Ice' ('Hawaii')
Brugmansia 'Variegata'
Caladium bicolor (C. × hortulanum)
Canna × generalis 'Stuttgart'
Clerodendrum thomsoniae 'Variegata'
Coleus blumei (Solenostemon scutellarioides)
Costus amazonica 'Variegata'
Cyperus alternifolius 'Variegata'
Duranta erecta (D. repens) 'Variegata'
Euphorbia marginata
Ficus pumila 'Variegata'

Gardenia augusta (G. jasminoides) 'Radicans Variegata'
Kaempferia gilbertii '3-D'
Musa basjoo 'Variegata'
Musa × paradisiaca 'Ae-Ae'
Osteospermum × hybrida 'Gweek Variegated'
Pelargonium crispum 'French Lace' and 'Variegatum'
Pelargonium graveolens 'Lady Plymouth'
Plectranthus amboinicus
Plectranthus forsteri (P. coleoides) 'Marginatus'
Plectranthus madagascarensis 'Minimus Variegatus'
Pseuderanthemum atropurpureum 'Albo-marginatum'
Saccharum officinarum 'California Stripe'
Setaria palmifolia 'Variegata'
Tradescantia fluminensis 'Variegata'
Xanthosoma lindenii (Caladium lindenii) 'Magnificum'

Leaves multicolored with combinations of green, white, yellow, gold, red, pink, orange, and/or bronze

Acalypha godseffiana 'Heterophylla'
Acalypha wilkesiana
Acalypha wilkesiana 'Kilavea'
Acalypha wilkesiana 'Macrophylla'
Alternanthera dentata 'Krinkle'
Alternanthera dentata 'Tricolor'
Ananas bracteatus 'Tricolor'
Breynia disticha (Breynia nivosa) 'Roseapicta'

Caladium bicolor (C. × hortulanum)
Canna × generalis 'Durban'
Canna × generalis 'Pink Sunburst'
Canna × generalis 'Tropicana' ('Phasion')
Cissus discolor
Codiaeum variegatum var. pictum 'Andreanum'

Codiaeum variegatum var. *pictum*
  'Big Dipper'
Codiaeum variegatum var. *pictum*
  'Carrieri'
Codiaeum variegatum var. *pictum*
  'Fascination'
Codiaeum variegatum var. *pictum*
  'Reidii'
*Coleus blumei (Solenostemon
  scutellarioides)* cvs.
Colocasia esculenta 'Illustris'
Cordyline terminalis 'Calypso Queen'
Cordyline terminalis 'Firebrand'
*Cordyline terminalis (C. fruticosa,
  Dracaena terminalis)* 'Tricolor'
Ficus elastica 'Doscheri'
Ficus elastica 'Tricolor'
Fuchsia 'Island Sunset'
Graptophyllum pictum
Guzmania spp.
Heliconia indica 'Spectabilis'

Hibiscus rosa-sinensis
  'Cooperi' ('Checkerboard')
Ipomoea batatas 'Pinkie'
  ('Pink Frost', 'Tricolor')
Ipomoea tricolor 'Roman Candy'
Kaempferia pulchra
Kaempferia pulchra 'Bronze Peacock'
Kaempferia pulchra 'Silver Spot'
Lysimachia congestiflora
  'Outback Sunset'
Neoregelia spp.
Pelargonium quercifolium 'Fair Ellen'
Pelargonium × *zonale* 'Skies of Italy'
Pelargonium × *zonale*
  'Vancouver Centennial'
Phormium 'Pink Stripe'
Phormium 'Sundowner'
Pseuderanthemum atropurpureum
  'Variegatum' ('Tricolor')
Tradescantia fluminensis 'Orchid Frost'
  ('Variegata')

Leaves solid, tinged, or variegated with purple or bronze

Alocasia 'Black Velvet'
Alocasia plumbea
Alternanthera dentata 'Rubiginosa'
Alternanthera polygonoides 'Purple
  Select'
Canna × *generalis* 'Intrigue'
Canna × *generalis* 'Red King Humbert'
Canna × *generalis* 'Wyoming'
*Coleus blumei (Solenostemon
  scutellarioides)*
Colocasia esculenta
Colocasia esculenta 'Jet Black Wonder'
  ('Black Magic')
Cordyline australis 'Atropurpurea'
Cordyline invidisa (Dracaena indivisa)
  'Purpurea'
Crinum asiaticum 'Procerum'
Ensete ventricosum 'Maurelii'
Eucomis bicolor 'Sparkling Burgundy'
Euphorbia cotinifolia
Ficus elastica 'Burgundy Knight'
Fuchsia triphylla 'Gartenmeister
  Bonstedt'
Gynura aurantiaca (G. sarmentosa)
Gynura bicolor
Hibiscus acetosella 'Red Shield'

Ipomoea batatas 'Blackie'
Ipomoea batatas 'Vardman'
Leea amabilis 'Splendens'
Musa acuminata var. *sumatrana*
Oxalis hedysaroides 'Rubra'
Oxalis regnellii
Oxalis vulcanicola 'Red Velvet'
Pennisetum setaceum 'Rubrum'
  ('Atropurpureum')
Phormium 'Atropurpureum'
Phormium 'Bronze Baby'
Pseuderanthemum alatum
Pseuderanthemum atropurpureum
Pseuderanthemum atropurpureum
  'Rubrum'
Ricinus communis 'Carmencita'
Saccharum officinarum 'Violaceum'
Setaria palmifolia 'Rubra'
Solanum atropurpureum
Solanum quitoense
Strobilanthes dyeranus
*Tradescantia pallida (Setcreasea
  purpurea)* 'Purple Heart'
Xanthosoma violaceum

TROPICAL PLANTS WITH FRAGRANT FLOWERS

Often intensifying at night, the sweet perfume of these tropical flowers adds another dimension to the tropical-style garden, a dimension that to some is the essence of paradise.

Acidanthera bicolor var. *murieliae*
   (*Gladiolus callianthus*)
Alpinia zerumbet
Brugmansia spp.
Cestrum spp.
Cestrum nocturnum
Datura inoxia (*D. metaloides*)
Datura metel
Eucharis × *grandiflora*
Gardenia augusta (*G. jasminoides*)
Hedychium coccineum

Hedychium coronarium
Ipomoea alba
Jasminum nitidum
Jasminum officinale
Jasminum polyanthum
Jasminum sambac
Melianthus spp.
Passiflora spp.
Plumeria spp.
Senna (*Cassia*) spp.
Zingiber zerumbet

TROPICAL VINES FOR A JUNGLY LOOK

Choose among these vines to grow overhead in a wild tangle to create the layered planting style that characterizes a tropical-style garden.

Abutilon spp.*
Abutilon megapotamicum 'Variegata'*
*Acalypha hispida**
Acalypha repens (*A. pendula*)*
Allamanda blanchetii (*A. violacea*)
Allamanda cathartica
Argyreia nervosa
Aristolochia elegans (*A. littoralis*)
Aristolochia grandiflora
Bougainvillea spp.*
Cissus antarctica
Cissus discolor
Clerodendrum × *speciosum*
Clerodendrum splendens
Clerodendrum thomsoniae
Clerodendrum ugandense
Ficus pumila
Gynura aurantiaca (*G. sarmentosa*)
Gynura bicolor
Ipomoea alba
*Ipomoea batatas**
Ipomoea coccinea
Ipomoea × *multifida*
Ipomoea purpurea
Ipomoea quamoclit
Ipomoea tricolor
Jasminum officinale

Jasminum polyanthum
Lantana montevidensis
Mandevilla × *amabilis* (*Dipladenia*
   × *amabilis*)
Mandevilla boliviensis (*Dipladenia*
   boliviensis)
Mandevilla sanderi (*Dipladenia sanderi*)
Nepenthes mirabilis
Passiflora alata
Passiflora caerulea
Passiflora coccinea
Passiflora incarnata
Passiflora × 'Incense'
Passiflora × 'Jeanette'
Passiflora trifasciata
*Plumbago auriculata**
Senecio confusus (*Pseudogynoxys*
   chenopodioides)
Solanum jasminoides
Solanum rantonnetii (*Lycianthes*
   rantonnetii)*
Stigmaphyllon ciliatum
Thunbergia alata
Thunbergia battiscombei
Thunbergia grandiflora
Vigna caracalla

* These plants are not true vines because they do not climb by twining or tendrils; however, you can easily train their sprawling or weeping branches to grow like a vine or climber by tying them to a support such as a post, fence, or arbor.

TROPICAL PLANTS WITH ARCHITECTURAL SHAPES

Because of their dramatic height or striking silhouette, these tropicals make a strong architectural statement when used as specimens or focal points in a planting.

Acidanthera bicolor var. *murieliae*
    (*Gladiolus callianthus*)
Aechmea fasciata
Agave spp.
Alpinia zerumbet
Ananas bracteatus
Archontophoenix cunninghamiana
Billbergia nutans
Blechnum brasiliense
Chamaedorea elegans
Cocos nucifera
Costus amazonica 'Variegata'
Crinum spp.
Cyathea cooperi
Cycas spp.
Cymbopogon citratus
Cyperus spp.
Dicksonia antarctica
Dioon edule
Ensete ventricosum
Euphorbia spp.
Guzmania spp.
Hedychium coccineum
Hedychium coronarium
Heliconia spp.
Homalocladium platycladum
    (*Muehlenbeckia platyclada*)
Howea forsteriana

Kalanchoe beharensis
Kalanchoe daigremontiana
Leonotis leonurus
Melianthus major
Neodypsis decaryi
Neoregelia spp.
Nephrolepis acutifolia
Pennisetum setaceum 'Rubrum'
    ('Atropurpureum')
Phoenix dactylifera
Phoenix roebelinii
Phormium spp.
Platycerium bifurcatum
Plumeria spp.
Rhapidophyllum hystrix
Rhapsis excelsa
Rhipsalis spp.
Rhynchelytrum repens
Russelia equisetiformis
Saccharum officinarum
Senna (*Cassia*) spp.
Setaria palmifolia
Solanum atropurpureum
Strelitzia reginae
Syagrus romanzoffianum
    (*Cocos plumosa*)
Trachycarpus fortunei
Zamia fischeri

TROPICAL PLANTS FOR MIXED CONTAINERS

Although almost any tropical plant adapts well to container culture, the following ones are easy to grow and combine well with other plants. When designing a mixed container, use tall plants for height, filler plants for volume, and cascading plants to spill over the container's edge.

Plants for height

Abelmoschus manihot (*Hibiscus manihot*)
Acalypha hispida
Acidanthera bicolor var. *murieliae*
    (*Gladiolus callianthus*)
Anisodontea × *hypomandarum*
Brugmansia spp.
Canna × *generalis*
Clerodendrum ugandense
Cordyline spp.

Ensete ventricosum
Eucalyptus cinerea
Heliconia spp.
Hibiscus rosa-sinensis
Leonotis leonurus
Musa spp.
Phormium tenax
Saccharum officinarum
Tibouchina spp.

Plants for filler

Abutilon spp.
Angelonia angustifolia
Arctotis × *hybrida*
Begonia spp.
Caladium bicolor (C. × hortulanum)
Coleus blumei (Solenostemon
  scutellarioides)
Cuphea ignea
Duranta erecta (D. repens)
Fuchsia × *hybrida*
Jasminum spp.
Justicia carnea (Jacobinia carnea)

Kalanchoe spp.
Lantana camara
Orthosiphon stamenius
Osteospermum × *hybrida*
Oxalis vulcanicola
Pelargonium spp.
Pelargonium × *zonale*
Pentas lanceolata
Phygelius capensis
Plectranthus spp.
Strobilanthes dyeranus

Plants for trailing

Abutilon megapotamicum 'Variegata'
Acalypha repens (A. pendula)
Alternanthera spp.
Bougainvillea spp.
Cissus discolor
Ficus pumila
Gynura aurantiaca (G. sarmentosa)
Ipomoea batatas

Lantana montevidensis 'Lavender
  Cascade' and 'White Cascade'
Lotus spp.
Lysimachia congestiflora
Rhipsalis spp.
Russelia equisetiformis
Solanum jasminoides
Tradescantia spp.
Wedelia trilobata

COLD-HARDY TROPICAL-LOOKING TREES

Because of their exotic-looking foliage or flowers—or both—these Temperate Zone trees have a tropical look that you can exploit in your landscape design. Trees marked with * also have flowering interest. Those marked with ** have colorful foliage.

Compound, bold-textured leaves

Aesculus × *carnea* 'Briotii' and 'O'Neil
  Red', zones 5–8*
Ailanthus altissima, zones 4–9*
Aralia elata 'Aureovariegata' and
  'Variegata', zones 4–9* **
Cladrastis lutea, zones 4–8*

Fraxinus spp., zones 2–9
Gymnocladus dioicas 'Shademaster',
  zones 4–7
Koelreuteria paniculata, zones 5–9*
Phellodendron armurense, zones 4–7

Compound, lacy-textured leaves

Albizia julibrissin 'Charlotte' and
  'Tryon', zones 6–9*
Gleditsia triacanthos, zones 4–9
Gleditsia triacanthos 'Sunburst',
  zones 4–9**
Juglans nigra, zones 4–9

Laburnum × *watereri* 'Vossii',
  zones 6–8*
Robinia pseudoacacia, zones 4–9*
Robinia pseudoacacia 'Frisia',
  zones 4–9* **
Sophora japonica, zones 6–9*

Big, solid leaves

Catalpa bignonioides 'Aurea',
 zones 5–9* **
Catalpa speciosa, zones 4–8*
Cercidiphyllum japonicum, zones 5–9
Cercis canadensis, zones 4–9*
Cercis canadensis 'Forest Pansy',
 zones 4–9* **
Lagerstroemia indica, zones 6–10*
Liquidambar styraciflua 'Gold Dust',
 zones 5–9**
Liriodendron chinense, zones 7–9*
Liriodendron tulipifera, zones 5–9*

Liriodendron tulipifera 'Majestic Beauty'
 ('Aureomarginata'), zones 5–9* **
Magnolia grandiflora, zones 6–10*
Magnolia hypoleuca, zones 5–9*
Magnolia macrophylla, zones 6–9*
Magnolia × soulangiana, zones 5–9*
Magnolia virginiana var. australis,
 zones 6–9*
Oxydendrum arboreum, zones 5–9*
Paulownia tomentosa, zones 5–8*
Poncirus trifoliata, zones 6–9*
Styrax obassia, zones 6–9*

COLD-HARDY PALMS

Big, fan- or feather-shaped fronds characterize these Temperate Zone palms. The best of these are described in detail in the encyclopedia entry for the palm family, Palmae, on pages 172–74.

Chamaerops humilis, zones 7a–10
Rhapidophyllum hystrix, zones 5–10
Sabal etonia, zones 7a–10
Sabal minor, zones 6b–11
Sabal palmetto, zones 7b–10
Serenoa repens, zones 6b–11

Trachycarpus fortunei, zones 7a–10
Trachycarpus martianus, zones 7a–10
Trachycarpus takil, zones 6b–10
Trachycarpus wagnerianus, zones 7a–10
Trithrinax campestris, zones 7b–10

COLD-HARDY TROPICAL-LOOKING SHRUBS

Big, solid or entire leaves and exotic flowers give these shrubs a tropical look. Those marked with * have colorful leaves. Those marked with ** are grown only for their foliage and do not have showy blossoms.

Bold leaves and flowers

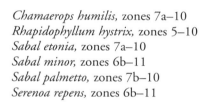

Acuba japonica 'Variegata', zones 7–9* **
Aesculus parviflora, zones 4–9
Buddleia davidii 'Harlequin', zones 5–10*
Camellia japonica, zones 7–9
Clerodendrum trichotomum, zones 7–9
Cotinus coggygria 'Notcutt's Variety' and
 'Royal Purple', zones 5–9*
Euonymus fortunei 'Emerald 'n Gold'
 and 'Silver Queen', zones 5–9* **
Forsythia 'Goldleaf', zones 5–9*
Hydrangea arborescens, zones 4–9
Hydrangea macrophylla, zones 6–9

Hydrangea macrophylla 'Maresii
 Variegata', zones 6–9
Hydrangea quercifolia, zones 5–9
Mahonia aquifolium, zones 5–9
Osmanthus heterophyllus 'Variegatus',
 zones 7–9*
Prunus laurocerasus, zones 7–9
Viburnum rhytidophyllum, zones 6–8
Yucca filamentosa, zones 4–10
Yucca filamentosa 'Gold Band',
 zones 4–10
Yucca rostrata, zones 6–11

Ferny or fine-textured leaves and flowers

Fuchsia magellanica, zones 6–9
Hibiscus syriacus, zones 5–9
Indigofera kirilowii, zones 5–7
Lespedeza thunbergii, zones 6–8
Nandina domestica, zones 7–9
Pieris japonica 'Variegata', zones 5–8*
Rhus typhina 'Laciniata', zones 3–8
Sambucus racemosa 'Laciniata',
   zones 3–8

Sambucus racemosa 'Plumosa Aurea',
   zones 3–8*
Sorbaria kirlowii, zones 3–8
Spiraea × bumalda 'Goldflame' and
   'Goldmound', zones 4–8*
Tamarix ramosissima, zones 4–8
Weigela florida 'Variegata', zones 5–9*

COLD-HARDY TROPICAL-LOOKING PERENNIALS

Boasting either big, lush leaves or exotic-looking flowers—or both—these cold-hardy perennials look tropical but return to your garden year after year. Those marked with * offer colorful leaves.

Low (under 2 ft tall)

Begonia grandis, zones 7–10;
   6 with winter mulch
Bergenia cordifolia, zones 3–8
Euphorbia epythiodes, zones 4–8
Helleborus spp., zones 3–8
Heuchera micrantha 'Palace Purple',

   zones 4–8*
Hosta spp., zones 3–9*
Houttuynia cordata 'Tricolor',
   zones 6–11*
Liriope muscari, zones 6–9
Liriope muscari 'Variegata', zones 6–9*
Ophiopogon planiscapus 'Nigrescens',

Medium-height (2 to 4 ft tall)

Acanthus spinosus var. *spinosissimus*,
   zones 5–9
Alstroemeria aurantiaca, zones 7–10
Asphodeline lutea, zones 5–8
Crocosmia × crocosmiiflora, zones 6–10
Darmera peltata, zones 5–9*
Equisetum spp., zones 3–11*
Eryngium alpinum, zones 4–8
Filipendula rubra, zones 3–9
Iris ensata, zones 4–9
Iris pseudacorus, zones 5–8
Kniphofia uvaria, zones 5–9
Ligularia stenocephala, zones 5–8

Lobelia cardinalis, zones 2–9
Penstemon digitalis 'Husker Red',
   zones 2–8*
Petasites japonicus 'Giganteus',
   zones 5–7
Phlomis russeliana, zones 4–8
Polygonatum commutatum, zones 3–9
Polygonatum odoratum 'Variegatum',
   zones 3–9*
Rheum palmatum 'Atrosanguineum',
   zones 5–9*
Rodgersia spp., zones 5–7
Sedum spectabile, zones 4–9

Tall (over 4 ft tall)

Aconitum spp., zones 3–7
Alcea rosea, zones 3–8
Angelica archangelica, zones 3–9
Aruncus dioicus, zones 5–7
Astilbe chinensis var. *taquetii* 'Superba',
   zones 4–7
Cimicifuga simplex, zones 3–8

Crambe cordifolia, zones 6–9
Cynara cardunculus, zones 6–8
Eupatorium fistulosum, zones 4–8
Gunnera manicata, zones 8–10*
Hibiscus coccineus, zones 6–11
Hibiscus moscheutos, zones 5–9
Macleaya cordata, zones 3–8

COLD-HARDY TROPICAL-LOOKING FERNS

These are some of the best hardy ferns to use when designing a tropical-looking garden. Those marked with * spread rapidly to form thick stands.

Adiantum pedatum, zones 2–8
Athyrium filix-femina, zones 2–9
Athyrium niponicum 'Pictum',
   zones 4–9
Cyrtomium falcatum, zones 6–10
Dennstaedtia punctilobula, zones 3–8*

Dryopteris crassirhizoma, zones 5–8
Dryopteris filix-mas, zones 4–8
Matteuccia struthiopteris, zones 2–6*
Osmunda cinnamomea, zones 2–10
Osmunda regalis, zones 2–10
Polystichum munitum, zones 6–9

COLD-HARDY TROPICAL-LOOKING VINES

Rampant and leafy, these big vines will make a big statement in your tropical-looking garden. Those with * have colorful leaves; those with ** bear showy flowers.

Actinidia kolomitka 'Arctic Beauty',
   zones 4–8*
Akebia quinata, zones 4–9
Ampelopsis brevipedunculata 'Elegans',
   zones 7–9*
Aristolochia durior, zones 4–8
Bignonia capreolata, zones 6–9**
Campsis radicans, zones 5–9**
Celastrus orbiculatus, zones 3–8
Clematis × *hybrida*, zones 4–8**
Clematis montana, zones 6–8**

Clematis ternifolia (*C. maximowicziana*),
   zones 4–9**
Hedera helix 'Buttercup' and 'Gold
   Heart', zones 6–9*
Humulus lupulus 'Aurea', zones 4–8*
Hydrangea petiolaris, zones 5–7**
Lonicera × *heckrottii*, zones 4–9**
Lonicera sempervirens, zones 4–9**
Parthenocissus quinquefolia, zones 3–9
Polygonum aubertii, zones 5–8
Wisteria spp., zones 5–9**

COLD-HARDY TROPICAL-LOOKING
BAMBOOS AND ORNAMENTAL GRASSES

Towering or ground-covering, these hardy bamboos and ornamental grasses bring architectural beauty to any garden, adding a wild, exotic mood. Those marked with * have colorful leaves. Bamboos marked with ** are aggressive and must be contained to prevent them from becoming invasive.

Bamboos

Fargesia murielae, zones 4b–10
Fargesia nitida, zones 4b–10
Phyllostachys aureosulcata,
   zones 4b–9**
Phyllostachys nigra, zones 5b–10**

Pleioblastus variegatus, zones 6a–9* **
Pleioblastus viridistriatus, zones
   5a–9* **
Sasa veitchii, zones 5a–10**

Ornamental grasses

Arundo donax, zones 6–10*
Arundo donax 'Variegata',
    zones 7–10*
Carex elata 'Bowles Golden',
    zones 7–9*
Carex morrowii 'Variegata', zones 7–9*
Cortaderia selloana, zones 8–10;
    protected site in 7
Cortaderia selloana 'Gold Band' and
    'Pumila', zones 8–10;
    protected site in 7
Erianthus ravennae, zones 6–10*
Hakonechloa macra 'Aureola',
    zones 6–9*

Imperata cylindrica 'Red Baron',
    zones 6–9*
Miscanthus giganteus, zones 5–9
Miscanthus sinensis, zones 4–9
Miscanthus sinensis 'Strictus',
    zones 6–9*
Miscanthus sinensis 'Variegatus',
    zones 5–9*
Pennisetum alopecuroides, zones 5–9
Pennisetum setaceum 'Rubrum',
    zones 8–10
Phalaris arundinacea 'Picta',
    zones 5a–9**
Stipa gigantea, zones 7–9

COLD-HARDY TROPICAL-LOOKING BULBS

Exotic-looking and often fragrant, these showy bulbs will put on their display for many years to come.

Allium christophii, zones 4–8
Allium giganteum, zones 4–8
Amaryllis belladonna, zones 5–8
Camassia leichtlinii, zones 3–11

Fritillaria imperialis, zones 5–8
Lilium × *hybridum*, zones 4–8
Lycoris squamigera, zones 5–9
Tulipa × *hybrida*, zones 5–8

TROPICALS TO OVERWINTER OUTDOORS

These tropicals and tender plants make good candidates for overwintering outdoors in a temperate climate by any of the methods described in chapter 5.

Abutilon spp.
Agapanthus spp.
Agave spp.
Alpinia zerumbet
Brugmansia spp.
Colocasia esculenta
Curcuma alismatifolia
Eucomis bicolor
Fuchsia spp.
Gardenia augusta (*G. jasminoides*)
Globba winitii

Hedychium coccineum
Melianthus major
Musa spp.
Nerium oleander
Osteospermum × *hybrida*
Palmae
Passiflora spp.
Phormium spp.
Phygelius × *rectus*
Tibouchina spp.

◆◆◆

Appendix
Two

Sources for Tropical and Tropical-Looking Hardy Plants

Plants for tropical-style gardens don't have to be gathered from the jungle or shipped to you from some exotic location. Most are propagated and grown by nurseries in Florida, California, or other mild-climate areas and are shipped to nurseries all over the country. Tropical plants aren't all that hard to find and are becoming increasingly available as their popularity in outdoor gardens grows. Your local garden center is likely to carry a selection of tropical and subtropical plants, although you may find many of those you intend to grow outdoors in the greenhouse or houseplant section. Most nurseries in the North offer the widest selection of tropical plants in spring after all danger of frost has passed.

If your local nursery doesn't have the plants recommended in this book, one of the mail-order nurseries listed below ought to be able to supply the flora on your wish list. Nurseries that specialize in tropicals can offer you an eclectic assortment of dreamy exotic plants. But many large mail-order operations that stock an assortment of hardy perennials, shrubs, and trees include tropicals in their offerings as well. Bulb catalogs sell tropical bulbs along with tulips and daffodils, so seek out these tender beauties among their wares.

If the catalogs from the firms listed here only whet your appetite, you can try searching for that rare tropical on the Internet. The World Wide Web is fast becoming a source for wondrous and exciting plant material. You can contact many mail-order nurseries or plant collectors through their Web pages, which have stunning photos of their offerings. There you can find thousands of listings for unusual plants from all over the world, most of which can be sent to you in a matter of days. Seeds of tropicals are easily obtained from specialty growers and collectors, and growing these novel plants from seed can be a rewarding and cost-effective way to acquire new plants. Some tropicals grow very fast when started from seed. This is especially true of most tropical vines, which can grow many feet in one season.

When you purchase a tropical plant, unless it's growing outside in full sun at the nursery, you'll probably need to acclimate it to its new location outdoors in your garden. Start off by keeping the plant in a partly shaded area for a week or so, then bring it out to a half-sun location for another week before gradually moving it into more sun.

Here are the names and contact information of some recommended nurseries that carry a variety of useful plant material and seeds.

Aloha Tropicals
P.O. Box 6042
Oceanside, CA 92054
(760) 631-2880
Fax: (760) 631-2880
E-mail: alohatrop@aol.com
Web: www.alohatropicals.com
plants and bulbs

Avant Gardens
710 High Hill Road
North Dartmouth, MA 02747
(508) 998-8819
Fax: (866) 442-8268
E-mail: plants@avantgardensne.com
Web: www.avantgardensne.com
unusual annuals, tender perennials

B & T World Seeds
Rue des Marchandes
Paguignan
Aigues-Vives, France 34210
+04 68 91 29 63
Fax: +04 68 91 30 39
Web: www.b-and-t-world-seeds.com
seeds

The Banana Tree Inc
715 Northampton Street
Easton, PA 18042
(610) 253-9589
Fax: (610) 253-4864
Web: www.banana-tree.com
plants, seeds, tubers, rhizomes

Black Jungle
6 Arch Street
Greenfield, MA 01301
(413) 774-4448
Orders: (800) 268-1813
E-mail: email072604@blackjungle.com
Web: www.blackjungle.com
Tropicals, terrarium plants

Brent and Becky's Bulbs
7900 Daffodil Lane
Gloucester, VA 23061
(804) 693-3966
Fax: (804) 693-9436
Web: www.brentandbeckysbulbs.com
tender and hardy bulbs

Buena Creek Gardens
418 Buena Creek Road
San Marcos, CA 92079-2033
(760) 744-2810
Fax: (760) 744-0510
E-mail: buenacreekgrdns@aol.com
Web: www.buenacreekgardens.com
plants

Cacti.com/Serra Gardens
3314 Serra Road
Malibu, CA 90265
(310) 456-1572
Web: www.cacti.com
Cacti, succulents

Chiltern Seeds
Bortree Stile, Ulverston
Cumbria LA12 7PB, England
+44 01 229 581-137
Fax: +44 01 229 584-549
E-mail: info@chilternseeds.co.uk
Web: www.chilternseeds.co.uk
extensive seed list

Cistus Nursery
22711 NW Gillihan Road
Sauvie Island, OR 97231
(503) 621-2233
Fax: (503) 621-9657
E-mail: josh@cistus.com
Web: www.cistus.com
unusual plants from around the world

Companion Plants
7247 N. Coolville Ridge Road
Athens, OH 45701
(614) 592-4643
Fax: (614) 593-3092
E-mail: complants@frognet.net
Web: www.companionplants.com
seeds, plants

Dutch Gardens
144 Intervale Road
Burlington, VT 05401
(802) 660-3500
E-mail: info-dg@dutchgardens.com
Web: www.dutchgardens.nl
plants, bulbs

Foliage Gardens
2003 128th Avenue SE
Bellevue, WA 98005
(425) 747-2998
Fax: (425) 643-6886
Web: www.foliagegardens.com
hardy and tropical ferns

The Fragrant Path
P.O. Box 328
Ft. Calhoun, NE 68023
seeds

Glasshouse Works
P.O. Box 97
Church Street
Stewart, OH 45778-0097
(740) 662-2142
Fax: (740) 662-2120
E-mail: info@glasshouseworks.com
Web: www.glasshouseworks.com
tropical plants

Heronswood Nursery Ltd
7530 NE 288th Street
Kingston, WA 98346
(360) 297-4172
Fax: (360) 297-8321
E-mail: info@heronswood.com
Web: www.heronswood.com
hardy and tropical plants

Highland Succulents
1446 Bear Run Road
Gallipolis, OH 45631
(740) 256-1428
E-mail: hsinfo@highlandsucculents.com
Web: www.highlandsucculents.com
succulents

Horn Canna Farm
Route 1 Box 94
Carnegie, OK 73015
(580) 637-2327
Fax: (580) 637-2295
E-mail: cannas@cannas.net
Web: www.cannas.net
canna tubers

J. L. Hudson, Seedsman
Star Route 2, Box 337
La Honda, CA 94020
no phone or fax
E-mail: inquiry@jlhudsonseeds.net
Web: www.jlhudsonseeds.net
seeds

Landcraft Environments Ltd
1160 East Mill Road
Mattituck, NY 11952-1289
(631) 298-3510
Fax: (631) 298-3514
E-mail: LandcraftE@aol.com
Web: www.landcraftenvironments.com
wholesale tropicals, tender perennials

Lilypons Water Gardens
P.O. Box 10
Buckeystown, MD 21717-0010
(800) 999-5459
E-mail: info@lilypons.com
Web: www.lilypons.com
water plants

Logee's Greenhouses Ltd
141 North Street
Danielson, CT 06239
(888) 330-8038
E-mail: logee-info@logees.com
Web: www.logees.com
plants

Maryland Aquatics Nurseries Inc
3427 North Furnace Road
Jarrettsville, MD 21084
(410) 557-7615
Fax: (410) 692-2837
E-mail: info@marylandaquatics.com
Web: www.marylandaquatic.com
water plants

Natural Selections Exotics
1401 SW 1st Avenue
Fort Lauderdale, FL 33315
(954) 523-2428
E-mail: nsexotics@bellsouth.net
Web: www.naturalselections.safeshopper.com
exotic tropicals

Neon Palm Nursery
3525 Stony Point Road
Santa Rosa, CA 95407
(707) 585-8100
email: mobuxup@earthlink.net
Web: www.palmislandnursery.com
subtropical plants

Out of Africa
1005 Eckard Road
Centerburg, OH 43011
(740) 625-5790
Fax: (740) 625-5900
E-mail: outofafrica@ecr.net
Web: www.out-of-africa-plants.com
succulents, caudiciforms

Park Seed Company
1 Parkton Avenue
Greenwood, SC 29647-0001
(800) 213-0076
E-mail: info@parkscs.com
Web: www.parkseed.com
plants, seeds

Plant Delights Nursery Inc
9241 Sauls Road
Raleigh, NC 27603
(919) 772-4794
Fax: (919) 662-0370
E-mail: office@plantdelights.com
Web: www.plantdelights.com
plants

The Plumeria People
P.O. Box 31668
Houston, TX 77231-1668
(713) 728-1228
E-mail: miltonp@botanictreasures.com
Web: www.plumeriapeople.com
plants, bulbs, seeds

Rainforest Seed Company
207 Howard Park Avenue
Toronto, Ontario
M6R 1V9
(416) 767-0649
Fax: (416) 767-2280
E-mail: rainseed@interlog.com
Web: www.interlog.com/~rainseed
seeds

Raintree Nursery
391 Butts Road
Morton, WA 98356
(360) 496-6400
Fax: (888) 770-8358
E-mail: customerservice@raintreenursery.com
Web: www.raintreenursery.com
plants

Silverhill Seeds
P.O. Box 53108
Kenilworth, 7745
Cape Town, South Africa
+27 21 705-0295
Fax: +27 21 706-7987
E-mail: info@silverhillseeds.co.za
Web: www.silverhillseeds.co.za
seeds

Singing Springs Nursery
8802 Wilkerson Road
Cedar Grove, NC 27231
Fax: (919) 732-6336
E-mail: Plants@singingspringsnurery.com
Web: www.singingspringsnursery.com
unusual annuals, tender perennials

Stokes Tropicals
4806 E. Old Spanish Trail
Jeanerette, LA 70544
(337) 365-6998
Orders: (800) 624-9706

Fax: (337) 365-6991
E-mail: info@stokestropicals.com
Web: www.stokestropicals.com
tropical plants, bulbs

Thompson & Morgan Seedsmen Inc
P.O. Box 1308
Jackson, NJ 08527-0308
(800) 274-7333
Fax: (888) 466-4769
E-mail: tminc@thompson-morgan.com
Web: www.thompson-morgan.com
seeds

Tropiflora
3530 Tallevast Road
Sarasota, FL 34243
(941) 351-2267
Orders: (800) 613-7520
Fax: (941) 351-6985
E-mail: sales@tropiflora.com
Web: www.tropiflora.com
tropical plants

Van Bourgondien Bulbs
P.O. Box 2000
Virginia Beach, VA 23450-2000
(800) 622-9959
Fax: (800) 327-4268
E-mail: blooms@dutchbulbs.com
Web: www.dutchbulbs.com
plants, bulbs

Wayside Gardens
1 Garden Lane
Hodges, SC 29695-0001
(800) 213-0379
E-mail: info@waysidecs.com
Web: www.waysidegardens.com
plants

White Flower Farm
P.O. Box 50
Route 63
Litchfield, CT 06759-0050
(800) 503-9624
Fax: (800) 503-9624
E-mail: custserv@whiteflowerfarm.com
Web: www.whiteflowerfarm.com
plants, bulbs

Woodlanders Inc
1128 Colleton Avenue
Aiken, SC 29801
(803) 648-7522
E-mail: woodland@scbn.net
Web: www.woodlanders.net
rare and native exotics

Acknowledgments

Writing and photographing this book absorbed much of our time for the better part of a year. We are especially grateful for our partners' understanding during this endeavor. Susan is particularly appreciative of the support and encouragement of her husband, Mark Schneider, whose gift for gab with garden owners proves just as valuable an addition to her photography work as his patience as a photographic assistant and notetaker. Dennis would like to thank his family and friends for their encouragement during this project and especially Bill Smith for holding the fort while Dennis traveled to distant gardens and worked on the manuscript many nights into the wee hours. And we thank each other for maintaining good humor throughout the project—we are grateful that we remain friends at its completion.

We extend our heartfelt thanks to the following garden owners, garden designers, public gardens, and botanical gardens for sharing their gardens with us and our camera. Without them, this book would not have been possible.

Garden owners and designers

- Mr. and Mrs. Michael Ashkin
- Tony Avent, Plant Delights Nursery, Raleigh, North Carolina
- Randy Baley
- Pierre Bennerup and Susan Sawicki
- John Bierne
- Michael W. Bowell, Flora Design Gallery, Kimberton, Pennsylvania
- Ben Caldwell
- Danny Cameron
- Linda Cochran
- Mr. and Mrs. Stanley Cohen
- Ellen Coster and Maurice Isaac, Moel Gardens, Mattituck, New York
- Conni Cross Garden Design, Cutchogue, New York
- David Culp and Mike Alderfer
- Harold H. Culton, Jr.
- Bill Dement and Ed Sessoms
- Kevin J. Doyle Garden Design, Dover, Massachusetts
- Joe Eck and Wayne Winterrowd
- Jenks Farmer

- Frank E. Galloway
- Ben Hammontree
- Richard Hartlage
- Dan Hinkley and Robert Jones, Heronswood Nursery, Kingston, Washington
- Richard Iversen
- Jeffrey Jabco
- Lee Link
- Little and Lewis Inc., Bainbridge Island, Washington
- Jeff Mendoza Garden Design, New York, New York
- Carol Mercer
- Debbie Munson
- Dave Murback
- Bill Pollard and Holly Weir, Rocky Dale Gardens, Bristol, Vermont
- Douglas Ruhren Garden Design, Durham, North Carolina
- Lisa Stamm and Dale Booher, The Homestead Garden and Design Collaborative, Shelter Island, New York
- Marco Polo Stufano
- Kelly Sweezey, Basin Harbor Club, Vergennes, Vermont
- Barbara Toll
- David Wierdsma, French Farm, Greenwich, Connecticut
- Bunny Williams
- Chris Woods

Gardens

- Bellevue Botanical Garden, Seattle, Washington
- Brooklyn Botanic Garden, Brooklyn, New York
- Bronx Zoo, Bronx, New York
- Callaway Gardens, Pine Mountain, Georgia
- Chanticleer, Wayne, Pennsylvania
- Hallockville Museum Farm, Riverhead, New York
- Longwood Gardens, Kennett Square, Pennsylvania
- New York Botanical Garden, Bronx, New York
- J. C. Raulston Arboretum, Raleigh, North Carolina
- Riverbanks Zoological Park and Botanical Garden, Columbia, South Carolina
- Rockefeller Center, New York, New York
- Scott Arboretum, Swarthmore College, Swarthmore, Pennsylvania
- The State University of New York at Farmingdale
- Washington Park Arboretum, Seattle, Washington
- Wave Hill, Riverdale, New York

✦✦✦

Index

Abutilon pictum 'Thompsonii'